T0319988

Asia-Pacific Issues in International Business

Asia-Pacific Issues in International Business

Edited by

Sidney J. Gray
Sara L. McGaughey
William R. Purcell

Australian Centre for International Business
University of New South Wales
Sydney, Australia

Edward Elgar
Cheltenham, UK • Northampton, MA, USA

© Sidney J. Gray, Sara L. McGaughey and William R. Purcell 2001

All rights reserved. No part of this publication may be reproduced, stored in a retrieval system or transmitted in any form or by any means, electronic, mechanical or photocopying, recording, or otherwise without the prior permission of the publisher.

Published by
Edward Elgar Publishing Limited
Glensanda House
Montpellier Parade
Cheltenham
Glos GL50 1UA
UK

Edward Elgar Publishing, Inc.
136 West Street
Suite 202
Northampton
Massachusetts 01060
USA

A catalogue record for this book is available from the British Library

Library of Congress Cataloguing in Publication Data

Asia-Pacific issues in international business / edited by Sidney J. Gray, Sara L. McGaughey, William R. Purcell.
A selection of papers presented at the annual conference of the Australia-New Zealand Business Academy, held September 30–October 2, 1999, and hosted by the Australian Centre for International Business at the University of New South Wales in Sydney, Australia.
Includes index.
1. East Asia—Foreign economic relations—Congresses. 2. Asia, Southeastern—Foreign economic relations—Congresses. 3. Pacific Area—Foreign economic relations—Congresses. 4. Australia—Foreign economic relations—Congresses. 5. New Zealand—Foreign economic relations—Congresses. I. Gray, S.J. II. McGaughey, Sara L., 1968– III. Purcell, William R., 1963– IV. Australia-New Zealand Busimess Academy. Conference (1999: Australian Centre for International Business at the University of New South Wales)

HF1600.5.A84 2001
337.5—dc21 00–069504

ISBN 1 84064 557 1

Printed and bound in Great Britain by
Biddles Ltd, Guildford and King's Lynn.

Contents

PART III: FOREIGN DIRECT INVESTMENT ISSUES

PART IV: MANAGING INTERNATIONAL BUSINESS RELATIONSHIPS

Contributors

Ali, M. Yunus	Queensland University of Technology, Australia
Bamberry, Geoff	Charles Sturt University, Australia
Chuang, Cheng-Min	Taiwan University, Taiwan
Fang, Shih-Chieh	I-Shou University of Taiwan, Taiwan
Fraser, Campbell	Griffith University, Australia
Gray, Sidney J.	University of New South Wales, Australia
Hsiao, Luke Y.C.	I-Shou University of Taiwan, Taiwan
Lin, Julia L.	I-Shou University of Taiwan, Taiwan
Lindsay, Val	University of Auckland, New Zealand
Maitland, Elizabeth	University of Melbourne, Australia
McGaughey, Sara L.	University of New South Wales, Australia
McGraw, Peter	Macquarie University, Australia
Nicholas, Stephen	University of Melbourne, Australia
Nielsen, Kim V.	PA Consulting, Copenhagen, Denmark
Petersen, Bent	Copenhagen Business School, Denmark
Purcell, William R.	University of New South Wales, Australia

Rose, Elizabeth L.	University of Auckland, New Zealand
Sim, A.B.	University of Wollongong, Australia
Srirojanant, Sirinuch	Victoria University of Wellington, New Zealand
Thirkell, Peter	Victoria University of Wellington, New Zealand
Welch, Lawrence S.	University of Western Sydney-Nepean, Australia
Wickramasekera, Rumintha	Charles Sturt University, Australia
Zarkada-Fraser, Anna	Griffith University, Australia

Preface

This collection of articles is a selection from among the best contributions to the annual conference of the Australia–New Zealand International Business Academy. The conference was held from 30 September to 2 October 1999 and hosted by the Australian Centre for International Business at the University of New South Wales in Sydney, Australia. The theme of the conference was 'International Business Dynamics of the New Millennium' and the articles chosen reflect this theme in respect of the Asia-Pacific context of international business.

We would like to thank all of the contributors to this volume for their promptness and efficiency in the rewriting and updating of their articles. Thanks are also due to Grace Setiawan for her help in preparing the manuscript for publication and to Francine O'Sullivan from Edward Elgar for her assistance and encouragement.

Sydney
2000

1. Introduction

Sidney J. Gray, Sara L. McGaughey and William R. Purcell

While the triad economies of North America, Japan and the European Union continue to dominate trade and investment flows, sweeping political, economic and social changes are shifting the locus of international business activity to other regions. Many argue that the twenty-first century will be the age of the Asia-Pacific. The chapters in this volume represent the latest research on a selection of key Asia-Pacific issues relevant to international business. The chapters are grouped according to topic area: the internationalisation process, export expansion and performance, foreign direct investment issues and, finally, the problems of managing international business relationships.

The first part of the book focuses on the internationalisation process. The chapter by Bent Petersen, Lawrence Welch and Kim Nielsen examines the establishment pattern of Danish companies in South–East Asia to illustrate a broader concept of foreign operation, or entry mode, development. They argue that this is closer to the original concept of incrementalism underlying some of the early studies of the internationalisation process. A dynamic growth process by US multinational enterprises (MNEs) is identified in the study by Elizabeth Maitland, Elizabeth Rose and Stephen Nicholas which reveals two different patterns of growth. While some firms display random variation in the timing of their first investments into a host country, others display different types of clustering strategies influenced by organisational learning, experience, internal architecture and the translation of tacit know-how into firm capabilities.

Export expansion and performance is the theme of the second part of the book. The chapter by Sirinuch Srirojanant and Peter Thirkell explores the impact of the Internet on export effectiveness and performance by Australian and New Zealand exporters. The key elements of a successful Internet export strategy were found to be an interactive web site, effective stakeholder communications, supportive top management and intensive

Internet usage to foster acceptance. Rumintha Wickramasekera and Geoff Bamberry examine the factors perceived as inhibiting or enhancing the export expansion of the Australian wine industry. The major inhibitor was found to be insufficient stocks to meet demand, while the key enhancement factors were perceived to be the quality and uniqueness of the wines produced. The focus of Val Lindsay's chapter is on the development and application of export performance measures. A multi-faceted approach to measuring export performance is recommended. Using three sales-related export performance measures, her empirical study of New Zealand manufacturing exporters suggests the relevance of a contingency perspective based on a firm's situational context.

The third part of the book addresses foreign direct investment issues. The chapter by Stephen Nicholas, Sid Gray and William Purcell analyses the impact of policy incentives and non-policy factors on the investment location decisions of Japanese MNEs in Singapore and the Asian region comprising Australia, Thailand, Malaysia, Indonesia and the Philippines. Their results suggest that incentives were not viewed as important by Japanese MNEs and perceived as little different from the incentives offered by other countries in the region. Anna Zarkada-Fraser and Campbell Fraser explore variations in the decision-making mechanisms produced by the different levels of experience of Australian manufacturing firms investing or considering investing in Indonesia. Their findings suggest that the way Australian firms perceive the risks associated with investing in Indonesia differs according to the international experience of the firm and the level of exposure to the country itself.

The theme of the final part of the book is problems associated with managing international business relationships. Cheng-Min Chuang, Shih-Chieh Fang, Julia Lin and Luke Hsiao examine the multinational knowledge acquisition modes of firms in the Taiwan electronics industry. Their findings suggest that knowledge characteristics, firm characteristics and the learning environment influence a firm's choice of knowledge acquisition mode. The chapter by Sara McGaughey addresses the issue of how MNEs may protect their intellectual property in nations deemed to have weak intellectual property rights protection. Drawing on the case of INCAT, an Australian manufacturer of high-speed car and passenger carrying catamarans, the dominant assumptions in the literature are challenged concerning the risks faced by MNEs. Yunus Ali and A.B. Sim focus on the use of performance measures in international joint ventures in developing countries. Based on a study of joint ventures in Bangladesh, they conclude that there is support for the use of partners' goal achievement as the preferred measure of joint venture performance. The final chapter of the book is by Peter McGraw who compares the human resource values and practices of ethnic Chinese owned enterprises and the subsidiaries of

Anglo-American MNEs in Hong Kong. The findings indicate that there are significant differences between these groups in terms of both the values and practices relating to human resource management.

The scope of the chapters is wide-ranging while at the same time providing an important focus on key issues in international business from an Asia-Pacific perspective. Hopefully, this book will be an important point of reference for businesses in the region as well as for scholars of international business and Asian studies.

PART I

The Internationalisation Process

2. Resource Commitment to Foreign Markets: The Establishment Patterns of Danish Firms in South-East Asian Markets

Bent Petersen, Lawrence S. Welch and Kim V. Nielsen

INTRODUCTION

In the development of theories explaining internationalisation by companies one important approach has been the so-called internationalisation process theory, initially associated with the work of Nordic researchers (Johanson and Vahlne, 1977; Luostarinen, 1979). Their early empirical research indicated that companies developed their international operations in a relatively evolutionary, sequential way. The pattern that this research revealed was one of movement from low to high commitment methods of foreign market operations over time. For example, for Swedish manufacturing companies, the general pattern of foreign operation mode development (referred to as the 'establishment chain') that emerged from the research was: (1) no regular exporting; (2) start of exporting via the use of a foreign agent; (3) a sales subsidiary; and (4), eventually, for some companies, establishment of a foreign production subsidiary. Similarly, there tended to be a movement from initial operations in culturally close countries to later operations in culturally more distant markets.

This seemingly simplistic result was the basis of theorising around the forces driving the internationalisation of the firm, with particular emphasis on the learning process as foreign operations evolved (Buckley and Ghauri, 1999). While there has been a variety of challenges to the basic model, and a number of extensions, for example, through the incorporation of network processes and influences, the model still stands as an important reference point in empirical and theoretical work on internationalisation (Johanson and Vahlne, 1990; Björkman and Forsgren, 1997; Buckley and Ghauri, 1999). It is rather surprising, therefore, to find that the basis of analysis in most internationalisation studies, as in earlier approaches, is still a rather crude representation of foreign operation mode development. The problem is that explanations of internationalisation have become increasingly sophisticated, but that this has not been matched by greater sophistication in empirical analyses of operation modes in longitudinal pattern studies, to the extent that it is difficult to argue very much at all on the basis of the empirical data. One might even say that it is difficult to know what the true pattern of internationalisation for companies is. This is because the recorded patterns in terms of establishment chains have only included very broad operation mode categories, which have therefore limited the ability to capture the true nature and extent of companies' international development processes. While the assumption of step-wise commitment is a useful approximation of incrementalism, there is a need for more sophisticated and precise measures of firms' commitment of resources to foreign markets.

In this chapter, therefore, we develop the basis for a more in-depth treatment of what internationalisation, as represented by foreign operation mode development, actually entails. We do this by building a framework for analysing *within mode changes*, for it is at this level that the more intricate process changes might be expected to have effect. Furthermore, we consider the role of *mode additions* to existing mode use, which have been almost completely ignored in internationalisation pattern studies, but clearly have the potential to change the whole way a company moves through its international establishment chain. After a literature overview, an empirical investigation of Danish companies' recent establishment patterns in the ASEAN countries is used to illustrate the potential importance of mode additions.

WHAT IS MEANT BY 'WITHIN MODE CHANGES'?

By within mode changes we refer to an entrant firm's increasing resource commitment[1] to a specific foreign market that takes place without a change of operation mode. Thus, the foreign operation mode remains the same in terms of *what* business function is carried out (manufacturing, marketing, R&D, management, etc.), by *whom* it is carried out (the entrant firm itself, an independent operator, or both in collaboration), and *where* it is carried out (in the home country or in the foreign country). In the definition a distinction is made between (broad) *business functions* and *activities* (see also Porter, 1985: 36). Hence, 'marketing' is a business function that comprises various activities such as market analyses, sales calls, sales force training, after-sales service, product modification and so forth.

As examples of within mode changes an entrant firm may increase the *scale* of the existing activities in one of its production subsidiaries through plant extension and hiring of more workers or an entrant firm may increase the *scope* of activities of its sales subsidiary by establishing local product modification facilities in addition to the existing local service/repair workshop. The new product modification workshop represents a resource commitment that facilitates a subsequent establishment of a full-scale local production plant (production subsidiary).

These two examples involve within mode changes of in-house activities of the entrant firm. However, within mode changes may also occur in relation to contractual arrangements. Quite often the contract with local sales agents obliges the exporting firms to co-finance those marketing assets that have a high degree of asset specificity. For example, the exporter incurs partly or fully the costs of translating manuals and promotional material, costs of organising sales pitches in trade fairs, or costs of training and educating the local sales staff. The exporter may even agree to co-finance individuals in the sales force of the foreign representative under the condition that the individuals pay special attention to the lines of the exporter (Petersen, 1996). Thus, the appointment of a product manager of the exporter's product line may represent an important within mode change.

Among the various within mode changes in internationalisation models particular attention has been paid to the learning activities of the entrant firm (Johanson and Vahlne, 1977, 1990; Luostarinen, 1979). The acquisition of knowledge about how to do business in the foreign market is typically an investment in human assets which is irreversible and, indeed, very country-specific. In international joint ventures the entrant firm is usually exchanging its process or production know-how for knowledge possessed by the partner about the local business environment including valuable knowledge about network relations. Network development involves the establishment of contacts and connections with persons and institutions of relevance to the foreign operation (Haakansson and Snehota, 1995). Thus in the course of the joint venture the resource commitment of the entrant firm increases in terms of irreversible learning costs. The acquisition of knowledge through the joint venture is an investment that pays back if or when the entrant firm switches to a single venture (wholly owned subsidiary). Similarly, an exporting firm may learn about the local business conditions through frequent visits to its local intermediary and close collaboration in general. By 'tapping' an intermediary's knowledge, the entrant firm eases the establishment of direct sales channels to the end-users.

Table 2.1 sums up the different appearances of within mode changes and includes examples of the four basic types.

Table 2.1 Different appearances of within mode change

Type of 'within mode change'	Example
Scaling up in-house activities	Production subsidiary enlarges its plant capacity
Broadening the scope of in-house activities	Sales subsidiary extends with product modification workshop
More support of contractual partner activity	Entrant firm agrees to co-finance product manager in local sales agency
Acquisition of local market knowledge	Entrant firm learns about local customers through frequent visits to sales agent

WHAT IS MEANT BY 'MODE ADDITION'?

By *mode addition* we refer to the situation where the entrant firm introduces a foreign operation mode in addition to an existing one. The addition is made not just in terms of activities (as is the case for *within mode changes*), but also includes:

(1) new broad business functions, *or*
(2) new control/ownership arrangements, *or*
(3) a new location.

Some examples will explain the three different appearances of mode addition.

Firstly, mode addition occurs when an entrant firm adds a new broad business function, sometimes referred to as 'functional migration'. For instance, a firm has licensed out its production know-how to a foreign operator, but notices opportunities for additional sales to the licensee in the form of related marketing know-how and relevant trade marks. As a result, the entrant firm and the local operator (the licensee) agree to enter a franchise contract as well. So, the entrant firm is hereafter employing two foreign market operation modes simultaneously, namely licensing and franchising.

Now imagine an entrant firm that on the basis of a franchise contract has handed over all marketing operations to a local operator (a franchisee). After a while the franchisor realises that some marketing responsibilities are under-performing in the foreign market. As a consequence, the franchisor insists on assuming responsibility for the under-performing marketing activities via a local sales subsidiary. As a result, the entrant firm (the franchisor) introduces ownership control in addition to contractual control to its organisational set-up in the foreign market, thereby practising mode addition (franchising + sales subsidiary). As one distinguishes between different export modes (see Table 2A.1 in Appendix) other similar examples of mode addition emerge. Export via independent intermediaries may be supplemented by export through own sales channels (internet sales, home-based sales force or locally-based sales subsidiary) as a result of vertical or horizontal division of marketing responsibilities (Williamson, 1992).

Third, the entrant firm may practise mode addition by adding a new location to the existing activity. Think of an exporting firm establishing its own production operation in the target country in addition to its existing domestic production. By doing this the entrant firm effectively combines two modes of operation: exporting and local production. Presumably, this form of mode addition precedes a lot of manufacturing subsidiaries or may even constitute a permanent arrangement. By definition any assembly plant operation in a foreign country will involve export as well, but sourcing from the home country is also common among fully-fledged production subsidiaries (Moxon, 1982). Table 2.2 sums up the different appearances of mode additions and indicates examples of the three basic types.

Table 2.2 Different appearances of mode addition

Type of 'mode addition'	Example
Adding new business function	Foreign licensee enters franchising contract with licensor
Adding new ownership	The entrant firm assumes responsibility for some franchisee activities
Adding new location	Assembly production in target country is added to existing export

LITERATURE REVIEW

Internationalisation process theory suggests that the incremental resource commitment (and market expansion) pattern evident in a number of empirical studies is driven by the accumulation of knowledge about foreign markets through experiential learning. Experiential learning, it is argued, allied with network development, which is a prerequisite for much of the information flow and knowledge development, is a time-consuming process, thus contributing to the evolutionary pattern of internationalisation. Furthermore, given the risk-averse character of decision-makers, and a certain tolerable risk level, resource commitment to a foreign market can only take place with successive reductions of perceived market risk and uncertainty.

Internationalisation process theory has been the subject of considerable criticism (for an overview, see Johanson and Vahlne, 1990), particularly when studies have shown numerous examples where sequential, incremental development was not found to apply. Especially in the advanced stages of internationalisation, when companies have widespread foreign establishments, they frequently undertake *instantaneous* high resource commitments in new foreign markets without preceding, low commitment operation modes, in other words, leapfrogging directly to high commitment foreign operation modes in some foreign markets. Likewise, recent research has shown the existence of the so-called 'born global' phenomenon, whereby some small firms move from no international involvement to global operations in a short period of time (Knight and Cavusgil, 1996; Madsen and Servais, 1997). Such findings challenge the internationalisation process model at both the operational and theoretical levels (Andersen, 1993). If firms, as a general rule, establish high commitment operation modes, such as production subsidiaries, without preceding knowledge-accumulating operation modes, other driving factors than experiential learning must have come into play (Hirsch and Meshulach, 1991). This is evident, of course, when foreign production units are established to gain access to cheap labour, raw materials and the like (Hagen and Hennart, 1995).

Clearly, though, much of the argument turns on the observed pattern of a company's operation mode development and how incrementalism is defined. As noted above, the traditional focus has been on singular, discrete steps, that is, from one distinct operation mode and level of resource commitment, with specific organisational and institutional arrangements, to another. This became known as 'stages theory', and was viewed by some researchers as implying a relatively fixed sequence of stages (Johanson and Wiedersheim-Paul, 1975). However, we argue in this chapter that this approach, and the establishment chain concept as applied, may well reflect an incremental internationalisation process, but it can only do this *partially*. This is because of the broader and deeper array of steps that a company often undertakes which are typically not counted as operation mode change. These can be significant contributors to incremental development – including the addition of another operation mode in support of the existing format. This is illustrated in Figure 2.1, which depicts three different, broad patterns of firms' resource commitment to foreign markets: instantaneous, stepwise (often referred to as the 'stages model') and incremental.

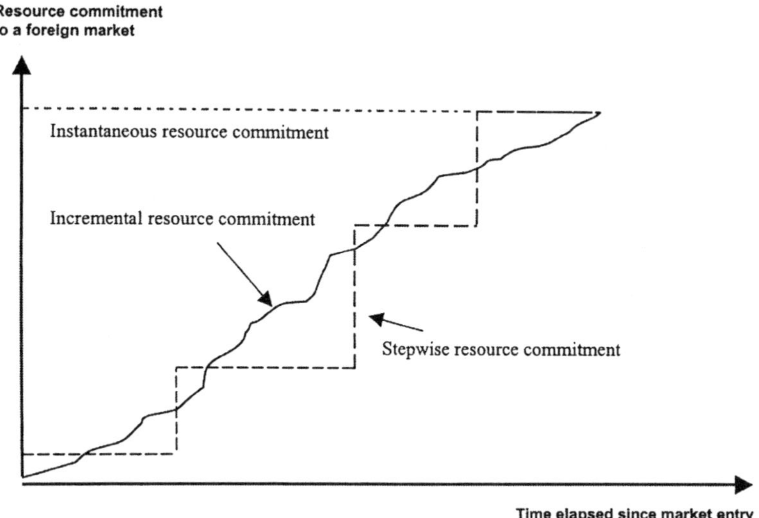

Figure 2.1 Three patterns of firms' resource commitment to foreign markets

The need to disaggregate the 'stages' or 'sequences' of resource commitment in internationalisation in order to elucidate the change process that takes place has been stressed by some researchers. For example, Beamish et al. (1997: 4–5) write:

> In the stages model, a firm might progress from (a) indirect/ad hoc exporting … to (b) active exporting and/or licensing to (c) active exporting, licensing, and joint equity investment in foreign manufacture to (d) full-scale multinational marketing and production. *These are, of course, broad-based stages. In practice, there are many more sub-categories.* Within exporting, for example, firms may start with order-filling only. Soon after, however, they may be confronted with questions of whether to use exporting middlemen who take ownership (distributors) or those who are commissioned agents; and whether to export directly (either through the firm's own sales force, an export department, or a foreign sales company) or indirectly (through brokers or export agents). Similarly, if an investment is to be made, there are questions regarding scale of investment (sales office, warehouse, packaging and assembly, or full-scale production), level of ownership (wholly, majority equity, equal, minority equity) and type of partner. (italics added)

In the same vein, Bonaccorsi and Dalli (1992) criticise 'stages' theory as being too mechanistic inasmuch as it is effectively assumed that situations between the stages are stable and free of changes and therefore important intra-stage evolution is ignored. Thus, in their study of the internationalisation of Italian firms Bonaccorsi and Dalli (1992) observe that the categories of agent and sales subsidiary are relatively broad, masking a wide range of feasible variation in types of operation within them. Reflecting on their study of the dichotomy between sales subsidiaries and outside agents Grønhaug and Kvitastein (1993) acknowledge that firms' choice of entry strategy counts, but changes are frequent, which calls for a more refined perspective on institutional arrangements to handle foreign business.

In a case study of the export channel development of a UK firm in the People's Republic of China, Easton and Li (1993) take a more micro look into the export stages. They focus on the changes that occur *within* rather than *between* modes of export: '... at a lower or more disaggregated level than much of the research that has been carried out into exporting' (p. 2). They develop a network framework for analysing some of these micro intra-stage changes, providing an indication of the possibilities for a new approach to the analysis of internationalisation patterns.

Benito and Welch (1994) in their review of past entry mode research also point out the deficiencies of a focus on major operation mode steps and argue for more subtle analysis of the steps:

> What is probably required is not just charting of the main steps in the process, but the measurement of smaller steps in between, such as the appointment of additional staff, which may be less apparent but nevertheless important in advancing the process, and in understanding more substantial and obvious changes in foreign market servicing. (p. 16)

In the same review article Benito and Welch note that foreign market servicing 'packages' may occur as a result of a firm adding new operation modes to the initial/entry mode in a foreign country. However, it is difficult to establish from the existing literature how frequently firms use mode addition in their internationalisation processes. Incidences of mode addition are chiefly reported from case studies (for an overview see Petersen and Welch, forthcoming), but to our knowledge only one survey study of internationalisation has reported registration of mode addition behaviour, namely the study by Clark et al. (1997) based on retrospective observations of foreign operation modes of 25 UK firms. Other authors have reported observations of firms operating more than one mode in foreign markets (for an overview see Petersen and Welch, forthcoming), but being static, cross-sectional surveys verification of mode *addition* is problematic. Nevertheless, in his cross-sectional study of the internationalisation of

French exporting firms Valla (1986) describes the observed mode combinations ('mixed approaches') as mode addition, and concludes that:

> . . . instead of changing the organisational arrangement to another one (as suggested by the available literature), the firms preferred to complement the existing organisational structure by additional marketing channels of distribution. This finding independently supports the idea of incremental decision processes as an important characteristic of the firms' internationalisation process, but not the sequential organisational stages theory. (p. 34)

Whereas we can conclude that no survey studies on firms' internationalisation have reported mode addition behaviour – with the important exception of Clark et al. (1997) – it is somewhat more complicated to settle the extent to which there exist internationalisation studies reporting within mode changes. To some degree any disaggregation of the conventional major operation mode steps captures within mode changes. As an example, a sub-classification of production subsidiaries into (a) assembly plants and (b) full production plants (Luostarinen, 1979) is effectively a way of registering within mode changes over a period of time. If we consider 'export' as one major operation step a number of internationalisation studies qualify as studies incorporating within mode changes. Thus, the seminal establishment chain study by Johanson and Wiedersheim-Paul (1975) divides 'export' into the categories of (a) 'no regular export', (b) sales agents and (c) sales subsidiaries. On the other hand, if we see 'export' as consisting of three individual major operation modes (see Table 2A.1 in Appendix) plus 'no regular export', very few survey studies of internationalisation explore within mode changes.

Table 2.3 presents the main data of 13 survey studies that retrospectively report 'establishment chains' of firms in the process of internationalisation. In terms of registration of within mode changes the 13 studies fall into three groups: the first and largest group consists of seven studies that have measured major operation modes exclusively. The observations of these studies are confined to 4–6 major operation modes – all included in the Appendix Table 2A.1 (except NX = no regular export).

No analysis of the individual operation mode has been carried out. This group includes the studies by Johanson and Wiedersheim-Paul (1975), Hedlund and Kverneland (1985), Van Den Bulcke (1986), Buckley et al. (1988), Millington and Bayliss (1990), Björkman and Eklund (1996) and Clark et al. (1997). The second group comprises five studies (Luostarinen, 1979; Juul and Walters, 1987; Bonaccorsi and Dalli, 1992; Luostarinen et al., 1994; Bell, 1995) containing elements of within mode change analysis in so far as disaggregation of one or two major operation modes has taken

Table 2.3 Survey studies on establishment chains

Author(s)	Number of entrant firms and country of origin		Number of host countries		Period of recorded mode development	Number of observations (at time of study/over time)	Number and types of operation modes studied *NX = no regular export, IX = indirect export DX = direct export, A = agent, D= distributor, L = licensing, JV = joint venture, SS = sales subsidiary, PS = production subsidiary*	
Johanson & Wiedersheim-Paul (1975)	4	Sweden	20	The world	1868-1970	89/165	**4**	NX, A, SS, PS
Luostarinen (1979)	997	Finland	n/a		- 1976	997/1432	**7**	NX,IX,DX,L,SS, assembling subsidiary, PS
Hedlund & Kverneland (1985)	18	Sweden	1	Japan	- 1981	43/138	**4**	NX, A, SS, PS
Van Den Bulcke (1986)	41	Belgium	n/a		1970-76	41/138	**6**	NX, DX, A, SS, L, PS
Juul & Walters (1987)	12	Norway	1	UK	-1985	12/24	**7**	NX, IX, DX, sales unit, SS, PS, service unit
Buckley et al. (1988)	43	UK	n/a		-1975	43/111	**5**	NX, DX, A, SS, PS
Millington & Bayliss (1990)	50	UK	12	EC	n/a	n/a	**6**	NX, L, DX, A, SS, PS
Bonaccorsi & Dalli (1992)	172	Italy	n/a		n/a	n/a	**8**	NX, A, DX, Italian resident intermediaries, foreign intermediaries resident in Italy, foreign D, consortia, subcontracting
Luostarinen et al. (1994)	494	Finland	n/a	The world	n/a	n/a	**7**	NX, IX, DX, L, SS, assembling subsidiary, PS
Bell (1995)	88	SF, IRL, N	10	The world	n/a	n/a	**8**	NX, IX, A-D, X sales staff, L, JV, SS, PS
Björkman & Eklund (1996)	114	Finland	1	W. Germany	1981-90	86/163	**4**	NX, X, SS, PS
Erminio & Rugman (1996)	1	USA		The world	1912-96	73/139	**10**	NX, D/A, Upjohn rep. office/local D, sales office/local D/local pharmaceutical firms, branch, SS, manufacturing contract with local pharmaceutical firm, JV in manufacturing, wholly-owned manufacturing plant with distribution capacity
Clark et al. (1997)	25	UK	n/a		n/a	679 (first move)/882	**6**	NX, X, L, SS, PS, JV

place. These studies have registered seven or eight operation modes. The study by Erminio and Rugman (1996) makes up the third 'group'. The study stands out through its registration of 10 types of operation modes – a disaggregration that partially opens up the 'black boxes' of the major operation modes. The study is also distinctive inasmuch as the observed organisational arrangements are those of a single company (Upjohn pharmaceutical firm). In general, though, it is clear that the extant body of research on internationalisation lacks the fine-grained treatment of foreign operation mode development that seems to be a basic prerequisite for theory building.

EMPIRICAL INVESTIGATION

Methodology

Company case studies were conducted in order to provide an in-depth understanding of the actual process of resource commitment to foreign markets (Yin, 1994). The study of Danish firms in the ASEAN region was based on company documentation and semi-structured interviews. The purpose of these interviews was to elicit an overview of the pattern and process of the companies' organisational arrangements in a foreign country/region. The study was exploratory in the sense that no particular patterns were anticipated. Accordingly, the interview consisted of open-ended rather than closed questions. The overall research aim was to investigate whether firms' increase of resource commitment to a foreign market *exclusively* takes place in connection to distinct shifts from one operation mode sequence (for example, a sales agent) to another (for example, a sales subsidiary). Potentially, increase of resource commitment may take place *within* a broadly defined operation mode sequence, and furthermore, *additions* rather than *replacements* of operation modes might be the case. For reasons of convenience (time constraints, better access to company information) the case companies were all domiciled in Denmark, the home country of two of the three authors at the point in time of the study.

More specifically, establishments of affiliates in the ASEAN region as of 1997 (including Brunei, Indonesia, Malaysia, the Philippines, Singapore and Thailand) by Danish manufacturing companies during the period 1994–97 were investigated. Being a high-growth market until the economic crisis emerged in the summer of 1997 the expectation of the researchers was that a considerable number of Danish firms would have established subsidiaries in ASEAN countries within the time period under observation. Moreover, spillover effects from one ASEAN country to another in terms of resource commitment should be observable. The affiliates involved subsidiaries or representative offices. With assistance from the Danish embassies in the region a search indicated that 22 companies had established 25 subsidiaries or representative offices in ASEAN countries during the period under observation. All of these companies were contacted and 16 were prepared to participate in the study. Two of the firms participated on a strategic business unit level and contributed two cases (subsidiary track records) each. So altogether the study included 18 cases. The average annual sales of the companies participating in the study were DKK 3830 million (in 1997 equal to approximately US$600 million), the average number of employees 3336, and the average number of countries with affiliates 12. Key data for the individual companies are included in Table 2A.2 in the Appendix. Interviews were held with either area or country managers for the companies in their respective offices in one of the ASEAN countries. All of the interviewees were either the actual decision-maker or heavily involved in the decision-making process. The interviews were conducted from August through December 1997. In Denmark the interviewer had familiarised himself with the basic data of the exporting firms. On the basis of the interviewer's hand notes or tape recordings the interviews were transcribed into a detailed indications summary.

Findings

The study demonstrated that mode additions are a common outcome of the attempt by the Danish companies to increase their penetration of the ASEAN market. In an overall sense the pattern can be described as an incremental expansion path, with movement from one level of commitment to a higher level (see Figure 2.2).

None of the cases exhibited an 'instantaneous' resource commitment behaviour of establishment without preceding activity in the form of appointing a local intermediary. However, apart from two cases, none of the observed establishment patterns fits the conventional, stepwise resource commitment (i.e. the establishment chain sequence of a local intermediary followed by a sales subsidiary). Seventeen out of eighteen recorded establishment patterns in individual markets were characterised by other than orthodox steps from one individual mode to that of another. As shown in Figure 2.2, 16 out of the 18 cases involved a mode shift that could be best described as mode addition – primarily through the creation of a regional headquarters, but with the retention in most cases of the existing foreign intermediary arrangements. In five cases a regional headquarters was already in place, so that the establishment of subsidiaries involved a deepening of existing within market arrangements. Intermediaries were, however, retained in three out of these five examples, emphasising again that mode addition rather than simple replacement may be used by companies as a way of easing the process of foreign market penetration.

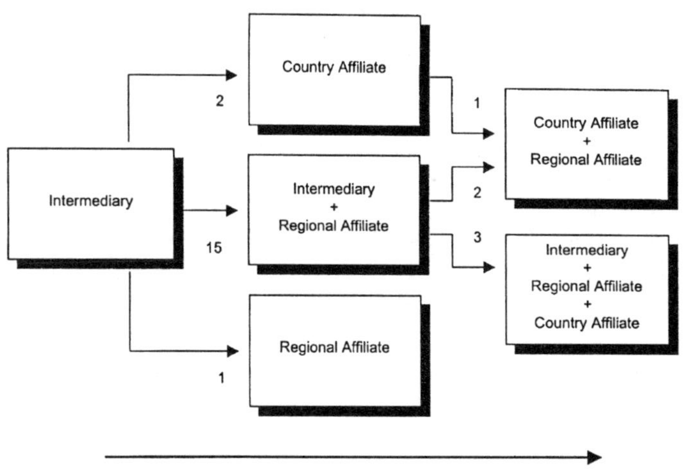

Figure 2.2 Establishment patterns of Danish companies in the ASEAN region 1994–97

The regional headquarters role, as a part of mode development, was perceived as an important step by the companies concerned in not only getting closer to intermediaries and customers in the various ASEAN markets, but also in improving intermediary networking capabilities between the various markets. This was seen as a way of improving the flow of information and knowledge between the various markets through the regional headquarters, which involved just one person from head office in Denmark in a number of cases. For Toftejorg, a producer of equipment for cleaning containers and tanks, this process was facilitated through the provision of training programmes at their Singapore regional HQ for sales personnel from their various ASEAN intermediaries. The 15 companies setting up regional HQs cited the improvement of intermediary networks through closer market proximity and greater direct ASEAN market involvement as a major factor in the decision-making process. Also, a number of companies mentioned the accumulation of local market knowledge as an important role of the regional HQs.

As an illustration of within mode change observed in the study, Lego, a toys producer, was making extensive use of independent distributors in the ASEAN countries. In two of the countries, Malaysia and Thailand, Lego had placed their own marketing officer with the independent distributor in order to accelerate sales of the Lego line.

DISCUSSION

As the Danish evidence indicates, mode additions are used in internationalisation, and their role may be important in extending the international penetration of companies in a particular market or on a broader basis. Apart from the role of a mode addition in supporting or extending an existing operation mode, the Danish companies also added modes as a way of providing a stepping stone to a later mode switch. In so doing, the mode addition is a critical step in the approach to internationalisation by the companies concerned, smoothing the process of expansion in the ASEAN market. One company clearly indicated that the dual mode operation in the foreign market was to be a stepping stone to an arrangement in which it would fully take over operations in the longer term. Whether deliberate or not, mode additions which involve two independent organisational entities servicing the same market and to some degree competitive are unlikely to be stable, long-term arrangements.

The changes within a given operation mode may be such that they move the company to the point where it is only a small step from one mode to the next 'higher' mode in the establishment chain. They may also permit an easy transfer to what might seem on the surface to constitute 'leapfrogging' in mode use. For example, the step from exporting via an agent to the use of a company-owned sales subsidiary is typically depicted as a 'step up' in the company's resource commitment to a foreign market, as indicated by the dotted, bold line in Figure 2.3. Hence, Figure 2.3 demonstrates the reality that a given mode switch may generate a wide range of outcomes in resource commitment by a company, some of which might be described as escalation, point A, as would typically be the conclusion drawn in establishment chain studies (Benito and Welch, 1997). In the Uppsala school tradition (Johanson and Wiedersheim-Paul, 1975; Johanson and Vahlne, 1977), a sales agency is considered to be a low commitment operation mode. In many cases the entrant firm allows the agent to drive the foreign market activity, only visiting the agent infrequently and relying on the agent to undertake translation of relevant manuals and promotional material. Such an approach is sometimes an outcome of the fact that it is the foreign agent who initiates initial involvement, spotting the local market potential for a foreign product or service (Roberts and Senturia, 1996). However, the way in which a company uses the agency operation prior to the overall mode switch may be very different from its starting pattern, even to the point of quasi-integration. A company may have actively developed

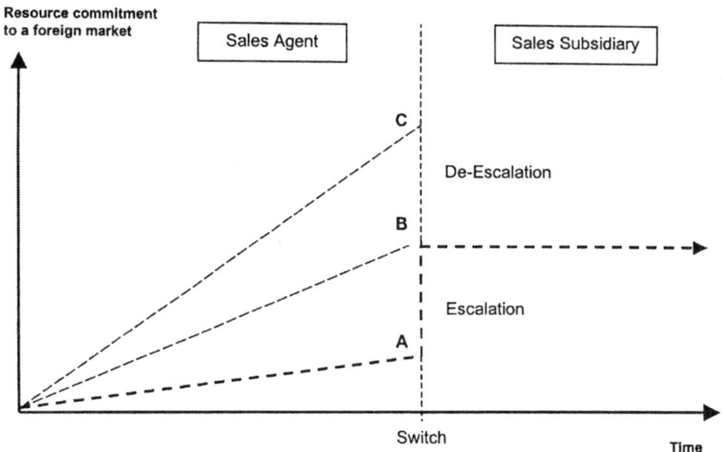

Figure 2.3 Resource commitment development and mode switch: three different developments

its operations in a foreign market in close cooperation with its agent. This may include extended promotional support for the agent, a training programme for agency staff, frequent visits and even placement of its own staff with the agent (as was the case for two of the Danish companies). In this situation, the establishment of a sales subsidiary may have negligible implications in terms of additional resource commitment. In effect most of the advance has already occurred within the existing mode format (see point B in Figure 2.3). The switch from sales agent to sales subsidiary may even entail a lower resource commitment by the exporter. Suppose the exporter has invested heavily in its agency operation as a base for export then switches to a sales subsidiary, but that this is poorly supported and is staffed on a part-time basis only, providing a very limited service to customers. In this situation it is conceivable that the switch to a sales subsidiary can be viewed as a de-escalation in terms of resource commitment of the entrant firm (point C in Figure 2.3). In our study of Danish companies' mode switches in South-East Asia, a highly minimalist approach to the establishment of sales offices in Singapore was found. In some cases the Danish company employee sent to staff the office was effectively working out of his apartment. Finnish research has indicated a wide range in types and uses of the sales subsidiaries of Finnish companies (Hentola, 1993). Thus, in assessing the significance of a mode switch from an internationalisation perspective, whatever the overt pattern much depends on the changes that have taken place prior to the formal switch, and also of the form of the 'new' mode. The essence of change is not simply captured by the existence of a mode switch.

Clearly, there is a danger in rushing to judgement about the nature of internationalisation processes based on only singular mode establishment chains that take no account of within mode changes. In general, there is a variety of ways of easing the path of mode switches that are not obvious in the overall form of operation mode. Thus, it was not uncommon among the observed Danish companies to hire staff from their former, or current, agent to facilitate the set-up and operation of a sales subsidiary. As reported in the study, cooperative forms of association with the agent may be used after the sales subsidiary set-up, representing a type of organic extension of the existing arrangement, as a way of easing the demands and risks associated with the mode switch. As indicated above, sales subsidiaries can also be set up in a form that minimises the degree of commitment of the company.

CONCLUSION

The nature of the establishment chain as it has been depicted, while a useful device for conceptualising and studying internationalisation in a broad sense, may be inadequate for exposing the nuances and character of firms' resource commitment to foreign markets. It may even have acted as an inhibitor on the analysis of the underlying processes that were the focus of the early research on internationalisation.

The study of Danish companies' internationalisation in South-East Asia indicated that they were using a number of approaches to easing the path of mode development, including within mode changes and mode additions, which would not have been apparent in normal establishment chain studies. In some cases this was part of a deliberate process of establishing the base for a later switch to another operation mode, preeminently foreign representative to sales subsidiary. The Danish experience demonstrated that incrementalism in internationalisation, as identified through mode development, may be an important component in the role of mode additions, and that therefore needs more thorough empirical investigation in internationalisation studies.

In general, there seems to be a need for more fine-grained entry mode studies where the level of analysis is the individual business activity rather than broad business functions. Such studies should come closer to the practice and decision-making of managers of international firms.

NOTES

[1] *Resource commitment* refers to the level of dedicated assets – physical or human – that cannot be transferred from one country to another without loss of economic value (Vernon, 1979; Randøy, 1997). As an example, an exporting firm may adapt its products to the specific needs of the customers or authorities in the importing country. The product adaptation represents a dedicated (country-specific) asset inasmuch as it generates additional sales revenue in one specific foreign country, but does not fit the demand requirements of other foreign countries.

REFERENCES

Andersen, Otto (1993), 'On the Internationalization Process of Firms: A Critical Analysis', *Journal of International Business Studies,* **24** (2), 209–31.

Beamish, Paul W., Allen Morrison and Philip M. Rosenzweig (1997), *International Management* (3rd edn), Chicago: Irwin.

Bell, Jim (1995), 'The Internationalisation of Small Computer Software Firms – A Further Challenge to "Stage" Theories', *European Journal of Marketing*, **29** (8), 60–75.

Benito, Gabriel R.G. and Lawrence S. Welch (1994), 'Foreign Market Servicing: Beyond Choice of Entry Mode', *Journal of International Marketing*, **2** (2), 7–27.

Benito, Gabriel R.G. and Lawrence S. Welch (1997), 'De-internationalisation', *Management International Review*, **37** (2), Special Issue, 7–25.

Björkman, Ingemar and Michael Eklund (1996), 'The Sequences of Operational Modes Used by Finnish Investors in Germany', *Journal of International Marketing*, **4** (4), 33–55.

Björkman, Ingemar and Mats Forsgren (1997), 'Nordic Contributions to International Business Research', in I. Björkman and M. Forsgren (eds), *The Nature of the International Firm*, Copenhagen: Copenhagen Business School Press.

Bonaccorsi, Andrea and Daniele Dalli (1992), 'Internationalisation Process and Entry Channels: Evidence from Small Italian Exporters', in J. Cantwell (ed.), *Proceedings of the 18th Annual EIBA Conference*, University of Reading, pp. 509–26.

Buckley, Peter J., Gerald D. Newbould and Jane C. Thurwell (1988), *Foreign Direct Investment by Smaller UK Firms: The Success and Failure of First-time Investors Abroad*, London: Macmillan Press.

Buckley, Peter J. and Pervez N. Ghauri (eds) (1999), *The Internationalization of the Firm*. London: Thomson International Business Press.

Clark, Timothy, Derek S. Pugh and Geoff Mallory (1997), 'The Process of Internationalisation in the Operating Firm', *International Business Review*, **6** (6), 605–23.

Easton, Geoff and Zhi X. Li (1993), 'The Dynamics of Export Channels – A Case Study of Exporting from the UK to The People's Republic of China', research paper presented at the 9th IMP Conference in Bath, UK.

Erminio, Fina and Alan M. Rugman (1996), 'A Test of Internationalization Theory: The Upjohn Company', *Management International Review*, **36** (3), 199–213.

Grønhaug, Kjell and Olav Kvitastein (1993), 'Distributional Involvement in International Strategic Business Units', *International Business Review,* **2** (1), 1–14.

Haakonsson, Haakon and Ivan Snehota (1995), *Developing Relationships in Business Network*, London: Routledge.

Hagen, James M. and Jean-Francois Hennart (1995), 'Foreign Production: The Weak Link in Tests of the Internationalization Process Model', competitive paper presented at the AIB 1995 meeting in Seoul, Korea.

Hedlund, Gunnar and Adne Kverneland (1985), 'Are Strategies for Foreign Markets Changing? The Case of Swedish Investment in Japan', *International Studies of Management & Organization*, **XV** (2), 41–59.

Hentola, Helena (1994), 'Foreign Sales Subsidiaries and Their Role Within the Internationalization of the Firm: A study of Finnish Manufacturing Companies', doctoral dissertation, The Helsinki School of Economics and Business Administration.

Hirsch, Seev and Avi Meshulach (1991), 'Towards a Unified Theory of Internationalisation', in *Proceedings of the 17th Annual EIBA Conference (Vol. 1),* Copenhagen Business School, pp. 577–601.

Johanson, Jan and Finn Wiedersheim-Paul (1975), 'The Internationalization of the Firm: Four Swedish Cases', *Journal of Management Studies*, **12** (3), 305–22.

Johanson, Jan and Jan-Erik Vahlne (1977), 'The Internationalization Process of the Firm: A Model of Knowledge Development and Increasing Foreign Market Commitment', *Journal of International Business Studies*, **8** (Third Quarter), 23–32.

Johanson, Jan and Jan-Erik Vahlne (1990), 'The Mechanism of Internationalisation', *International Marketing Review*, **7** (4), 11–24.

Juul, Monika and Peter G.P. Walters (1987), 'The Internationalisation of Norwegian Firms – A Study of the UK Experience', *Management International Review*, **27** (1), 58–66.

Knight, Gary A. and Tamer S. Cavusgil (1996), 'The Born Global Firm: A Challenge to Traditional Internationalization Theory', *Advances in International Marketing*, **8**, 11–26.

Luostarinen, Reijo (1979), *Internationalization of the Firm: An Empirical Study of the Internationalisation of Firms with Small and Open Domestic Markets, with Special Emphasis on Lateral Rigidity as a Behavioral Characteristic in Strategic Decision-making*, Helsinki School of Economics: Series A, No. 30.

Luostarinen, Reijo, Heli Korhonen, J. Jokinen and T. Pelkonen (1994), *Globalisation and SMEs*, Ministry of Trade and Industry, Finland, Helsinki.

Madsen, Tage K. and Per Servais (1997), 'The Internationalisation of Born Globals: an Evolutionary Process?', *International Business Review*, **6** (6), 561–4.

Millington, Andrew and Brian Bayliss (1990), 'The Process of Internationalisation: UK Companies in the EC', *Management International Review*, **30** (2), 151–61.

Moxon, Richard W. (1982), 'Offshore Sourcing, Subcontracting, and Manufacturing', in Ingo Walter (ed.), *Handbook of International Business*, New York: John Wiley and Sons.

Petersen, Bent (1996), 'Explaining Cost-effective Export Market Penetration via Foreign Intermediaries,' Ph.D. Thesis, Ph.D. Series 4.96, Copenhagen: Copenhagen Business School.

Petersen, Bent and Lawrence S. Welch (forthcoming), 'Foreign Operation Mode Combinations and Internationalisation', *Journal of Business Research*, Special Issue: Marketing in the Next Millenium.

Porter, Michael E. (1985), *Competitive Advantage*, New York: Free Press.

Randøy, Trond (1997), 'Towards a Firm-Based Model of Foreign Direct Investment', in I. Björkman and M. Forsgren (eds), *The Nature of the International Firm*, Copenhagen: Copenhagen Business School Press, pp. 257–80.

Roberts, E.B. and T.A. Senturia (1996), 'Globalizing the Emerging High Technology Company', *Industrial Marketing Management*, **25** (6), 491–506.

Valla, Jean-Paul (1986), 'The French Approach to Europe', in P.W. Turnbull and J-P. Valla (eds), *Strategies for International Industrial Marketing*, London: Croom Helm, pp. 11–41.

Van Den Bulcke, Daniel (1986), 'Role and Structure of Belgian Multinationals', in K. Marcharzina and W.H. Staehle (eds), *European Approaches to International Management*, Berlin: Walter de Gruyter, pp. 105–28.

Vernon, Raymond (1979), 'The Product Cycle Hypothesis in a New International Environment', *Oxford Bulletin of Economics and Statistics*, **41** (2), 255–67.

Williamson, Peter J. (1992), 'Europe's Single Market: The Toughest Test Yet for Sales and Distribution', *The Economist Intelligence Unit: Multinational Business,* (Summer), 57–76.

Yin, R.K. (1994), *Case Study Research: Design and Method* (2nd edn). Thousand Oaks: Sage Publications.

APPENDIX

Table 2A.1 Main characteristics of various foreign operation modes of market-seeking MNCs.

Foreign operation mode	Business function	Control/ operator	Location
Production subsidiary	Manufacturing operations etc.	Entrant firm	Foreign country
Licensing	Manufacturing operations	Outside agent	Foreign country
Joint venture	Manufacturing operations etc.	Entrant firm + outside agent	Foreign country
Turnkey contracts	Manufacturing set-up	Entrant firm	Home/Foreign country
Management contract	Management operations	Entrant firm	Foreign country
Franchising	Retail marketing	Outside agent	Foreign country
Export	Manufacturing operations	Entrant firm	Home country
Export via home-based sales force	Business marketing	Entrant firm	Home country
Export via sales subsidiary/ branch	Business marketing	Entrant firm	Foreign country
Export via agent/distributor	Business marketing	Outside agent	Foreign country

Table 2A.2 Key data of the companies participating in the study (1996)

Company	Main product(s)	Most recent establishment	Employees	Sales (m DKK)	Export (%)
A'Gramkow Group	Filling and recycling equipment for automotive industry	Regional HQ, Singapore (1996)	205	250	98
B-K Medical	Ultrasound scanners	Regional HQ, Thailand (1995)	241	229	95
Dampa	Ceiling systems	Regional HQ, Malaysia (1997)	180	104	> 80
Danfoss	Refrigeration, heating and motion control systems	Sales subsidiary, Philippines (1997) Sales branch, Indonesia (1997)	18 270	13 202	> 90
Densit	Industrial floors	Regional HQ, Malaysia (1995)	68	88	> 90
F.L.Schmidt & Co	Plants for cement production	Sales branch, Philippines (1997)	1 193	3 499	95
Grundfos	Pumps	Regional HQ, Thailand (1993)	9 154	6 682	> 95
Jensen Group	Equipment for flat-work and folders for towels and garments	Regional HQ, Singapore (1993)	450	375	> 95
Kompan	Toys for playgrounds	Regional HQ, Singapore (1996)	496	550	95
Lego Group	Toys	Regional HQ, Singapore (1997)	8 671	7 616	99
MD Foods	Dairy products	Regional HQ, Malaysia (1995)	13 122	23 141	65
Nikomed	EKG-electrodes and products used for fixation	Regional HQ, Singapore (1996)	227	n/a	90-95
Niro	Plants for processing liquid, particulate and solid materials	Sales subsidiary, Thailand (1994) Sales subsidiary, Philippines (1995)	423	946	95
RE Groups	Digital equipment, video/audio codec	Regional HQ, Malaysia (1995)	197	248	99
Skako	Plants for concrete production	Regional HQ, Malaysia (1996)	407	411	85-90
Toftejorg	Equipment for cleaning of containers and tanks	Regional HQ, Singapore (1995)	70	107	90

3. Patterned Growth? The Dynamics of Multinational Expansion

Elizabeth Maitland, Elizabeth L. Rose and Stephen Nicholas*

INTRODUCTION

After 25 years of research into internationalisation, the dynamics of MNE growth remain poorly understood. Firms internationalise by organising value-adding activities across national boundaries. Internationalisation thus requires the adaptation of firm strategy, resources, structure and organisation to new international environments (Welch and Luostarinen, 1988; Calof and Beamish, 1995). This process is inherently dynamic. Yet, internationalisation research has been focused on progression by stages. The empirical international business literature has been dominated by notions of 'transitioning', either through forms of overseas involvement (including exporting, agents, licences, alliances and hierarchy) or modes of market entry (the choice, within hierarchy, between greenfield investment and the acquisition of sales and production subsidiaries, whether joint ventures or wholly-owned). The theoretical models underpinning much of the empirical literature are comparatively static, focusing on the attributes of discrete arrangements within the internationalisation process.

The stages-based research has not dealt, explicitly, with the timing of investments. Understanding firm growth requires a multi-market and long-run time series approach, in order to uncover investment patterns. Using the Harvard Multinational Enterprises database, this chapter provides new empirical evidence on the timing of initial investments into host countries by US MNEs, and advances a new understanding of the dynamic patterns of MNE growth.

REVIEW OF THE LITERATURE

Johanson and Vahlne (1977) and Luostarinen (1977) initiated the stages approach, identifying sequential step models of overseas involvement. Based on case study evidence from Swedish steel, engineering and pulp and paper companies, Johanson and Vahlne explained the internationalisation of MNEs in terms of incremental increases in market-specific knowledge and experience and increased resource commitment to foreign markets. Archival work has uncovered similar patterns. For example, pre-1939 British MNEs switched from agency contracts to sales branches as foreign location information and market sales volumes grew (Nicholas, 1983; Wilkins, 1974). Recently, Andersson et al. (1997) placed acquisition within the process stages model. Acquisition behaviour was described as organic, building on the knowledge and relationships of previous involvement in an incremental fashion. Key variables in the acquisition process included the experiences shared between acquirer and acquired, and the acquirer's psychic distance, measured as the scope and depth of the acquirer's international experience.

There is contradictory evidence on whether MNEs routinely pass sequentially through the stages of exporting, agents, sales branches and production plants. Hedlund and Kverneland (1985) found that 44 per cent of the Swedish firms investing in Japan went from agents to production, without passing through intermediate stages. Newbould et al. (1978) noted that 84 per cent of a sample of firms investing in the USA formed a sales branch after investing in a production plant (cited in Calof and Beamish, 1995). A Bureau of Industry Economics (1984) report on 228 Australian FDIs found that only 39 per cent of the firms had prior country involvement. Ayal and Raben (1997), Turnbull (1987) and Millington and Bayliss (1990) also found little empirical support for the stages process, although Luostarinen (1979) and Kwon and Hu (1995) provided supporting empirical evidence for a staged internationalisation process (cited in Andersen, 1997). More recently, Calof and Beamish (1995), in a study of 38 Canadian firms, with 121 form changes, found that only 52 per cent were single-step incremental stages.

Scholars studying internalisation have also been concerned with the dynamics of selecting forms of overseas involvement. Within the Coasean paradigm, internalisation initially focused on the MNE as an alternative contractual form to transacting in the market (Hymer, 1976; Buckley and Casson, 1976; Dunning, 1977). Following Williamson (1979), Casson (1979), and Hennart (1982), internalisation was widened into a transaction cost-agency perspective, incorporating a range of intermediate forms of overseas involvement (such as licences, franchises, alliances and long-term contracting) as well as markets and hierarchy. Reviewing MNE and FDI theory, Calvert (1981) recognised the static nature of the internalisation paradigm, noting the need to analyse the forces that move economic transactions to be internalised or externalised. Buckley (1983, 1988, 1990) expanded on this deficiency, labelling the internalisation model a concept in search of a theory largely because of its failure to explain the transition from one mode (internal or external) to the other. Similarly, Teece (1985) argued that the literature on the MNE, whether emphasising market power or efficiency, suffered from a common deficiency: under emphasis on dynamics.

More recently, transaction cost models have been extended to entry mode choices, including greenfield subsidiaries and acquisitions, both joint venture and wholly-owned (Hennart 1988, 1991; Kogut, 1988). However, empirical work has not generally differentiated between choices of form and choices of entry mode, with most empirical studies focusing only on entry mode. In an early entry mode study, Dubin (1975) found that US MNEs tended to choose greenfield entry when the firm was large, had foreign experience and was targeting a developing country (cited in Kogut and Singh, 1988; Wilson, 1980). Using the Harvard MNE database, Davidson (1980) and Davidson and McFetridge (1984) discovered that internal versus market transfer depended on experience, the nature of the technology, R&D intensity and host country characteristics. Also using the Harvard database, Wilson (1980) noted that greenfield entry was facilitated by experience and the capacities to deal with host governments, adjust technology and production techniques and reformulate marketing strategies. Collecting firm-specific data on 138 foreign entrants into the USA, Caves and Mehra (1986) found the entrant's corporate organisation and the structural traits of its product market drove entry mode choice. Experience favoured acquisition over greenfield, due to the parent's knowledge of routinised processes of international expansion through seeking and making acquisitions.

In a study of new ventures versus acquisitions by Swedish MNEs, Zejan (1990) argued that product line diversification encouraged, and industry growth discouraged, acquisition, while experience was insignificant. Using data on 1000 Swedish affiliates over three decades, Andersson and Svensson (1994) discovered that firms with relatively more organisational skills favoured acquisition, while those with relatively higher technological skills favoured greenfield investments. Andersson and Svensson's results were consistent with Caves and Mehra's (1986) argument that experience in routinised processes of expanding internationally encouraged acquisitions. Along similar lines, Belderbos and Sleuwaegen (1996) tested a choice model on Japanese domestic firms that exported, MNEs investing in Asia, and MNEs investing in the West, using firm-specific data. They found that inter-firm horizontal and vertical links replaced firm-specific experience for

Japanese MNEs investing in Asia and explained location-specific form choices within a transaction cost framework.

In a study of greenfield investment versus acquisition for Japanese manufacturers in the USA, Hennart and Park (1992) provided a full model of entry mode choice, including governance factors (knowledge, experience and scope economies), location factors (scale economies, transport, production and tariff and non-tariff costs), and strategic factors (collusion, follow-the-leader, competitive dynamics and exchange of threat). In that study, greenfield investment was favoured when the scale of the US operation was small, the product was already produced in Japan and the parent firm was more research intensive. When market growth was rapid, permitting assets to be accumulated quickly without adding to industry capacity, acquisition was favoured. This finding supports those of Caves and Mehra (1986). Diversification and experience were not significant in the Hennart and Park study, counter to the results of Caves and Mehra (1986) and Wilson (1980), but consistent with those of Zejan (1990).

The choice between partially and wholly-owned subsidiaries has also been studied. Using the Harvard MNE database, Gatignon and Anderson (1988) modelled, sequentially, the choice between wholly-owned (integration) and partnership (shared ownership) entry and the choice among various levels of partial ownership. This study showed that wholly-owned subsidiaries were preferred to shared ownership when the firm had higher R&D and advertising intensities, a smaller scale of operations and faced lower country risk (see also Anderson and Gatignon, 1986). Kogut and Singh (1988) investigated Wilson's (1980) finding regarding the impact of nationality, studying joint ventures and acquisitions for MNEs investing in the USA between 1981 and 1985, and found that cultural distance and asset size were significant in the choice of entry mode, but that prior experience was not. Considering Japanese subsidiaries in the USA, Hennart (1991) found that joint ventures were preferred when market growth was rapid and the firm was diversified, but that wholly-owned subsidiaries were favoured when the Japanese MNEs were experienced in the USA. Hennart concluded that Japanese MNEs were driven by the same general factors as their US counterparts in terms of investment strategies. This conclusion differs from those of Wilson (1980), Kogut and Singh (1988), and Belderbos and Sleuwaegen (1996).

While much of the empirical literature has focused on initial entry form and mode choices, Kogut (1983) differentiated between decisions regarding the initial establishment of a subsidiary in a host country and those associated with subsequent investments. Rejecting the more narrow focus in which FDI is viewed as a decision made at a discrete point in time, Kogut (1983, 1993) and Kogut and Chang (1991) viewed the MNE as a set of resource options that can be allocated to different locations, depending on the firm's organisational experience gained through coordinating a network of international subsidiaries. Expanding on the sequential approach, Chang's (1995) empirical results showed that Japanese electronic firms in the USA generally made small core investments before moving into more distant lines of business on a larger scale, utilising learning gained from prior entries. Chang and Rosenzweig (1998) showed that industry effects dominated region of origin effects for European and Japanese chemical and electronic MNEs making sequential investments into new lines of business.

By emphasising that the initial investment generates future options for subsequent investments, the sequential approach identified the importance of incorporating strategic decision-making and international rivalry into models of firm growth. This has also been recognised in the empirical work on form and entry mode choice. For example, the disappointing results of their partial ownership model led Gatignon and Anderson (1988) to argue that the long-term versus short-term nature of executives' decision-making approaches should be integrated into models. Kogut and Singh (1988) called for further studies of culturally-based decision-making criteria and Hennart and Park (1992)identified the need to assess the judgements of top executives. Kim and Hwang (1992), who introduced global strategic variables to explain the choice of wholly-owned firms over licensing, suggested that their results reinforced in executives' minds the importance of expanding entry decision variables to include global strategic factors. Kogut and Singh (1988) and Hennart and Park (1992) argued that executives were already well aware of this concept. More recently, Calof and Beamish (1995) found that changes in managers' attitudes provided strong explanatory power for mode choice changes.

Strategic FDI decision-making turns not only on internal dynamics, but also on the dynamics of market competition. The taxonomies of inter-firm rivalry address strategic motivations for firms' seeking involvement in foreign markets. Approaches such as Knickerbocker's (1973) 'follow-the-leader', Graham's (1978) 'exchange of threats', Sann-Randaccio's (1990) 'non-provocative firm growth' and Acocella's (1991) 'monopolisation' describe the behaviour of MNEs in oligopolistic markets, which provide opportunities for the appropriation of rents. Vernon (1966), Flowers (1976), Graham (1974, 1978), Yu and Ito (1988) and Rose and Ito (1999) investigated firms in oligopolistic industries and found that those operating in domestic oligopolies have a high propensity for investing overseas. Recent research in multiple-point competition has considered the multi-market actions of rivals and indicates that MNEs devise strategies of both 'mutual forbearance' and head-on competition (Ito and Rose, 1998). As MNE oligopolistic rivals match or avoid each others' investments, consolidating international markets provide dynamic evidence of MNE growth and decline.

While the extant literature has highlighted many aspects of firms' international expansion paths, a necessary, but neglected, precursor to modelling the dynamics of internationalisation is an examination of patterns in the timing of MNEs' initial FDI entries into individual countries. There are two possibilities: firms display 'standard' patterns in their initial investments in countries, or firms exhibit different timing with respect to their first investments. Several authors have identified bunching in investment activities. The early studies on inter-firm rivalry by Knickerbocker (1973) noted the bunching of foreign investment by US MNEs. Using a sample of 448 pre-1939 British MNEs, Nicholas (1991) found that nearly 60 per cent invested in two or more countries in the same year. Archival case studies of British MNEs revealed that plant investment decisions were concentrated within a very few years (Nicholas and Maitland, forthcoming). Preliminary studies of Japanese MNEs in the 1950s-80s also uncovered evidence that some firms tended to invest in several countries in the same year (Nicholas and Maitland, 1999).

The notion of bunching of initial investment is the focus of this chapter. We use the methodology of statistical process control to identify non-random patterns in the initial manufacturing investments of US MNEs through time. Initial investments are operationalised as the firm's first direct manufacturing investment in a country. If a parent firm has established multiple manufacturing subsidiaries (subsequent investment) in a particular country, only the oldest of the subsidiaries is included in the study. Our analysis uncovers two patterns of investment behaviour. Some firms display no systematic patterns in the distribution of their initial investments. Other firms cluster their investments, which results in non-random variation. The clustering provides clues to the dynamics of firm growth. We demonstrate the methodology for identifying degrees of clustering, and advance preliminary explanations for the clustering phenomenon, or variations of investment strategies, based on a long-run perspective.

METHODOLOGY

Methodological Issues and Statistical Process Control

Strictly qualitative assessment of patterns in initial overseas investment through time has severe limitations. The visual assessment of patterns in time series data is notoriously difficult, and the resulting low inter-rater reliability casts considerable uncertainty on any conclusions derived from such an approach. Therefore, this study proposes a quantitative measure of clustering. A well-established numerical measure and an understanding of its distributional properties will permit statistically justifiable comparisons of clustering levels across firms, along with the development of models to investigate the determinants of clustering activities. This research takes the first steps toward the development of such a measure.

A useful quantitative measure of clustering must capture the dynamic nature of the problem, and it must incorporate a consideration of both within- and between-year clustering. Within-year clustering is typified by a firm's establishing several new subsidiaries in a single year. Between-year clustering considers the time series nature of the data and is characterised by a firm's making repeated consecutive annual investments. A robust measure must also incorporate variation in the time periods of firms' multinational operations (for example, one firm with a 10-year history of overseas investment and another with a 50-year history).

The methodology used to develop the clustering measure employs control charts, which form the basis of statistical process control (SPC). Although there is a strong tendency to think of SPC only in the context of quality control in a manufacturing environment, the analytic tools are applicable to virtually any type of process (Roberts, 1993). FDI through time is readily viewed as a process. The SPC methodology is particularly appropriate for this application, because it identifies the presence of non-random patterns over time by incorporating the time series aspect of the data and both the location and variation of the process.

Statistical process control is a well-established methodology, originally developed for manufacturing applications by Shewhart (1931). Its fundamental concept is the differentiation between two different types of variation: 'special cause' and 'common cause'. Common cause variation represents the dispersion that is inherent in the process when it is running at steady state. Special cause variation is associated with non-random behaviour in the process.[1] SPC is based on striking a reasonable balance between over-reacting to common cause variation and under-reacting to special cause variation.[2] In the context of the clustering application, over-reacting to common cause variation would result in identifying a non-existent cluster.

Development of the Clustering Measure

Of the many types of control charts in the SPC repertoire, the zone chart is used for this application. The zone chart is an adaptation of more widely employed control charts (for example, *X*-bar (means) and *I* (individuals) charts) for studying process data, and was selected because its structure permits the development of a numerical measure of clustering for individual parent firms.

Construction of a zone chart for initial investments by an MNE begins with a time series plot of the number of investments in each year. Only the firm's first investments in each country are considered; subsequent investments in a country are omitted. For each firm, year 1 is the year of the MNE's first overseas subsidiary establishment, and year *n* is that of the last initial investment in the sample. The mean value of the firm's initial investments per year is computed, along with the standard error. The standard error is computed based on the average moving range of pairs of consecutive observations, which is regarded as a robust measure of dispersion.

On the time series plot, the following seven lines are added: the mean, and the mean ± one, two and three estimated standard errors. Each observation (number of investments in a given year) contributes points that are used to compute the clustering measure. The points are based on both the individual observation's distance from the mean and its contribution to a potential non-random pattern in the time series. The points based on distance from the mean are assigned as follows:

Location of observation	Points
Within one standard error of mean	0
Between one and two standard errors above or below mean	2
Between two and three standard errors above or below mean	4
More than three standard errors above or below mean	8

This point allocation has been demonstrated to be robust, in terms of the trade-off between over-reacting to common cause variation and under-reacting to special cause variation (Davis et al. 1990).

The points scheme shown above captures the within-year variation in investment. Considering each observation in the context of those close to it captures the between-year variation. For consecutive observations on the same side of the mean, the points for each observation are added to those associated with the previous point. The accumulation continues until an observation falls on the other side of the mean. When the mean is crossed, the accumulation process recommences from zero.

An example may clarify the points scheme. Figure 3.1 shows a zone chart constructed for initial foreign direct investments by Company A. Its first overseas subsidiary was established in the United Kingdom in 1952. Subsequent FDI activities resulted in subsidiaries in Europe, Japan, Central and South America, Canada and Australia.

Figure 3.1 covers a 22-year time span. The mean number of new investments by Company A over the time period was 0.727 subsidiaries per year, with an estimated standard error for the number of new subsidiaries per year of 0.675. The chart indicates that Company A made no new overseas investments in years 2, 3, 5, 10, 11 and 15-21. One new foreign subsidiary was established in each of the following years: 1, 4, 6, 8 and 22.

Years 7 and 12–14 each saw the establishment of two new overseas subsidiaries and year 9 was the firm's most active year for FDI, with three new subsidiaries.

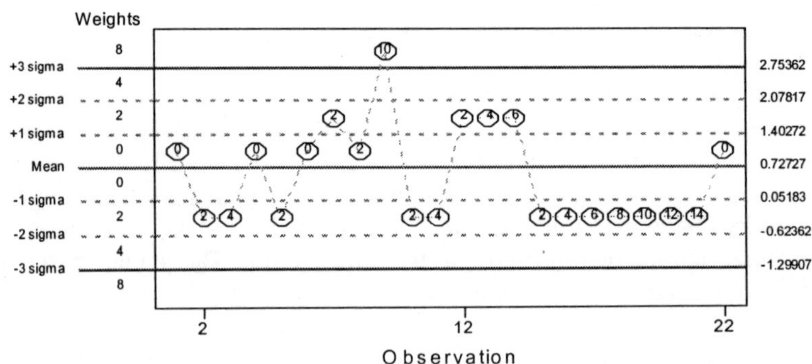

Figure 3.1 Zone chart for Company A

The points associated with each observation are shown on the zone chart. Table 3.1 details the point allocation scheme for this data set. For example, the single investment in year 1 is within one standard error of the mean, so the observation attracts no points. Year 2 had no new investment, which is between one and two standard errors below the mean, so it attracts two points. Year 3 was also without investment. As the observation falls on the same side of the mean as its predecessor, its own two-point contribution is added to that from year 2, resulting in a point total for year 3 of four points. The summation for this 'run' is stopped at year 4, when the mean line is crossed. Similar summations occur in years 6–9, 10–11, 12–14 and 15–21.

Following the construction of the zone chart, using the Minitab statistical package, the clustering measure, *C*, is computed as the mean of the points associated with each year. For Company A, the sum of the points (i.e., the sum of the far right column in Table 3.1) is 96, yielding $C = 96/22 = 4.36$. Theoretically, $0 \leq C \leq \infty$, where higher values represent stronger clustering of investments. This simple measure can be seen to meet the desirable criteria discussed earlier. It captures the dynamic nature of the process by incorporating the effects of both within- and between-year variation, and is comparable for firms with different numbers of years of FDI experience.

Table 3.1 Point allocation for Company A

Year	Number of investments in that year	Standard errors from the mean	Points associated with individual observation	Cross the mean?	Total points associated with observation
1	1	0–1	0		0
2	0	1–2	2	Yes	2
3	0	1–2	2	No	2 + 2 = 4
4	1	0–1	0	Yes	0
5	0	1–2	2	Yes	2
6	1	0–1	0	Yes	0
7	2	1–2	2	No	0 + 2 = 2
8	1	0–1	0	No	2 + 0 = 2
9	3	3+	8	No	2 + 8 = 10
10	0	1–2	2	Yes	2
11	0	1–2	2	No	2 + 2 = 4
12	2	1–2	2	Yes	2
13	2	1–2	2	No	2 + 2 = 4
14	2	1–2	2	No	4 + 2 = 6
15	0	1–2	2	Yes	2
16	0	1–2	2	No	2 + 2 = 4
17	0	1–2	2	No	4 + 2 = 6
18	0	1–2	2	No	6 + 2 = 8
19	0	1–2	2	No	8 + 2 = 10
20	0	1–2	2	No	10 + 2 = 12
21	0	1-2	2	No	12 + 2 = 14
22	1	0–1	0	Yes	0

DATA ANALYSIS

A subset of the Harvard Multinational Enterprises database is employed to demonstrate the use of the clustering measure, *C*. This database includes information on US-based multinational firms and their FDI activities, covering a period of pre-1901 through 1975. The database is well established, and has been employed in many previously published studies (e.g., Gatignon and Anderson, 1988; Gomes-Casseres, 1989). For this exploratory analysis, we consider only subsidiaries established to operate primarily in the manufacturing sector, including manufacturing, assembling and packaging activities.

We are interested in studying the phenomenon of clustering in MNEs' initial entry into countries, based on annual data. This subset of the Harvard database yields data on 181 parent firms. The initial investments, all prior to 1976, consist of a total of 3444 manufacturing subsidiaries in 119 different nations, with Canada, the UK, Mexico, France, Germany and Australia as the six most frequent destinations. The time span between first and last investments ranges from 3 years to over 74, with a mean of 44.3 years.

It should be noted that this analysis represents a first step toward investigating two issues. First, we need to evaluate whether or not the proposed clustering measure functions well. This process will involve extensive qualitative comparisons of the numerical cluster measure with plots of the number of annual investments for individual MNEs. Second, we need to develop an understanding of the empirical sampling distribution of the clustering statistic to enable statistically defensible assessments of which values of C correspond to 'high' and 'low' levels of clustering. Studying a sample of 181 firms represents the necessary first step in this development process.

The clustering measure, C, is computed for each of the 181 parent firms. A histogram of the computed measures is shown as Figure 3.2. The sample distribution of the clustering measure is quite skewed, with large variation. For this sample, the mean value of C is 3.59, the median is 1.21 and the

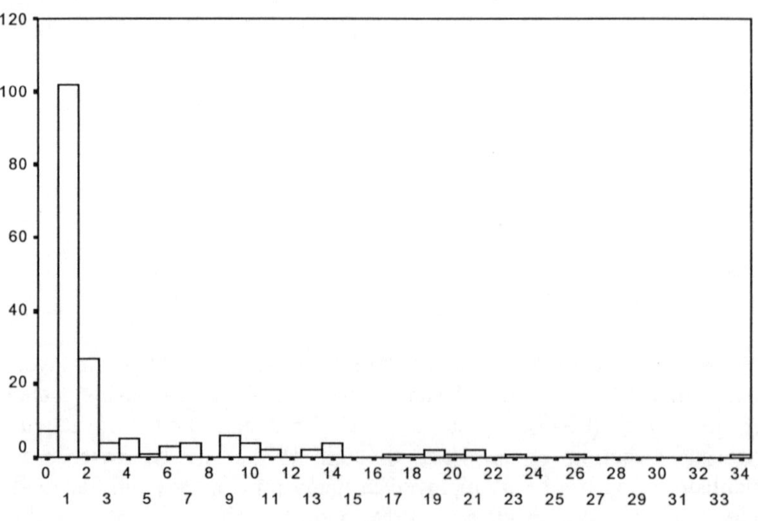

Figure 3.2 Histogram of computed values of C

standard deviation is 5.54. A 95 per cent confidence interval for the mean is (2.78, 4.40). The computed values of C range from 0.17 to 34.47, and the 25th and 75th percentiles are 0.90 and 2.45, respectively. In the context of this sample, Company A, with $C = 4.26$, shows fairly strong evidence of clustering.

Some examples of higher and lower levels of clustering, based on this measure, may be enlightening. Parent firm #41 in the Harvard MNE database has a 24-year span between the establishment of its first overseas manufacturing subsidiary and its last one prior to 1976. Figure 3.3 shows a bar chart of the firm's initial investment pattern, which reveals a fairly even spread across the 24 years. This pattern corresponds to a clustering measure of $C = 0.5$, which is in the lowest quartile of the sample distribution. In contrast, parent firm #139 has a 47-year span for its initial investments, as shown in Figure 3.4. The pattern for this firm, which shows a flurry of FDI activity in the last quarter of the time frame, yields $C = 17.1$, indicating a high degree of clustering.

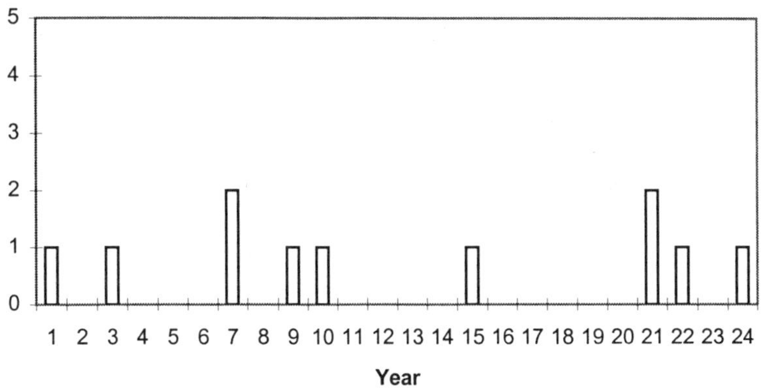

Figure 3.3 Initial investment history for parent firm #41

Study of the patterns for highly-clustered firms indicate the existence of three different modes of clustering, which we call 'concentration', 'hibernation' and 'hybrid'. The concentration mode refers to multiple investments in single years. For example, parent firm #139 made three initial investments in year 34 and four in year 35 (see Figure 3.4); this is evidence of concentration clustering. Figure 3.5 shows the bar chart for parent firm #593. With $C = 11.5$, this MNE shows evidence of very strong clustering activity. Inspection indicates that the form of the clustering is quite different. This firm displays the hibernation mode of clustering, with small clusters of initial FDI, surrounded by periods in which no initial investments were made. The chart for parent firm #509, shown in Figure 3.6, displays the hybrid mode, with evidence of both concentration and hibernation.

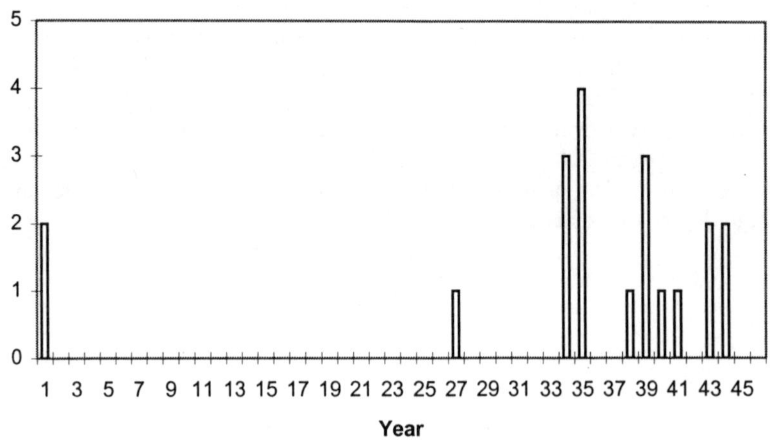

Figure 3.4 Initial investment history for parent firm #139

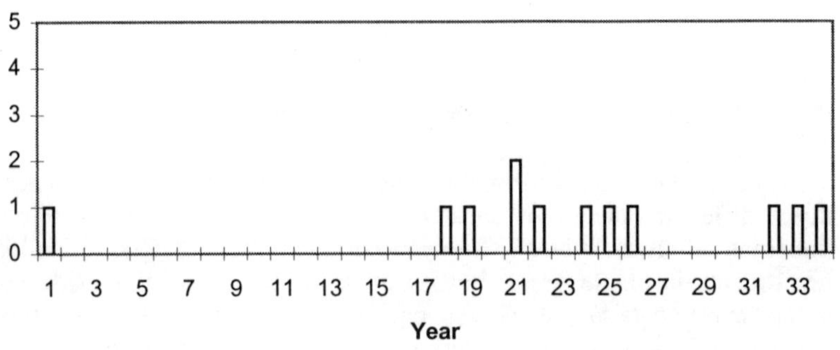

Figure 3.5 Initial investment history for parent firm #593

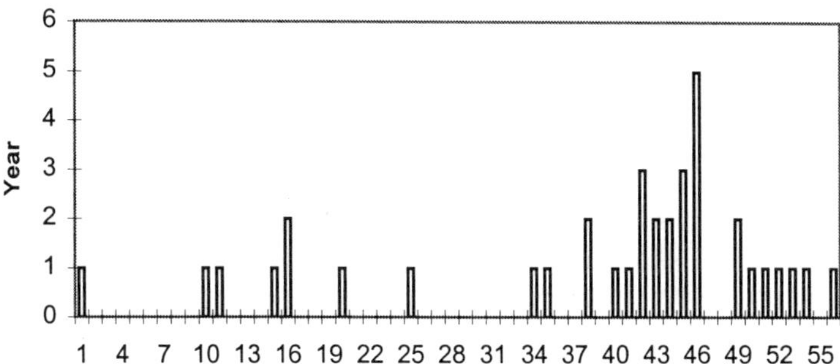

Figure 3.6 Initial investment history for parent firm #509

WHY DO FIRMS CLUSTER THEIR INVESTMENTS?

For the 181 US-based MNEs in our sample, there is a marginally significant relationship ($p < 0.10$) between *C* and the elapsed time between the first and the most recent (pre-1976) initial investment. A 1 per cent increase in the number of years of FDI experience is associated with an approximately 0.3 per cent increase in *C*. This result is consistent with a dynamic element implicit in much of the stages-based empirical literature, with its emphasis on experience and learning.

Several types of learning have been measured in the empirical literature. Knowledge can be gained through learning-by-doing in a specific market (measured by the number of subsidiaries or years operating in one country); such knowledge may well be transferable to new operations in different countries. There is also form-specific learning, proxied, for example, by the number of overseas branches operated by a firm. Finally, there is experience related to being an MNE, which is typically represented by the number of years a firm has operated internationally. Kogut (1990) used the concept of multinational coordination and network flexibility advantages to explain sequential investment within a country. However, network advantages are scope economies that also allow MNEs to make subsequent investments in other countries. In short, these different types of knowledge capabilities may allow a firm to cluster its investments.

The experience that allows clustering is likely to be tacit knowledge embodied in teams of managers. Our research on Australian investment in Asia provides evidence on decision-making related to new market FDI. A recent survey of Australian firms revealed that 67 per cent of those investing in Indonesia and 71 per cent of those investing in India used their experience in these markets to facilitate investment in other overseas projects. Market entry in each country was part of a broader global strategy for 76 per cent of the sample firms. The transfer of staff from one foreign operation to another by 19 per cent of the firms in the sample provides evidence that tacit learning was embedded in the human capital of the MNEs' managers. The study indicated that learning about investing in one country provided experience and information that were difficult to codify and were used for subsequent FDI in other countries.

The learning process by management teams and the firm is opaque, especially its relationship to the foreign investment decision (Aharoni, 1966). The concept of transnational firms, developed by Bartlett and Ghoshal (1989), emphasises path dependent growth related to the MNE's administrative heritage and organisational structures. Organisational designs that allow the development of cross-unit learning and network flexibility facilitate the acquisition of know-how that can be applied to international expansion.

The linkage between organisational history and learning in the FDI decision is an under-researched area. Recent organisational learning models have emphasised the practice of the firm's formal and informal routines, procedures, norms and culture (for example, Hedberg, 1981; Winter, 1987; Huber, 1991; Kim, 1993; Inkpen, 1995; Leroy and Ramanantsoa, 1997). Headquarters–subsidiary contact is likely to provide the opportunity for learning through frequent interactions, allowing new information to be generated and experiments to be undertaken. When knowledge related to organising, monitoring and assessing markets and subsidiaries is routinised within the firm, the ability to 'go abroad' can be institutionalised.

In line with these arguments, we posit that undertaking FDI creates serious administrative disruptions for firms, both in terms of changes to the parent's structure and the development of links with the new subsidiaries. These stresses would explain the stages of administrative structures that Stopford and Wells (1972) identified for MNEs. The administrative stresses should have differential impacts on firms. For example, the administrative disruption is likely to be more serious for integrated MNEs than for more national responsive MNEs. Further, some internal structures are more able to deal with administrative disruption. Under these circumstances, it is logical for management to embark on clustered FDI, in order to reduce the disruption and allow for a period during which the MNE 'digests' its new investments. This notion is consistent with evidence from our empirical results described above, where many clustering firms have long periods of hibernation.

In an effort to understand the possible rationales for clustering, some preliminary modelling was undertaken, using our sample of 181 parent firms. No simple industry effect was apparent; analysis of variance revealed no significant differences in the mean of C as a function of the parent firm's 2-digit SIC code. Further, clustering does not appear to be related to the aggregate US or global business cycles. Clustering MNEs did not tend to make multiple investments during the same years.

Evidence about the role of nationality and the generalisability of the measure awaits consideration of data from parent firms based outside the USA. Some very preliminary work on this issue has been encouraging, showing that the results from 20 large Japanese multinationals (Nicholas and Maitland, 1999) are consistent with those of the 181 US-based parent firms.

SUMMARY

This chapter has identified a dynamic process of MNE growth. Analysis using the methodology of statistical process control revealed two different patterns of growth. While some firms display random variation in the timing of their first investments into a host country, others display non-random variation, clustering their investments. Three types of clustering strategies were identified: concentrating, hibernating and hybrid (concentrate and hibernate). Preliminary arguments, based on organisation learning, experience, internal architecture and the translation of tacit know-how into firm capabilities, have been advanced to explain these findings. The use of the tools of statistical process control represents a unique application of this methodology in the international business literature, providing a statistical measure for the dynamics of MNE growth.

This research is preliminary in nature. The next step is to model the clustering process using firm-specific data on headquarters and subsidiaries. While the measure is only applied to first investments in this chapter, the clustering measure is applicable to other FDI processes, particularly sequential investment in a country.

NOTES

* The authors would like to thank Professor Lou Wells for access to the Harvard Multinational database. Research grants from the Australian

Research Council and the Economics and Commerce Faculty of the University of Melbourne provided the financial support for the research.

[1] Special and common cause variations are conceptually analogous to statistically significant and statistically insignificant differences, respectively, in sample data.

[2] In a manufacturing environment, over-reacting to common cause variation might result in excessive adjustment of machinery based on nonsignificant differences in the weight of a product. Unfortunately, such over-adjustment actually increases the process variation in the long run.

REFERENCES

Acocella, N. (1991), 'Strategic Foreign Investment in the EC', in J. Cantwell (ed.), *Multinational Investment and Modern Europe: Strategic Interaction in the Integrated Community*, Aldershot: Edward Elgar.

Aharoni, Y. (1966), *The Foreign Investment Decision Process*, Cambridge, MA: Harvard University Press.

Anderson, E. and H. Gatignon (1986), 'Modes of Foreign Entry: A Transaction Cost Analysis and Propositions', *Journal of International Business Studies*, **17** (3) 1–26.

Andersen, O. (1997), 'Internationalization and Market Entry Mode', *Management International Review*, **37** (2), 27–42.

Andersson, T. and R. Svensson (1994), 'Entry Modes for Direct Investment Determined by the Composition of Firm-specific Skills,' *Scandinavian Journal of Economics*, **98** (4), 551–60.

Andersson, U., J. Johanson and J.-E. Vahlne (1997), 'Organic Acquisitions in the internationalization process of the business firm', *Management International Review,* **37** (2) , 67–84.

Ayal, I. and J. Raban (1997), 'Export Management Structure and Successful High Technology Innovation', in S. Reid and P.J. Rosson (eds), *Managing Export Entry and Expansion,* New York: Praeger.

Bartlett, C.A. and S. Ghoshal (1989), *Managing Across Borders: The Transnational Solution,* Cambridge, MA: Harvard Business School Press.

Belderbos, R. and L. Sleuwaegen (1996), 'Japanese Firms and the Decision to Invest Abroad: Business Groups and Regional Core Networks', *Review of Economics and Statistics*, **78** (2), 214–20.

Buckley, P.J. (1983), 'New Theories of International Business: Some Unresolved Issues', in M. Casson (ed.), *The Growth of International Business,* London: George Allen and Unwin.

Buckley, P.J. (1988), 'Organisational Forms and Multinational Companies', in S. Thompson and M. Wright (eds), *Internal Organisation, Efficiency and Profit,* Oxford: Philip Allan.

Buckley, P.J. (1990), 'Problems and Developments in the Core Theory of International Business', *Journal of International Business Studies*, **21** (4), 657–66.

Buckley, P.J. and M. Casson (1976), *The Future of the Multinational Enterprise,* London: Macmillan.

Bureau of Industry Economics (1984), *Australian Direct Investment Abroad,* Canberra: Australian Government Printing Service.

Calof, J. and P. Beamish (1995), 'Adapting to Foreign Markets: Explaining Internationalization', *International Business Review,* **4** (2), 115–31.

Calvert, A. (1981), 'A Synthesis of Foreign Direct Investment Theories and Theories of the Multinational Firm', *Journal of International Business Studies*, **12** (1), 43–60.

Casson, M. (1979), *Alternatives to the Multinational Enterprise*, London: Macmillan.

Caves, R.E. and S.K. Mehra (1986), 'Entry of Foreign Multinationals into U.S. Manufacturing Industries', in M.E. Porter (ed.), *Competition in Global Industries,* Cambridge, MA: Harvard Business School Press.

Chang, S.-J. (1995), 'International Expansion Strategy of Japanese Firms: Capability Building through Sequential Entry', *Academy of Management Journal*, (38), 383–407.

Chang, S.-J. and P. Rosenzeig (1998), 'Industry and Regional Patterns in Sequential Foreign Market Entry', *Journal of Management Studies*, **38** (2), 797–822.

Davidson, W.H. (1980), 'The Location of Foreign Direct Investment Activity: Country Characteristics and Experience Effects', *Journal of International Business Studies*, **11** (2), 9–22.

Davidson, W.H. and D.G. McFetridge (1984), 'International Technology Transactions and the Theory of the Firm', *Journal of Industrial Economics,* **32** (3), 255–64.

Davis, R.B., A. Homer and W.H. Woodall (1990), 'Performance of the Zone Control Chart', *Communications in Statistics: Theory and Methods*, **19** (5), 1581–87.

Dubin, M. (1975), 'Foreign Acquisitions and the Spread of the Multinational Firm,' D.B.A. Thesis, Graduate School of Business Administration, Harvard University.

Dunning, J.H. (1977), 'Trade, Location of Economic Activity and the MNE: A Search for an Eclectic Approach', in B. Olin, P. Hesselborn and P. M. Wijkman (eds), *The International Allocation of Economic Activity: Proceedings of a Nobel Symposium held at Stockholm,* London: Macmillan.

Flowers, E.B. (1976), 'Oligopolistic Reactions in European and Canadian Direct Investment in the United States', *Journal of International Business Studies*, **7** (2), 43–55.

Gatignon, H. and E. Anderson (1988), 'The Corporation's Degree of Control over Foreign Subsidiaries: An Empirical Test of a Transaction Cost Explanation', *Journal of Law, Economics, and Organization*, **4** (2), 305–36.

Gomes-Casseres, B. (1989), 'Ownership Structures of Foreign Subsidiaries', *Journal of Economic Behavior and Organization*, **11** (1),1–25.

Graham, E. (1978), 'Transatlantic Investment by Multinational Firms: A Rivalistic Phenomenon', *Journal of Post-Keynesian Economics*, **20** (1), 82–99.

Graham, E. (1974), *Oligopolistic Imitation and European Direct Investment in the United States,* Cambridge, MA: Graduate School of Business Administration, Harvard University.

Hedberg, B. (1981), 'How Organizations Learn and Unlearn', in P. Nystrom and W. Starbuck (eds), *Handbook of Organizational Design,* London: Oxford University Press.

Hedlund, G. and A. Kverneland (1985), 'Are Strategies for Foreign Markets Changing? The Case of Swedish Investment in Japan', *International Studies of Management and Organization*, **15** (2), 41–59.

Hennart, J.-F. (1982), *A Theory of Multinational Enterprise,* Ann Arbor: University of Michigan Press.

Hennart, J.-F. (1988), 'A Transaction Cost Analysis of Equity Joint Ventures', *Strategic Management Journal*, **9** (4), 361–88.

Hennart, J.-F. (1991), 'The Transaction Costs Theory of Joint Ventures: An Empirical Study of Japanese Subsidiaries in the United States', *Management Science,* **37** (4), 483–97.

Hennart, J.-F. and Y.R. Park (1992), 'Location, Governance and Strategic Determinants of Japanese Manufacturing Investments', *Strategic Management Journal*, **15** (6), 419–36.

Huber, G.P. (1991), 'Organizational Learning: The Contributing Processes and a Review of the Literature', *Organization Science*, **2** (2), 88–117.

Hymer, S.H. (1976), *The International Operations of National Firms: A Study of Direct Foreign Investment,* Cambridge, MA: MIT Press.

Inkpen, A. (1995), *The Management of International Joint Ventures: An Organizational Learning Perspective,* New York: Routledge.

Ito, K. and E.L. Rose (1998), 'Multiple Market Competition in the Global Tyre Industry', in S.J. Gray and S. Nicholas (eds.) *Proceedings of the Inaugural Conference of the Australia-New Zealand International Business Academy Meeting*, pp. 155–70. Melbourne: Australia-New Zealand International Business Academy.

Johanson, J. and J.-E. Vahlne (1977), 'The Internationalization Process of the Firm: A Model of Knowledge Development and Increasing Foreign Market Commitments', *Journal of International Business Studies*, **8** (1), 23–32.

Kim, D. (1993), 'The Link Between Individual and Organizational Learning', *Sloan Management Review*, **35** (1), 37–50.

Kim, W.C. and P. Hwang (1992), 'Global Strategy and Multinationals' Entry Mode Choice', *Journal of international Business Studies*, **23** (1), 29–53.

Knickerbocker, F.T. (1973), *Oligopolistic Reaction and Multinational Enterprise*. Cambridge, MA: Division of Research, Graduate School of Business Administration, Harvard University.

Kogut, B. (1983), 'Foreign Direct Investment as a Sequential Process', in C.P. Kindleberger and D. Audretsch (eds), *The Multinational Corporation in the 1980s,* Cambridge, MA: MIT Press.

Kogut, B. (1988), 'Joint Ventures: Theoretical and Empirical Perspectives', *Strategic Management Journal*, **9** (4), 319–32.

Kogut, B. (1990), 'International Sequential Advantages and Network Flexibility', in C.A. Bartlett, Y. Doz, and G. Hedlund (eds), *Managing the Global Firm,* London: Routledge.

Kogut, B. (1993), 'Learning, or the Importance of Being Inert: Country Imprinting and International Competition', in S. Ghoshal and D.E. Westney (eds), *Organization Theory and the Multinational Corporation,* New York: St Martin's Press.

Kogut, B. and H. Singh (1988), 'The Effect of National Culture on the Choice of Entry Mode', *Journal of International Business Studies*, **20** (2), 411–32.

Kogut, B. and S.-J. Chang (1991), 'Technological Capabilities and Japanese Foreign Direct Investment in the United States', *Review of Economics and Statistics*, **73** (1), 401–13.

Kwon, Y.-C. and M.Y. Hu (1995), 'Comparative Analysis of Export-oriented and Foreign Production-oriented Firms' Market Entry Decisions', *Management International Review*, **36** (4), 325–36.

Leroy, F. and B. Ramanantsoa (1997), 'The Cognitive and Behavioural Dimensions of Organizational Learning in a Merger: An Empirical Study', *Journal of Management Studies*, **34** (6), 871–94.

Luostarinen, R. (1977), *The Internationalization of the Firm,* Helsinki: Acta Academic Oeconomica Helsingiensis.

Luostarinen, R. (1979), *Internationalisation of the Firm*. Helsinki: Acta Academica Series A.

Millington, A. and B. Bayliss (1990), 'The Process of Internationalization: UK Companies in the EC', *Management International Review*, **30** (2), 151–61.

Newbould, G., P. Buckley and J. Thurwell (1978), *Going International: The Experience of Smaller Companies Overseas,* New York: John Wiley and Sons.

Nicholas, S. (1983), 'Agency Contracts, Institutional Modes, and the Transition to Foreign Direct Investment by British Manufacturing Multinationals Before 1939', *The Journal of Economic History*, **43** (3), 675–86.

Nicholas, S. (1991), 'The Expansion of Multinational Firms: New Evidence from British Foreign Direct Investment', in J. Foreman-Peck (ed.), *Reinterpreting the Nineteenth Century British Economy: Essays in Quantitative Economic History,* Cambridge: Cambridge University Press.

Nicholas, S. and E. Maitland (1999), 'Do Multinational Corporations Cluster Their Investments?: Evidence from British and Japanese MNEs', in J.-F. Hennart (ed.), *Global Competition and Market Entry Strategies,* Amsterdam: Elsevier Science.

Roberts, H.V. (1993), 'Using Personal Checklists to Facilitate TQM', *Quality Progress*, **26** (6), 51–56.

Rose, E.L. and K. Ito (1999), 'Competitive Interactions: The International Investment Patterns of Japanese Automobile Manufacturers', in J.-F. Hennart (ed.), *Global Competition and Market Entry Strategies,* Amsterdam: Elsevier Science.

Sann-Randaccio, F. (1990), *European Direct Investment in US Manufacturing,* Rome: Edizioni Kappa.

Shewhart, W.A. (1931), *Economic Control of Quality of Manufactured Product,* New York: Van Nostrand.

Stopford, J.M. and L.T. Wells (1972), *Managing the Multinational Enterprise,* New York: Basic Books.

Teece, D.J. (1985), 'Multinational Enterprise, Internal Governance, and Industrial Organization', *The American Economic Review*, **75** (2), 233–44.

Turnbull, P. (1987), 'A Challenge to the Stages Theory of the Internationalization Process', in P. Rosson and S. Reid (eds), *Managing Export Entry and Expansion,* New York: Praeger.

Vernon, R. (1966), 'International Investment and International Trade in the Product Cycle', *Quarterly Journal of Economics*, **80** (2), 190–207.

Welch, L. and R. Luostarinen (1988), 'Internationalization: Evolution of a Concept', *Journal of General Management*, **14** (2), 34–57.

Wilkins, M. (1974), *The Maturing of Multinational Enterprise: American Business Abroad from 1914 to 1970,* Cambridge, MA: Harvard University Press.

Williamson, O. (1979), 'Transaction-cost Economics: The Governance of Contractual Relations', *Journal of Law and Economics*, **22** (2), 233–61.

Wilson, B.D. (1980), 'The Propensity of Multinational Companies to Expand through Acquisitions', *Journal of International Business Studies*, **11** (1), 59–65.

Winter, S.G. (1987), 'Knowledge and Competence as Strategic Assets', in D. Teece (ed.), *The Competitive Challenge,* Cambridge, MA: Ballinger.

Yu, C.-M. and K. Ito (1988), 'Oligopolistic Reaction and Foreign Direct Investment: The Case of the U.S. Tire and Textile Industry', *Journal of International Business Studies,* **19** (3), 449–60.

Zejan, M.C. (1990), 'New Ventures or Acquisitions: The Choice of Swedish Multinational Enterprises', *Journal of Industrial Economics*, **38** (3), 349–55.

PART II

Export Expansion and Performance

4. Driving International Business Performance through Use of Internet Technologies: A Survey of Australian and New Zealand Exporters

Sirinuch Srirojanant and Peter Thirkell

INTRODUCTION

Since the mid 1990s, the explosive growth of the Internet has dominated the popular press and academic discussions. For marketers, the Internet has been an important focus since commercial use of the Internet has been the fastest growing part of the WWW (Hamill and Gregory, 1997). However, apart from a number of Internet books described as the 'get rich quick' type, there are few serious academic studies covering Internet-based marketing (Hamill and Gregory, 1997). In particular, Hamill (1997) comments that there has, to date, been little attempt to examine the specific role of the medium within the international marketing arena.

Hence, it is the intention of this study to offer some insight into New Zealand's and Australia's Internet-based international marketing activities and approaches. The main focus of this research was upon how this medium supports export success factors, that is, 'export barrier overcoming', 'export strategies', 'organisational competencies' and 'export performance'.

This chapter argues that exporters who use the Internet effectively can gain 'a low cost gateway' to international markets and be able to overcome many important export barriers which have historically been known to hinder SMEs' internationalisation (Hamill, 1997; Hamill and Gregory, 1997; Quelch and Klein, 1996). It also contends that the Internet helps improve export strategy formulation and implementation (Hamill, 1997; Hamill and Gregory, 1997) and organisational competencies (Marquardt, 1996; Slay, 1997; Tapscott, 1996; Thirkell, 1997). Since the Internet has the ability to help exporters improve across a set of 'critical export success factors' in their international business ventures (Hamill, 1997), these Internet-based international marketers should consequently achieve better financial performance overall.

The objectives of this research were:

- to study the state of development of Internet usage among New Zealand and Australian small- to medium-sized exporters
- to identify the impact of an Internet presence and use upon exporting activities and success
- effective export barrier overcoming
- different electronic export strategies
- various dimensions of organisational competency

LITERATURE REVIEW

The Internet and International Marketing

Writing on Internet marketing has dominated both the popular press and academic literature over the last two to three years. Most of the work in the popular press is of the 'get rich quick' type (Hamill, 1997). A review of the academic literature in the area, however, reveals diverse and interesting strands of literature.

Some of these strands feature, for example, the effect of the Internet on today's commerce and market, such as the Internet as a new form of 'marketspace' (Rayport and Sviokla, 1994); of 'hyper media computer-mediated environments' (Hoffman and Novak, 1996); of virtual 'communities' (Armstrong and Hagell III, 1996); as a new 'market maker' (Klein and Quelch, 1997); as a new electronic shopping channel (Burke, 1997; Jones, 1998; Keeling and McGoldrick, 1997; Stephens et al., 1996); its effects on retail shopping (Stevens and Howson, 1997); its influence on reducing importance of traditional intermediaries (Quelch and Klein, 1996) and introducing the new 'cybermediaries' (Sarkar et al., 1998).

Internet-related effects on marketing approaches have been explored in the areas of, for instance, relationship marketing (Thirkell, 1997; Srirojanant and Thirkell, 1998); networking (Nouwens and Bouwan, 1995); organisational learning (for example, Roberts, 1998; Young and Sauer, 1996); the marketing concept (Brannback, 1997a, b), and micro marketing (Sivadas et al., 1998a). Moreover, the Internet has been seen as a new form of marketing communication medium (Hoffman and Novak, 1996), needing a new marketing communication framework (Stanners, 1997), and different advertising attributes (Gordon and De Lima-Turner, 1997).

Another group of authors asserts that the Internet has the potential to make a profound impact on international marketing (see, for example, Bennett, 1997, 1998; Cronin, 1996; Hamill, 1997; Hamill and Gregory, 1997; Poon and Jevons, 1997; Poon and Swatman, 1997; Quelch and Klein, 1996; Sterne, 1995). Hamill (1997) and Hamill and Gregory (1997) state that the Internet provides a completely new international marketing environment within which business will be conducted as part of the emerging electronic age. Consequently, the international marketing discipline will need to refocus its theoretical and teaching direction by recognising the importance of and embracing Internet-enabled international marketing approaches.

Research Gap on Internet Use among Small to Medium-sized Exporters (SMEs)

Internet-enabled international marketing is of great importance to smaller businesses as they are traditionally ones that have fewer resources to conduct international businesses. As never before, the medium provides 'a low cost gateway' to global markets (Hamill, 1997; Hamill and Gregory, 1997; Quelch and Klein, 1996). Hence, increasing numbers of worldwide researchers are now specifically focusing on the impact of the Internet on small- to medium-sized businesses (Abell and Lim, 1996; Cragg, 1996; Hamill and Gregory, 1997; Poon and Jevons, 1997; Poon and Swatman, 1997).

In New Zealand itself, Stevens (1996) provides preliminary insights into Internet usage by local firms. Abell and Lim (1996) investigated New Zealand's business use of the Internet and the benefits perceived by managers in relation to their business activities generally, and for marketing and advertising. Srirojanant and Thirkell (1997b, 1998) empirically established important links between level of Internet use and the adoption of relationship marketing principles among New Zealand firms.

There have not, however, been many studies done on New Zealand's Internet-enabled SMEs. Only the work of Hamill and Gregory (1997), and Bennett (1997) has provided some descriptive empirical evidence on UK Internet-enabled exporters. Hence, it was the intention of this study to examine the linkage between Internet and international marketing in New Zealand and Australia.

INTERNET INTERACTIVITY FACTORS

In implementing Internet-based international marketing strategies, some common tools that can be used by exporters include: Web sites, e-mail and other forms of on-line communications; information search and retrieval software (Hamill and Gregory, 1997). This section examines different aspects of company Web sites in support of exporting.

The Web Page Aspects: Web Site Types and Site Interactivity Measures

Srirojanant and Thirkell (1998) empirically determined that the development of existing Web sites in New Zealand can be classified broadly into five categories according to level of interactivity. They are: passive representation sites, interactive representation sites, interactive experiential sites, response relationship sites and true relationship sites. The Web site classifications represent a continuum from passive to dynamically interactive representation. Conceptually, the site categories specifically allow for different levels of interaction between companies and customers (Srirojanant and Thirkell, 1998).

A further site interactivity measure was also identified, with two dimensions: 'commitment to site development' and 'customer responsiveness'. In this study, it was posited that the Web site types and site interactivity are two important components of Web sites allowing exporters not only to be more in touch with customers and stakeholders but also with the ever-changing market environment at a more interactive and meaningful level. With highly interactive sites, exporters are able to learn about and interact with customer and market stakeholders faster and on a one-to-one level. Furthermore, if exporters are more committed to the ongoing development of their Web sites, such as being interactively responsive to customer queries, constantly collecting customer and other useful information through the Internet, and continually adding more value-added content to the Web sites, they will be able to attract revisits to their sites, learn more about their customers on an individual basis, and identify threats and opportunities from the surrounding environment more effectively. Hence, this study argues that, the more technically interactive a Web site, the more an exporter will be able to learn about both customer-specific needs and the market environment.

Apart from the Web page aspects, exporters' abilities to maximise the benefits of the Internet also depend upon how well they make use of various Internet applications. The following section examines dimensions of Internet aspects argued to be important in assisting exporting activities.

Internet Aspects

Two dimensions of the Internet important to assist exporters' Internet-based international marketing activities are the Internet applications deployed and the intensity of Internet use.

Internet applications

Three main Internet applications that SME exporters use the Internet for are network communications, market intelligence and sales promotion (Hamill, 1997; Hamill and Gregory, 1997).

Communications – In the era of relationship marketing, maintaining effective foreign customer communications with suppliers, agents and distributors has been found to be critically important to successful internationalisation (Payne et al., 1996; Gronroos, 1994; Gummerson, 1996; Hamill and Gregory, 1997). It is found that the Internet provides various tools for improving or supporting communications with different stakeholders in the firm's network (Hamill and Gregory, 1997; Poon and Swatman, 1997; Srirojanant and Thirkell, 1997b). The most used tools to support communication strategies are e-mail; Usenet and Listserv groups; Internet Relay Chat (IRC); Multi-User Dialogues (MUDS) and MUD Object Oriented (MOOS); and video conferencing (Hamill and Gregory, 1997). Most commonly used among these is e-mail.

Marketing Intelligence – In the international market setting, firms need effective management of information as they operate in diverse and complex environments subject to rapid and often unexpected change (Hamill and Gregory, 1997). Effective export marketing research is empirically proven to be a critical success factor discriminating between successful and unsuccessful SME exporters (Aaby and Slater, 1989; Hamill and Gregory, 1997). However, few SMEs adopt systematic procedures for market research (Cavusgil, 1985; Hamill and Gregory, 1997). Reasons contributing to the phenomenon include the view that export marketing research is too expensive; and that SMEs lack in-house marketing research personnel, knowledge or resources (Hamill and Gregory, 1997). It is argued that Internet connectivity can assist SME internationalisation, and the WWW is an invaluable source of low cost but up-to-date market research (Hamill and Gregory, 1997; Quelch and Klein, 1996). The Web offers exporters extensive amounts of relevant international marketing information, including on-line newspapers and journals; an extensive list of country and government contacts; details on host country legislation covering imports, agency agreements, joint ventures and so on; relevant international marketing Listserv and discussion groups; and numerous other sources of information (Hamill and Gregory, 1997; Larson, 1996).

Sales promotion – Increasingly, SMEs are setting up their own World Wide Web homepages as a means of disseminating company and product information to potential customers and encouraging customer feedback and interaction (Hamill and Gregory, 1997; Srirojanant and Thirkell, 1997b). A Web homepage can provide an attractive, low cost method of sales promotion for SMEs to global customers (Ellsworth and Ellsworth, 1995, 1996; Hamill and Gregory, 1997). The tools available for designing Web sites are becoming lower in price and easier to use, while the quality is increasingly sophisticated (Hamill and Gregory, 1997).

Apart from various Internet applications used among exporters (such as communications, market intelligence and marketing and sales promotion), intensity of Internet use was seen as a second important aspect that companies should consider if they choose the Internet as a medium to assist their international business ventures.

Intensity of Internet use

Intensity of Internet use is the second component of Internet aspects which complement the previous aspect of Internet applications. It is argued that without intense use of the Internet, the various applications will not yield maximal benefits to users. If staff spend more time searching for useful information on the World Wide Web and interacting with customers and other parties via the Internet, it follows that they will become more familiar with various resources on the Internet and more confident about using the medium to its fullest capacity. This would include: communicating effectively with stakeholders, conducting market research and updating information on the market and improving the marketing strategies of their Web sites.

Management Attitude towards Contributions of the Internet

Previous research has shown that management support and enthusiasm is important for IT success among small businesses (Cragg and King, 1993; Martin, 1989; Yap et al., 1992) and that management enthusiasm and commitment is a precondition of continuous Internet use (Poon and Swatman, 1997). A positive management attitude towards the values of the Internet is also correlated with the operation of highly interactive Web sites, which in turn enhances customer relationship building efforts (Srirojanant and Thirkell, 1997b, 1998). Without a positive management attitude towards the Internet contributions, it is unlikely that Internet-enabled exporters can maximise the advantages of their Web site and Internet use. A positive management attitude and enthusiasm will encourage staff to see the Internet in a positive light, fully use the medium, and try to improve and benefit from Internet-based international marketing strategies.

EXPORT MARKETING DETERMINANTS

Effective Export Barrier Overcoming

If companies aim to leverage the value of their assets, they must strive for global expansion to create growth (Chang, 1996). Many companies however, especially smaller firms which have limited resources to overcome financial and operational barriers, have reported various obstacles barring them from successful internationalisation (Hamill, 1997; Hamill and Gregory, 1997). Chang (1996) argues that businesses can benefit from international expansion if the management is effective in overcoming perceived difficulties and barriers. Hamill and Gregory's (1997) study of previous work in export barriers reveals four main export barriers for SMEs, which are:

Psychological barriers – This type of barrier relates to SMEs' perceptions concerning the costs, risks and profitability of exporting.

Operational barriers – These refer to the problems in dealing with company paperwork, language problems, delays in payment and so on.

Organisational barriers – These barriers come from the fact that SMEs usually have limited resources for export effort and limited international experience.

Product/market barriers – These relate to the suitability (or lack of suitability) of the firm's product or service for foreign markets and the country selection decision.

The Internet may not be a remedy for all export problems faced by SMEs, but if used effectively can be a powerful tool to assist them in overcoming export barriers, resulting in more rapid internationalisation. (Hamill, 1997; Hamill and Gregory, 1997). Bennett (1997: 327) argues that: 'the use of the Internet for global marketing enables firms to leap-frog the conventional stages of internationalisation, as it removes all geographical constraints, permits the instant establishment of virtual branches throughout the world, and allows direct and immediate foreign market entry to the smallest of businesses'. Use of the Internet and Web sites should in turn assist SMEs effectively to reduce export barriers. If the Internet is used to do market intelligence and support international networking, it can lead to a more positive attitude and an orientation towards global business, thus reducing psychological export barriers. Electronic trading also can help overcome operational barriers relating to export documentation. The establishment of a Web presence, in conjunction with a well designed marketing strategy, can be used to overcome barriers relating to product selection.

Thus, this chapter argues that if exporters utilise Internet resources and applications to the fullest extent, employ highly interactive Web sites and have a positive attitude and enthusiasm towards Internet usage, they will be better able to learn about the markets and general business environment. Consequently, they were expected to be better at overcoming various export barriers.

H1: Internet interactivity factors, which are (a) Internet aspects and (b) management attitude towards the Internet are positively related to SMEs' ability to overcome export barriers in the areas of:
(i) psychological barriers
(ii) operational barriers
(iii) organisational barriers
(iv) market barriers.

Internet-enabled Export Strategies

The selection of distribution channels for delivery and service is regarded by many authors to be one of the most critical decisions in international marketing (Aaby and Slater, 1989; Beamish et al., 1993; Rosson and Ford, 1982; Yaprak, 1985). Distribution strategies found to be positively related to export performance included ongoing evaluation and improvement of the distribution system (Cavusgil and Nevin, 1981); close channel relationships (Rosson and Ford, 1982); personal relationship with and frequency of visits to foreign agents (Anglemar and Pras, 1984; Craig and Beamish, 1989); and emphasis on the importance of ongoing distribution arrangements (Beamish et al., 1993, Rosson and Ford, 1982).

In respect of product and product line strategy in influencing export performance, other researchers have explored its importance (Aaby and Slater, 1989; Beamish et al., 1993; Cavusgil and Zou, 1994; Chetty and Hamilton, 1996; Cooper and Kleinschmidt, 1985). Different dimensions of product strategy investigated included: the degree of product adaptation, ranging from minimum adaptation to product specifically adapted for its export markets (Cooper and Kleinschmidt, 1985; Koh, 1990; Dau, 1991); product uniqueness and product competitive advantages (Beamish et al., 1993); and width of product line in the export market (Christensen et al., 1987).

This study argues further that the Internet can support Internet-enabled exporters to achieve effective *electronic* export strategies, specifically in respect of distribution and the product mix. Traditionally, SMEs have lacked adequate financial resources and personnel to carry out various exporting activities, such as formal international market research and country screening, or to establish branches overseas. With Internet technologies, businesses of any size can penetrate unfamiliar foreign markets and sell anywhere in the world (Cronin, 1994, 1996; Ellsworth and Ellsworth, 1995, 1996; Quelch and Klein, 1996; Sterne, 1995). Through online export market research available on the Internet, electronic market selection is significantly simplified and makes market selection decisions easier (Hamill, 1997).

Concerning electronic product mix strategies, Internet facilities not only help firms introduce and create sales leads for new products and services to global customers (Quelch and Klein, 1996) and facilitate goods order processing (for example through Internet-enabled EDI), but also allow exporters to interact with customers on inputs on new product ideas (Cronin, 1994, 1996; Wikstrom, 1996). Hence, Internet-enabled exporters are better able to allow customers to be part of this company–customer cooperation and co-production process (Srirojanant and Thirkell, 1998). The medium also helps exporters to create interactive product mix strategies evolving from micro marketing or niche marketing responding to individuals or small groups of customers in a truly customer-focused and individually customised way, at comparatively low cost (Quelch and Klein, 1996; Sivadas et al., 1998a).

In short, many Internet tools supporting export activity electronically coincide with success factors found in the export literature. Export planning and strategy development, market selection activities, distribution strategies and management and product mix strategies can all be conducted effectively through appropriate Internet use.

H2: Internet interactivity factors, which are (a) Internet aspects and (b) management attitude towards the Internet are positively related to Internet-enabled export strategies:

- (i) distribution strategy
- (ii) product mix

Organisational Competencies

Export and market knowledge

Research on internationalisation indicates that a major part of the firm's competence is based on less tangible areas such as experience, knowledge and skills (Welch and Welch, 1996) which can be related to export performance (Aaby and Slater, 1989; Chetty and Hamilton, 1996). Market knowledge, distinguished as experiential knowledge and market-specific knowledge, plays an important role in the international business planning process (Johanson and Vahlne, 1977; Dau and Thirkell, 1998). Using Internet tools, SMEs can improve their ability to conduct extensive marketing research, gather various types of export information and access extensive online marketing research resources which are usually free or come at very low cost (Hamill, 1997). Some of these tools include web browsers and information search and retrieval software: Netscape,

Microsoft, Gopher, Archie, WAIS, Veronica and so on (Hamill, 1997). Being able to participate in relevant discussion groups or international marketing online assistance also helps SMEs in developing their market knowledge and international contacts.

For New Zealand and Australian exporters, online export assistance offers a wide variety of export-related services. These offerings include information on export opportunities, news and analysis, currency briefing, export statistics, country information, assistance for companies to tackle technology and new product development, and export networking management by pooling resources and skills from companies in the same industry. This information mostly comes free of charge.

Communication capability

Apart from market knowledge, many export researchers have examined the role of exporters' communication capability and propensity to export (Bello and Barksdale, 1986; Czinkota and Johnston, 1982; Joynt, 1982). It was found that the most important export barrier for small and medium-sized businesses was communication difficulties. Effective communication with markets is important for exporters as it improves their understanding of individual customers, business practices of different markets, ability to negotiate, psychological advantage in selling and effective management of overseas subsidiaries. Effective communication can directly contribute to international business success (Turnbull and Welham, 1985) or enhance effective internal communications which in turn contributes to better performance (Dau and Thirkell, 1998).

Hamill (1997) argues that with the various Internet tools exporters can now obtain, they can improve communication with customers and different stakeholders in the international business environment. Using electronic communication generates interactive enquiries and feedback from actual and potential global customers worldwide (Srirojanant, 1997); effectively enhances small business network relationships (Poon and Jevons, 1997); facilitates complex export documentation procedures (Hamill, 1997); and also reduces the costs of communication (Ellsworth and Ellsworth, 1995, 1996; Sterne, 1995; Cronin, 1994, 1996; Poon and Swatman, 1997). It also supports and improves ongoing and one-to-one relationships with customers (Srirojanant and Thirkell, 1998). Its interactive and one-to-one communications and services also help increase customer satisfaction.

International orientation of management and staff

Closely linked to international market knowledge of the organisation is a firm's international orientation. Unless people in the organisation, especially emphasised by the management, have an international orientation and positive perception of exporting, the firm as a whole will not be able fully to exploit export market opportunities (Aaby and Slater, 1989; Chetty and Gray, 1996). Indeed, international orientation of top management was found to be an important determinant of export marketing behaviour (Cavusgil and Nevin, 1981). Specifically, managers with positive impressions of the desirability of international marketing will be more responsive to strategies that exploit international opportunities (Khan, 1978; Buatsi, 1980; Lim et al., 1993).

Regular use of the Internet to access various types of exporting information and international news and to participate in relevant discussion groups allows exporters to become more oriented towards the international business environment. In turn, users will be more psychologically encouraged to gather relevant information, and more confident about their international knowledge.

H3: Internet interactivity factors, which are (a) Internet aspects; and (b) management attitude towards the Internet; are positively related to Internet-enabled organisational competencies in the areas of:
(i) market knowledge
(ii) communication capacity
(iii) international orientation

EXPORT PERFORMANCE AND RESEARCH MODEL

Ultimately, the goal of any business is to perform well financially. In addition to examining the direct benefits of effective Internet use in support of export activity, this study examined whether it yielded any discernible performance benefit to Internet-enabled exporters. The aim was also to clarify whether some success factors identified in the exporting literature were applicable to the Internet-related context. The expected effects of the main independent constructs upon export performance were codified by use of three additional hypotheses, and are summarised in Figure 4.1.

H4: Companies' export barrier overcoming abilities, in the areas of: (a) psychological barriers; (b) operational barriers; (c) organisational barriers; and (d) market barriers are positively related to better export performance.

H5: Companies' electronic export strategies, which are (a) distribution strategy; and (b) product mix strategy are positively related to better export performance.

H6: Companies' organisational competencies in the areas of: (a) market knowledge; (b) communication capacity; and (c) international orientation are positively related to better export performance

In summary, the main focus of this research was upon how the 'Internet interactivity' factors support export success factors of 'export barrier overcoming', 'export strategies' and 'organisational competencies', and in turn how these factors relate to 'export performance'.

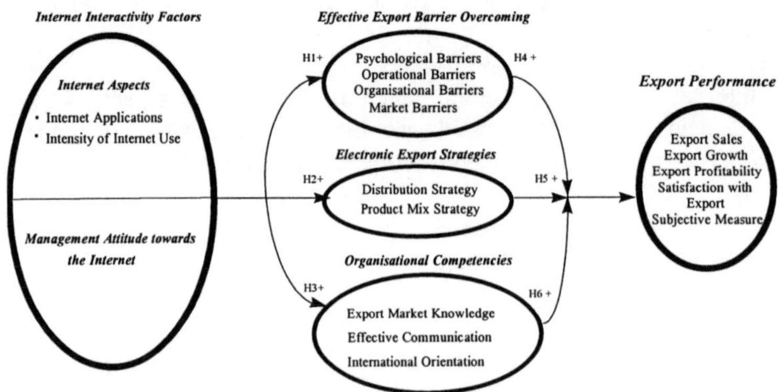

Figure 4.1 Research model

OPERATIONAL DEFINITIONS

Internet Aspects

A new measurement for 'Internet applications' was constructed using the framework of Hamill (1997) and Hamill and Gregory (1997). The 'intensity of Internet use' concept was adapted from Zeffane's (1992) concept of extent of computer functional use and the frequency of use.

Attitude towards the Internet Contributions

This construct drew directly upon the measures and scales formulated in Srirojanant (1997).

Overcoming Export Barriers

The study drew in part from Leonidou's (1995a) work, supplemented by new items reflecting exporter ability to overcome export barriers as identified by Hamill (1997) and Hamill and Gregory (1997). These constituted four types of export barriers: psychological, operational, organisational, and market barriers.

Electronic Export Strategies

To operationalise electronic 'distribution strategy' and 'product mix strategy' measures as derived from Internet use, some new items were developed, with the remainder being adapted from Bennett (1998).

Organisational Competencies

Items developed by Bennett (1998) were used to reflect contributions towards the organisational competencies described in this study, supplemented by further new items fully to reflect the Internet-based context of the study.

Export Performance

Export performance used five different dimensions: 'export sales volume', 'profitability', 'export growth', 'satisfaction with export operation' and 'subjective measurement of export performance'. They were adapted from Souchon and Diamantopoulos' (1997) dimensions of export performance.

METHODOLOGY

The data for this study were collected by means of a three-wave mail survey and one online survey (conducted between November 1998 and January 1999) of New Zealand and Australian exporters known to have had active Web sites at the time the survey was conducted. The survey instrument was subject to expert evaluation and pre-testing procedures before being released for the main study, using academics with experience in both international marketing and/or Internet marketing and also export practitioners. Care was taken to ensure identical wording in the chapter and Web-based survey instruments, although the physical form of each was clearly somewhat different given the different delivery media employed. A comparison of results from each of the two data collection approaches did not suggest any substantive differences attributable to the different instruments, although the possibility is acknowledged that some variability in results could occur depending on how the data were collected.

The majority of responses received were completed by either marketing/export managers or CEOs. The response rate across all the surveys was 17.5 per cent (153 responses of 873 surveyed firms). Sixty per cent of the respondents were New Zealand firms and the balance were Australian. Respondents represented a broad range of industries and firm sizes. Completion of questionnaires by senior managers did leave the possibility of bias or over-statement in some of the responses. No specific tests were undertaken in this regard, and future research could explore for this possibility across a sample composed of managers from various levels within the participating firms.

Scale Development and Testing

The development of each measure required four distinct steps. Firstly, items used to operationalise each scale were subjected to principle axis factor analysis with varimax rotation, forcing all items into a single factor to determine the degree of unidimensionality. Items that did not load at or above 0.40 were excluded from further analysis. Items that loaded above 0.40 on other factors with an unconstrained analysis (using an eigenvalue of 1 as the cut-off level) were also excluded, on the rationale that they were primarily reflecting another dimension apart from the intended primary construct of interest. These tests did not unduly stress the data, with only 4 of 58 items across the five main constructs of interest needing to be dropped from further analysis.

Second, reliability analysis was conducted on all remaining items to assess internal consistency (positive and high item-to-total correlations), and to ensure that Cronbach alpha values exceeded the recommended minimum of 0.70 (Nunnally, 1978).

Third, the content of each scale used in this study was assessed for face validity at the time of item selection to determine whether they measured what was intended to be measured. All items were also assessed in this way by academic staff with expertise in the area and during a pretest conducted among practitioners and exporters in the field. The face validity of the items finally employed appeared to be high.

Fourth, composite scale scores were converted to averages in a five point range rather than using the straight summation of all items. This had no effect on subsequent correlation and regression analysis and allowed for a more straightforward comparison of scale characteristics and levels across each of the main independent and dependent constructs.

Scale items typically employed five point Likert measures. The individual items used to measure Internet interactivity are summarised in

Appendix Table 4A.1. Items used to construct the export performance measure are summarised in Appendix Table 4A.2. Items used to construct scales for the remaining three independent constructs are reported exactly as used in the original questionnaires, in Tables 4.1 to 4.3. A visual inspection of the data after scale construction did not reveal any specific concerns about outliers in the dataset.

The main characteristics of the major five scales used for hypothesis testing are shown below in Table 4.1. All Cronbach alpha measures were in the range 0.84 to 0.91, and all scales exhibited acceptable normality based on use of the Kolmogorov–Smirnoff normality test. It was concluded that each scale demonstrated sufficient reliability and validity to be used in subsequent analysis.

Table 4.1 Scale descriptors

Scale	N of items	Mean	SD	Alpha	n
Internet interactivity	10 (from 12)	3.73	0.66	0.86	136
Export barrier overcoming	12 (from 14)	3.87	0.61	0.84	136
Electronic export strategies	11	3.14	0.67	0.87	136
Organisational competencies	12	3.58	0.51	0.85	136
Export performance	9	3.06	0.87	0.91	136

HYPOTHESIS TESTING AND RELATED FINDINGS

Relationships between Internet Interactivity and Export Benefits

Before conducting the formal hypothesis testing, all variables were examined for linearity and normality. The distributions of the four main scales used approached normality. A visual inspection of the scatterplots also suggested that the relationships in question were essentially linear.

Testing H1

Hypothesis 1 proposed that there was a positive relationship between a firm's interactive Internet strategy and its ability to overcome four types of export barriers: psychological, operational, organisational and market barriers.

The result of testing H1 is shown in Table 4.2. The Pearson correlation was not significant indicating that the hypothesised positive relationship between Internet Interactivity and a firm's ability to overcome export barriers was not confirmed. On this basis, Hl could not be accepted.

Table 4.2 Pearson correlations

Hypothesis		Internet interactivity
H1	Overcoming export barriers	.041
H2	Electronic export strategies	.609**
H3	Organisational competencies 1	.632**

** Correlation is significant at the 0.01 level (1-tailed).

This outcome was contrary to expectations, and may have simply reflected the stage at which New Zealand and Australian firms were with respect to the development of their Internet use in overcoming traditional export barriers. During the data collection phase, many marketing managers contacted said that their firms used the medium mainly for providing company information rather than to 'trade or export'. If this is the case, it suggests these firms were not yet using the Internet actively to explore business and export opportunities, meaning in turn that the medium was not up to this point assisting them in coping with export barriers.

Interestingly, the partial correlation analysis summarised in Table 4.3 reveals that the relationship between a firm's Internet interactivity and its ability to overcome export barriers was negative among larger firms and positive among medium-sized firms. The finding contradicts previous findings that larger businesses are less likely to experience impediments to export because of larger resources (e.g., Burton and Schlegelmilch, 1987; Cavusgil and Naor, 1987; Czinkota and Johnston, 1981; Leonidou, 1995a; Yaprak, 1985). This may reflect less activity by large firms seeking new ways to overcome export barriers, or higher levels of inertia in fully adopting Internet technologies.

The lower half of Table 4.3 indicates that there was also a significant positive relationship between Internet Interactivity and the ability to overcome barriers among firms which had highly interactive distribution strategies. Whether or not a firm had a high electronic distribution strategy was measured by the extent to which the firm used the Internet to distribute products/services and manage its overseas distributors. This finding

Table 4.3 Further investigation of relationship between Internet interactivity and overcoming export barriers, moderated respectively by firm size and distribution strategy

Firm size	Pearson *r*	Sig.	n
Small (1–7 employees)	0.165	0.155	41
Medium (8–35 employees)	0.249	0.061	41
Large* (36–700 employees)	-0.298	0.039	41
Distribution strategy			
Low distribution strategy	0.103	0.248	49
Mod distribution strategy	-0.091	0.322	30
High distribution strategy	0.374	0.008	42

* Outliers were excluded from the category so that the data distribution of the category approximates normality.

appears plausible, considering that if a firm actively uses the Internet for distribution, it is less deterred by export barriers in establishing a viable base for its international business and will be more likely to have a better interactive capability in the Web site deployed. Further research could more fully explore these preliminary insights.

Testing H2

Hypothesis 2 proposed that there was a positive relationship between a firm's interactive Internet strategy and its implementation of electronic export strategies. Electronic export strategies included electronic distribution and product strategies. Table 4.1 shows that the relationship between Internet interactivity and electronic export strategies were positively correlated ($r = 0.609$, $p < 0.01$). These findings confirmed the expectation that firms employing highly interactive sites were inclined to achieve a higher level of electronic export strategies. Therefore H2 was accepted.

Testing H3

Hypothesis 3 proposed that there was a positive relationship between Internet interactivity and organisational competencies: export market knowledge, communications capability and international orientation. As shown in Table 4.1, the relationship between Internet interactivity and organisational competencies was found to be positive ($r = 0.632$; $p < 0.01$). Hence, H3 was accepted.

Relationships between Export Benefits and Export Performance

The second objective of this study was to confirm an expected positive relationships between high export performance and three Internet-export critical success factors:

(a) ability to overcome export barriers;
(b) electronic export strategies;
(c) organisational competencies.

A multi-regression analysis was used to investigate the relationships.

In testing H4, H5 and H6 the regression was specified in the form of the following model:

$$Y_{PERFi} = A_i + B_1 X_{BARRi} + B_2 X_{STRATi} + B_3 X_{CPTNCYi}$$

Where for firm i -

Y_{PERFi}	=	Estimated export performance
X_{BARRi}	=	Ability to overcome export barriers
X_{STRATi}	=	Electronic export strategies
$X_{CPTNCYi}$	=	Organisational competencies

Testing H4

Table 4.4 provides a summary of the finding for the antecedents to export performance. An R square of 0.350 was achieved in the regression equation indicating that the proposed model is capable of predicting about 35 per cent of the variation in the performance score. As expected, it was found that the firm's ability to overcome export barriers had a significant positive effect on export performance ($p < 0.001$). Therefore, H4 was accepted.

Table 4.4 Regression analysis results

Dep. var.: export performance R = 0.591 $R^2 = 0.350$ Adj $R^2 = 0.335$
F = 23.641 Sig = 0.000

Independent variables	Beta	*Beta*	*T*	Sig.	Tol.	VIF	H
Overcoming export barriers	0.773	0.540	7.68	0.000	0.998	1.002	H4
Electronic export strategies	-0.014	0.011	–0.12	0.900	0.685	1.460	H5
Organisational competencies	0.450	0.230	2.71	0.008	0.684	1.461	H6

Testing H5

Contrary to expectations, electronic export strategies were not found to be significantly associated with export performance across the sample as a whole. The test resulted in a non-significant finding (p = 0.900), therefore H5 could not be accepted.

Table 4.5 shows an additional analysis however designed to explore more fully the relationship between electronic strategies and performance, taking into account the time since Web site establishment. By dividing the sample into three groups on the basis of how long the company has had a Web site, it was found that there was a positive relationship between electronic export strategies and export performance (Pearson $r = 0.482$, p = 0.008) among firms with mature Web sites (25–120 months old). This suggests that firms which had been on the Internet for over two years were more experienced in using the medium, and also that sufficient time had passed to demonstrate performance benefits from their implementation of electronic export strategies.

Table 4.5 Further investigation of relationship between export performance and electronic export strategies, moderated by time since Web site establishment

Young (1–12 months)	0.020	0.446	51
Intermediate (13–24 months)	-0.006	0.484	52
Mature (25–120 months)	0.482	0.004	29

Testing H6

From Table 4.4, organisational competencies can be seen to have had a significant positive relationship with export performance ($p < 0.008$). Therefore, H6 was accepted.

Furthermore, it can be concluded from Table 4.4 that, comparatively among the three Internet export benefits, the ability to overcome export barriers had the strongest relative impact on export performance as indicated by its standardised beta coefficient (0.540). This conclusion does need to be moderated however by the more subtle findings made in relation to electronic export strategies.

DISCUSSION

Internet Interactivity Factors

The Internet is a global window to information and international business opportunities, but the challenge is to find the important components of an Internet-based export strategy that will lead to improved performance. Among the surveyed firms it was found that the more successful firms (those that experienced the highest levels of export benefits and performance) shared five main success components:

Highly interactive Web sites

Firms that deploy Web sites which are more towards the interactive end of the continuum are better placed to provide two-way dialogue and interaction with customers, leading in turn to better performance. The more interactive Web sites allow exporters a fuller and deeper understanding of the customers on a one-to-one level, providing a foundation for firms to create marketing initiatives that add value to their individual customers.

Good Web site management

The more successful firms appear to have better Web site management processes, which are reflected in the level of their responsiveness to customers and their commitment to site development. While the Web site itself can be compared to an electronic front office, the management of a Web site is similar to the back office of a firm. Both are key aspects that continuously add value and attract a greater number of repeat visits to sites. Good management requires:

- Systematic and swift management of customer questions that come via the Web
- Facilitation of customer information gathering via the Web
- Frequent updates of content

Effective communications

The more successful firms intensively use the Internet to support and improve communications with different customers and stakeholders, as well as for internal communications. Many other studies have also found that effective communications are critically important to successful export activities. Apart from e-mail, there is an extremely large number of mailing lists and specialised discussion groups that exporters can subscribe to free of charge. These groups can be very useful for making industry contacts and keeping up to date with industry developments.

Positive management attitude

Top managers of the more successful companies demonstrated a stronger belief in the potential of Internet commerce. A positive management attitude and commitment to the firms' Internet strategy is the main precursor to establishing and maintaining a successful Web site. Enthusiastic managers tend to encourage staff to use the medium fully and think about the benefits resulting from implementation of specific Internet-based international marketing strategies.

Intensive use of the Internet

Finally, it was found that a successful Internet marketing strategy is reflected in the level of Internet use by all company staff. When staff are allowed to spend more time exploring the Internet for useful information and interacting with customers and stakeholders, they naturally become more familiar with various resources on the Internet. This in turn improves their ability to use the medium to communicate with stakeholders, find market information, and improve their ideas on Web marketing and sales promotion strategies.

Export-related Benefits and Improved Performance

Electronic distribution and product export strategies

Table 4.6 reports on the specific distribution and product related benefits that surveyed firms reported based on their Internet usage experience. Among the product distribution related benefits, the fact that the Internet helps them sell anywhere in the world is the most significant reported benefit. In the area of product mix related benefits, managers rated the Internet as benefiting them most in creating sales leads and finding information on other competitive products.

The subsequent question was whether the above strategies led to better export performance. The findings suggested that only firms with longer-established Web sites (two years or greater) were able to demonstrate benefits ultimately translating into better export performance. The finding here amplifies the importance of gaining Web-related experience as early as possible. Hence, firms should attempt to acquire 'experiential learning' in promoting exports through the Internet or other electronic commerce media.

Table 4.6 Electronic export strategy profiles

	Please indicate the extent to which you agree or disagree with each of the following contributions of the Internet towards export marketing activities... (1) Strongly disagree (2) Disagree (3) Neither agree nor disagree (4) Agree (5) Strongly agree	Mean score Low (1) High (5)	Std Dev	n
Distribution related benefits	• The Internet helps our firm sell anywhere in the world.	3.6	1.0	135
	• The Internet lowers the cost of international and export marketing activities.	3.3	1.1	135
	• The Internet allows us to avoid having to set up foreign branches.	2.3	1.0	132
	• The Internet reduces our dependence on foreign or export agents by allowing us to sell/market directly to customers.	3.1	1.1	135
	• The Internet assists us in finding new overseas agents or distributors.	2.6	1.1	136
	• The Internet helps facilitate faster and more flexible product order and delivery to customers.	2.9	1.2	136
Product mix related benefits	• The Internet assists in the introduction of new products/services.	3.3	1.0	136
	• The Internet helps create sales leads for our products/services.	3.7	.9	135
	• Through our Internet capabilities (such as our Web site, discussion groups), we get customer input on new product/ service ideas.	2.7	1.0	135
	• The Internet assists in finding information on competitive products in specific markets/countries.	3.7	.8	135
	• The Internet assists in finding information on new promotional methods in the market.	3.2	.9	135

This kind of experience can be cultivated through staff training and strategic personnel selection. Additionally, managers should ensure that employees leverage off their existing export experience by identifying what added value can be provided to customers through using the Internet. It appears that integrating Internet technologies into export business processes takes time, but the results support the promise of better performance for firms that persevere.

Increasing competencies

The findings suggest that firms deploying an Internet-based marketing strategy (with specific characteristics as described earlier in this section) are also characterised by improved competencies in market knowledge, communications capability and international orientation. Table 4.7 summarises reported benefits on specific aspects of Internet usage. In the area of market knowledge, it was found that the Internet helps firms most by identifying new sources of export marketing information. In the communications area, managers agreed most strongly that electronic communication tools such as e-mail allow them to reduce their communications cost. Firms also reported that the Internet helped their staff to enhance their international outlook and knowledge.

Consistent across all industries and firm sizes, it was found that firms scoring higher across the set of competencies were found to have higher average levels of export performance.

Table 4.7 Organisational competency profiles

	Please indicate the extent to which you agree or disagree with each of the following contributions of the Internet towards export marketing activities... (1) Strongly disagree (2) Disagree (3) Neither agree nor disagree (4) Agree (5) Strongly agree	Mean score Low (1) High (5)	Std Dev	n
Export market knowledge	• The Internet helps us to identify new sources of export marketing information.	3.3	0.8	135
	• Internet-based export market research helps us with decisions on selecting target countries/markets.	2.8	0.9	134
	• The Internet helps us to gather specific information on sales opportunities.	3.1	1.0	135
	• The Internet helps us to gather specific information on legislation/regulations.	3.0	9	133
	• Information gathered from the Internet helps us plan or anticipate future needs of export customers.	2.9	.9	135

Effective communica-tions	• Internet communication tools (e-mail) allow cost savings over traditional communication tools (tel, fax, etc).	4.3	0.8	134
	• Internet communication generates enquiries and feedback from actual and potential global customers.	3.8	9	135
	• Internet communication enhances one-to-one relationships with customers.	3.6	1.1	135
	• Internet communication helps establish networks of business partners.	3.4	1.0	133
International orientation	• The Internet generates better awareness of the international business environment among staff.	3.3	0.9	135
	• The Internet enhances the global knowledge and understanding of our staff.	3.4	0.9	135
	• The Internet assists us in understanding foreign business practices.	2.7	0.9	134

Overcoming export barriers

Firms that demonstrated a better capacity to overcome perceived export barriers also appeared to enjoy higher levels of export performance. The data further suggested that firms which were seriously committed to distributing their products electronically tended to be better at overcoming export barriers, and in a uniformly consistent manner. Table 4.8 summarises reported results in respect of listed barriers.

Managers of larger firms should be aware of possible difficulties arising from the implementation of an Internet strategy. It was found that firms with over 35 staff that had an Internet marketing strategy appeared to be less capable in overcoming export barriers in the reported areas. This suggests that the successful introduction of new Internet-based systems requires a change in organisational approach, both in attitude and perhaps in the relative level of resources committed to such developments. The organisational change required by big firms to embrace new IT may also be more difficult and painful than in small firms, which are generally more agile and able to implement change quickly.

In summary, to increase a firm's ability to tackle export barriers through use of Internet-based international business approaches, innovative ways to enhance electronic distribution strategies must be found. Big firms must also be aware of possible organisational barriers to an Internet-led export strategy, and ensure that the incorporation of Internet marketing into the firm's strategies is strategically facilitated.

Table 4.8 Export barrier profiles

	Please indicate the extent to which each of the following is a *constraint* on your firm's export growth and development... (1) Extreme constraint (2) Major constraint (3) Moderate constraint (4) Slight constraint (5) Not a constraint	Mean score Extreme (1) Not (5)	Std Dev.	n
Psychological barriers	• The risks involved in exporting.	3.7	1.0	136
	• Additional risks in exporting compared to domestic sales.	3.8	1.0	135
	• Profitability of exporting.	4.2	1.0	136
Operation barriers	• Export procedures and documentation.	4.3	1.0	136
	• Difficulties in collection of payments from export markets.	3.9	0.9	135
	• Difficulties in understanding the business practices of potential foreign markets or foreign customers.	3.6	0.8	136
	• Difficulties in understanding the culture of potential foreign markets or foreign customers.	3.6	0.9	136
Organisational barriers	• Lack of capital to finance export activities.	3.6	1.3	136
	• General lack of exporting knowledge or experience.	4.3	0.9	136
	• Lack of management time to devote to exporting .	3.9	1.1	135
	• Obtaining foreign representation (such as: agents, distributors, sales outlets).	3.6	1.1	135
Market barriers	• Identifying or selecting the most appropriate foreign markets.	3.9	1.0	136

CONCLUSION

This survey has sought to describe the state of development of Internet usage among primarily small to medium-sized exporters. It has determined that there is a wide diversity of adoption approaches and degrees of usage, from tentative and half-hearted applications to full-fledged strategies aimed at harnessing the power of the new medium to enhance and create new business opportunities in offshore markets. It has been further determined that a commitment to electronic export strategies and competencies appears to impact favourably upon subsequent levels of export performance, after allowing for adequate lead times and organisational learning to ensure solid adoption.

The findings are clearly preliminary, but they do suggest that adapting previous findings on critical export success factors is a fruitful basis for exploring the performance effects of Internet technologies in an international business context. Managers need to move systematically and at a senior level within the organisation if they are to harness what in this study appear to be clear beneficial effects from building an Internet-based business strategy.

Future research needs to draw more fully on a range of paradigms applicable to the new international business order that appears to be emerging in a wired world. Previous work in international business using relationship and network perspectives is well suited to Internet-based research, and should allow for confirmation and amplification of the findings in this study.

REFERENCES

Aaby, N.E. and S.F. Slater (1989), 'Management Influences on Export Performance: A Review of the Empirical Literature 1978–1988', *International Marketing Review*, **6** (4), 7–26.

Abell, W. and L. Lim (1996), 'Business Use of the Internet in New Zealand: An Exploratory Study', Lincoln University Applied Computing, Mathematics and Statistics Group Research Report No. 96/03.

Akoorie, M., K. Barber and P. Enderwick (1993), 'Europe 1992: Implications for New Zealand Business', *European Journal of Marketing*, **27** (1), 22–34.

Anglemar, R. and B. Pras (1984), 'Product Acceptance by Middleman in Export Channels', *Journal of Business Research*, **12**, 227–40.

Armstrong, A.G. and J. Hagel III (1996), 'The Real Value of On-line Communities', *Harvard Business Review*, May–June, 134–41.

Ashill, N.J., L. Casagranda and P. Stevens (1997), 'Using the Internet to Create Competitive Advantage: Cases from the New Zealand Primary Sector Industry', in Reed, P.W., S.L. Luxton and M.R. Shaw (eds) *Proceedings of the 1997 Australia New Zealand Marketing Educators' Conference*, **2** (December), 885–903.

Beamish, P.W., R. Craig and K. McLellan (1993), 'The Performance Characteristics of Canadian versus U.K. Exporters in Small and Medium Sized Firms', *Management International Review*, **33** (2), 121–37.

Bell, J., S. Chetty and B. Gray (1997), 'A Comparison of Export Promotion in Ireland and New Zealand', in Reed, P.W., S.L. Luxton and M.R. Shaw (eds) *Proceedings of the 1997 Australia New Zealand Marketing Educators' Conference*, Melbourne, **2** (December), 431–52.

Bello, D.C. and H.C. Barksdale (1986), 'Exporting at Industrial Trade Shows', *Industrial Marketing Management*, **15**, 197–206.

Bennett, R. (1997), 'Export Marketing and the Internet: Experiences of Web Site Use and Perceptions of Export Barriers among UK Businesses', *International Marketing Review*, **14** (5), 324–44.

Bennett, R. (1998), 'Using the World Wide Web for International Marketing: Internet Use and Perceptions of Export Barriers among German and British Businesses', *Journal of Marketing Communications*, **4**, 27–43.

Brannback, M. (1997a), 'Is the Internet Changing the Dominant Logic of Marketing', *European Management Journal*, **15** (6), December, 698–707.

Brannback, M. (1997b), 'The Knowledge-based Marketing Concept – A Basis for Global Business', *Journal of Management Studies*, **16** (4), 293–300.

Buatsi, S.N. (1980), 'The Influence of Organizational Factors on the Export Potential and Export Growth of Firms', Ph.D. Dissertation, University of Manchester, UK.

Burke, R.R. (1997), 'Do You See What I See? The Future of Virtual Shopping', *Journal of the Academy of Marketing Science*, **25** (4), Fall, 352–60.

Burton, F.N. and B.B. Schlegelmilch (1987), 'Profile Analysis of Non-exporters Versus Exporters Grouped by Export Involvement', *Management International Review*, **27** (1), 38–49.

Cavusgil, S.T. (1984a), 'Organizational Characteristics Associated with Export Activity', *Journal of Management Studies*, **21** (1), 3–22.

Cavusgil, S.T. and J. Naor (1987), 'Firm and Management Characteristics as Discriminators of Export Marketing Activity', *Journal of Business Research*, **15** (3), 221–35.

Cavusgil, S.T. and S. Zou (1994), 'Marketing Strategy-Performance Relationship: An Investigation of the Empirical Link in Export Market Ventures', *Journal of Marketing*, **58** (January), 1–21.

Cavusgil, T. (1985), 'Guidelines for Export Market Research', *Business Horizons*, **28** (6), 27–33.

Cavusgil, S.T. and J.R. Nevin (1981), 'Internal Determinants of Export Marketing Behavior: An Empirical Investigation', *Journal of Marketing Research*, **18**, 114–19

Chang, T.L. (1996), 'Cultivating Global Experience Curve Advantage on Technology and Marketing Capabilities', *International Marketing Review*, **13** (6), 22–42.

Chetty, S. (1994), 'Business Networks as a Determinant of Export Performance', *Journal of International Marketing*, **2** (4), 11–15.

Chetty, S. and B. Gray (1996), 'Exporting Success: Key Success Factors for Smaller Exporters', *New Zealand Strategic Management*, **2** (3), Winter, 45–9.

Chetty, S.K. and R.T. Hamilton (1993b), 'The Export Performance of Smaller Firms: A Multi-case Study Approach', *Journal of Strategic Marketing*, **1**, 247–56.

Chetty, S.K. and R.T. Hamilton (1996), 'The Process of Exporting in Owner-controlled Firms', *International Small Business Journal*, **14** (2), 12–25.

Christensen, C.H., A. da Rocha and R.K. Gertner (1987), 'An Empirical Investigation of the Factors Influencing Exporting Success of Brazilian Firms', *Journal of International Business Studies*, **18** (Fall), 61–77.

Cooper, R.G. and E.J. Kleinschmidt (1985), 'The Impact of Export Strategy on Export Sales Performance', *Journal of International Business Studies*, (Spring), 37–55.

Coviello, N. and H. Munro (1997), 'Network Relationships and the Internationalisation Process of Small Software Firms', *International Business Review*, **6** (4), 361–86.

Cragg, P. (1996), 'Adoption of the Internet by Small Firms', *Proceedings to AusWeb96 Conference* URL: http://www.scu.cdu.au/sponsored/ausweb.ausweb96/ business/cragg/, accessed on 21/05/98.

Cragg, P.B. and M. King (1993), 'Small-firm Computing: Motivations and Inhibitors', *MIS Quarterly*, (March), 47–60.

Craig, R. and P.W. Beamish (1989), 'A Comparison of the Characteristics of Canadian and UK Exporters by Firm Size', *Journal of Global Marketing*, **2** (4), 49–63.

Cronin, M.J. (1994), *Doing Business on the Internet*, New York: Van Nostrand Reinhold.

Cronin, M.J. (1995), *Doing More Business on the Internet*, New York: Van Nostrand Reinhold.

Cronin, M.J. (1996), *Global Advantage on the Internet*, New York: Van Nostrand Reinhold.

Czinkota, M. and W.J. Johnston (1981), 'Segmenting U.S. Firms for Export Development', *Journal of Business Review*, **9** (4), 353–65.

Czinkota, M. and W.J. Johnston (1982), 'Exporting: Does Sales Volume Make a Difference? – A Reply', *Journal of International Business Studies*, (Summer), 157–61.

Dau, R. (1991), 'Marketing Orientation and Export Performance in the New Zealand Manufacturing Industry', unpublished Ph.D Dissertation, Victoria University of Wellington, New Zealand.

Dau, R. and P.C. Thirkell (1996), 'The Relationship between Marketing Orientation and Export Performance: Further Empirical Evidence', in Martin, A.M. and R.G. Starr Jnr (eds) *Proceedings of the 1996 Australia New Zealand Marketing Educators' Conference*, 369–86.

Dau, D. and P.C. Thirkell (1998), 'Export Performance: Success Determinants for New Zealand Manufacturing Exporters', *European Journal of Marketing*, **32**, (9/10), 813–29.

Diamantopoulos, A. and A. Souchon (1998), 'The Impact of Export Information Utilisation on Export Performance', *Proceedings of the Academy of Marketing Annual Conference*, 598–99.

Eighmy, J. and L. McCord (1998), 'Adding Value in the Information Age: Uses and Gratifications of Sites on the World Wide Web', *Journal of Business Research*, **41** (3), March, 187–94.

Ellsworth, J.H. and M.V. Ellsworth (1995), *The Internet Business Book*, New York: John Wiley

Ellsworth, J.H. and M.V. Ellsworth (1996), *Marketing on the Internet – Multimedia Strategies for the WWW*, New York: John Wiley.

Enderwick, P. and M.E.M. Akoorie (1994), 'Pilot Study Research Note: The Employment of Foreign Language Specialists and Export Success – The Case of New Zealand', *International Marketing Review*, **11** (4), 4–19.

Flint, J. and R. Walker (1997), 'Export Marketing of Primary Produce: Implications for Development of International Marketing Theory', *Proceedings of the 1997 Australia New Zealand Marketing Educators' Conference*, Melbourne, December 1–3, 453–67.

Fontes, M. and R. Coombs (1997), 'The Coincidence of Technology and Market Objectives in the Internationalisation of New Technology-based Firms', *International Small Business Journal*, **15** (4), 14–35.

Fortin, D.R. and T.B. Greenlee (1998), 'Cybermediaries in Electronic Marketspace: Toward Theory Building', *Journal of Business Research*, **41** (3), March, 205–14.

Gordon, M.E. and K. De Lima-Turner (1997), 'Consumer Attitudes towards Internet Advertising: A Social Contract Perspective', *International Marketing Review*, **14** (5), 362–75.

Gronroos, C. (1994), 'From Marketing Mix to Relationship Marketing: Towards a Paradigm Shift in Marketing', *Management Decision*, **32** (2), 4–20.

Gummerson, E. (1996), 'Why Relationship Marketing is a Paradigm Shift: Some Conclusions from the 30Rs Approach', *MCB Electronic Conference on Relationship Marketing*, www.mcb.co.uk/confhome.htm.

Hagel, J. and A.G. Armstrong (1997), *Net Gain: Expanding Markets through Virtual Communities*, Boston, MA: Harvard Business School Press.

Hamill, J. (1997), 'The Internet and International Marketing', *International Marketing Review*, **14** (5), 300–23.

Hamill, J. and K. Gregory (1997), 'Internet Marketing in the Internationalisation of UK SMEs', *Journal of Marketing Management*, **13**, 9–28.

Hammond, R. (1996), *Digital Business: Surviving and Thriving in an On-line World*, Hodder & Stoughton.

Hoffman, D.L. and T.P. Novak (1996), 'Marketing in Hypermedia Computer-mediated Environments: Conceptual Foundations', *Journal of Marketing*, **60**, 50–68.

Jaworski, B. and A. Kohli (1993), 'Market Orientation: Antecedents and Consequences', *Journal of Marketing*, **57** (July), 53–70.

Johanson, J. and J.-E. Vahlne (1977), 'The Internationalization Process of the Firm - A Model of Knowledge Development and Increasing Foreign Market Commitments', *Journal of International Business Studies*, **8** (1), 23–32.

Jones, J.M. (1998), 'Internet Shopping: Findings from an Exploratory Study and Research Propositions', *Developments in Marketing Science*, **11**, 349.

Journal of Business Research (1998), Special Issue on Conducting Business in the New Electronic Environment: Prospects and Problems, **41** (3), March.

Joynt, P. (1982), 'An Empirical Study of Norwegian Export Behaviour', in M.R. Czinkota and G. Tesar (eds), *Export Management: An International Context*, New York: Praeger, pp. 55–69.

Keeling, K. and P. McGoldrick (1997), 'The Acceptance of Electronic Shopping: A Question of Control?', *Proceedings of 26th European Marketing Academy Conference*, **2**, 669–88.

Khan, M.S. (1978), 'A Study of Success and Failure in Exports', Department of Business Administration, University of Stockholm, Sweden.

Klein, L.R. and J.A. Quelch (1997), 'Business-to-Business Market Making on the Internet', *International Marketing Review*, **14** (5), 345–61.

Koh, A.C. (1990), 'Relationships among Organisational Characteristics, Marketing Strategy and Export Performance', *International Marketing Review*, **8** (3), 46–60.

Larson, B.D. (1996), 'Information Technology and International Trade: Resources for the Modern Exporter', *Business America*, **117** (5), May, 13.

Leong, E.K.F. and P.-J. Stanners (1997), 'Back to Basics for Marketers on the Web', *Proceedings of Australia New Zealand Marketing Educators' Conference*, **2**, 771–79.

Leonidou, L.C. (1995a), 'Export Barriers: Non-Exporters' Perceptions', *International Marketing Review*, **12** (1), 4–25.

Leonidou, L.C. (1995b), 'Export Stimulation: A Non-Exporter's Perspective', *European Journal of Marketing*, **29** (8), 17–36.

Lim, J.-S., T.W. Sharkey and K.I. Kim (1993), 'Determinants of International Marketing Strategy', *Management International Review*, **33** (2), 103–20.

Marquardt, Michael J. (1996), *Building the Learning Organization,* New York: McGraw-Hill.

Martin, C.J. (1989), 'Information Management in the Smaller Business: The Role of the Manager', *International Journal of Information Management*, **9**, 187–97.

Negroponte, N. (1995), *Being Digital*, New York: Alfred A Knopf Inc.

Normann, R. and R. Ramirez (1993), 'From Value Chain to Value Constellation: Designing Interactive Strategy', *Harvard Business Review,* (July–August), 65–77.

Nouwens, J. and H. Bouwan (1995), 'Living Apart Together in Electronic Commerce: The Use of Information and Communication Technology to Create Network Organizations', *Journal of Computer-Mediated Communication*, **1** (3). Web: http://www.ascusc.org/jcmc/vol1/issue3/nouwens.html

Nunnally, J.C. (1978), *Psychometrics Methods*, New York: McGraw-Hill.

Payne, A., M.C. Christopher and M.H. Peck (1996), *Relationship Marketing for Competitive Advantage: Winning and Keeping Customers*, Oxford: Butterworth-Heinemann.

Peterson, R.A., S. Balasubramanian and B.J. Bronnenberg (1997), 'Exploring the Implications of the Internet for Consumer Marketing', *Journal of the Academy of Marketing Science*, **25** (4), Fall, 329–46.

Pine, B.J. II, D. Peppers and M. Rogers (1995), 'Do You Want to Keep Your Customers Forever?', *Harvard Business Review*, (March–April), 103–14.

Poon, S. and C. Jevons (1997), 'Internet-enabled International Marketing: A Small Business Network Perspective', *Journal of Marketing Management*, **13**, 29–41.

Poon, S. and P.M.C. Swatman (1997), 'Small Business Use of the Internet: Findings from Australian Case Studies', *International Marketing Review*, **14** (5), 385–402.

Quelch, J.A. and L.R. Klein (1996), 'The Internet and International Marketing', *Sloan Management Review*, (Spring), 60–75.

Rayport, J.F. and J.J. Sviokla (1994), 'Managing in the Marketspace', *Harvard Business Review*, (November–December), 141–50.

Roberts, G. (1998), 'Electrifying learning in marketing?', in C. Gilligan et al. (eds) *Proceedings of the UK Academy of Marketing Annual Conference*, Academy of Marketing, Sheffield Hallam University, Sheffield, (July 8-10), pp. 652–53.

Robertson, C. and S.K. Chetty (1997), 'Enhancing Export Performance: A Contingency Based Approach', *Proceedings of 26th European Marketing Academy Conference*, 20–23 May, 1084–100.

Rosson, P.J. and L.D. Ford (1982), 'Manufacturer–Overseas Distributor Relations and Export Performance', *Journal of International Business Studies*, **13** (Fall), 57–72.

Sarkar, M., B. Butler and C. Steinfield (1998), 'Matching Electronic Distribution Channels to Product Characteristics: The Role of Congruence in Consideration Set Formation', *Journal of Business Research,* **41** (3), March, 215–21.

Sheth, J.N. and R.S. Sisodia (1997), 'Consumer Behaviour in the Future', in R.A. Peterson, *Electronic Marketing and The Consumer*, Beverly Hills, CA: Sage Publications Inc., 17–38.

Sivadas, E., R. Grewal and J. Kellaris (1998), 'The Internet as a Micro Marketing Tool: Targeting Consumers through Preferences Revealed in Music Newsgroup Usage', *Journal of Business Research*, **41** (3): 179–86.

Slay, J. (1997), 'The Use of the Internet in Creating an Effective Learning Environment', *Proceedings of AUSWEB 97.*

Souchon, A.L., A. Diamantopoulos (1997), 'Use and Non-use of Export Information: Some Preliminary Insights into Antecedents and Impact on Export Performance', *Journal of Marketing Management*, **13**, 135–51.

Srirojanant, S. (1997), 'Synergy of Relationship Marketing and the Internet', Unpublished Honours' Dissertation, Victoria University of Wellington, NZ.

Srirojanant, S. and P.C. Thirkell (1997a), 'Interactive Web Site Improves Relationships', *NZ InfoTech Weekly*, Monday 8 December.

Srirojanant, S. and P.C. Thirkell (1997b), 'Relationship Marketing as Bits and Bytes', *Proceedings to Australia and New Zealand Educators' Conference*, **1**, Melbourne, 1–3 December, pp. 395–96.

Srirojanant, S. and P.C. Thirkell (1998), 'Relationship Marketing and Its Synergy with Web-based Technologies', *Journal of Market-Focused Management*, **3** (1), 23–46.

Stephens, D.L., R.P. Hill and K. Bergman (1996), 'Enhancing the Consumer-Product Relationship: Lessons from the QVC Home Shopping Channel', *Journal of Business Research*, **37**, 193–200.

Sterne, J. (1995), *World Wide Web Marketing: Integrating the Internet into Your Marketing Strategy*, New York: John Wiley.

Stevens (1996), http://aorangi.vuw.ac.nz/webresearch/Survey/Survey.html.

Stevens, P.M. and L. Howson (1997), 'The Internet as a Retail Channel: Costs and Benefits for Consumers and Marketers', *Proceedings of Australia New Zealand Marketing Educators' Conference*, **1**, pp. 208–21.

Tapscott, D. (1996), *The Digital Economy: Promise and Peril in the Age of Networked Intelligence*, New York: McGraw-Hill.

Thirkell, P. (1997), 'Caught by the Web: Implications of Internet Technologies for the Evolving Relationship Marketing Paradigm', in T. Meenaghan (ed.), *Emerging Forces, Proceedings of the American Marketing Association Conference on Relationship Marketing*, American Marketing Association: Dublin, (June), 334–48.

Turnbull, P. and G. Welham (1985), 'The Characteristics of European Export Marketing Staff', *European Journal of Marketing*, **19** (2), 31–41.

Welch, D.E. and L.S. Welch (1996), 'The Internationalization Process and Networks: A Strategic Management Perspective', *Journal of International Marketing*, **4** (3), 11–28.

Wikstrom, S. (1996), 'Value Creation by Company–Consumer Interaction', *Journal of Marketing Management*, **12**, 359–74.

Yap, C.S., C.P.P. Soh and K.S. Raman (1992), 'Information Systems Success Factors in Small Business', *OMEGA International Journal of Management Sciences*, **20** (5-6), 597–609.

Yaprak, A. (1985), 'An Empirical Study of the Differences between Small Exporting and Non-exporting US Firms', *International Marketing Review*, **2** (Summer), 72–83.

Young, M.A. and P.L. Sauer (1996), 'Organizational Learning and Online Consumer Information Services', *Journal of Consumer Marketing*, **13** (5), 35.

Zeffane, R. (1992), 'The Dual Character of Computer-related Achievements in an Organization Context', in Urs. E. Gattiker (ed.), Technological Innovation and Human Resources, Vol. 3, *Technology-Mediated Communication*, Chapter 1, pp. 15–62.

APPENDIX

Table 4A.1 Internet interactivity scale items

Internet applications

• It is easy for customers to email staff in our organisation.	(1) Strongly agree (2) Agree (3) Neither agree nor disagree (4) Disagree (5) Strongly disagree
• In your company, to what extent is the Internet used to communicate with or provide information to customers and other stakeholders?	(6) Not at all (7) To a minor extent (8) Moderately (9) Somewhat significantly (10) Significantly
• What is the proportion of office staff who use the Internet regularly?	[%]

Management attitude towards the Internet

In your company, senior management believes that being on the Internet… • is an essential component of an effective IT strategy. • gives an image of being modern and involved in high technology. • adds value to customers in terms of product and service offerings. • allows our organisation to be on par or better than our main competitors. • is a less expensive way to promote and advertise products. • will result in financial benefits to our organisation in the near future. • allows our organisation to satisfy customer needs better.	(1) Strongly agree (2) Agree (3) Neither agree nor disagree (4) Disagree (5) Strongly disagree

Table 4A.2 Export performance scale items

Please evaluate your export market performance over the last three years on these criteria: • Export sales volume • Export profitability • Rate of new market entry • Market diversification • Market awareness of product and company • Customer service enhancement	(1) Poor (2) Somewhat poor (3) Moderate (4) Good (5) Excellent
Thinking about the performance of your company as an exporter, how would you rate its export performance ... • Three years ago? • At present • Three years from now?	(1) Poor (2) Somewhat poor (3) Moderate (4) Good (5) Excellent

Table 4A.3 Sample characteristics

	Distribution of ranges			Data distribution		No. of responses	Missing
	Range	Category ranges	% of all firms	Mean	Std Dev.		
Number of employees	1-10 000 employees	1-15 16-80 over 80	47.7 % 29.2% 23.1%	221.4	967.6	130	6
Number of export employees	0-500 people	0-2 3-5 6-500	34.4% 30.4% 35.2%	25.5	74.6	125	11
Years of export experience	0-133 years	0-4.90 5-11.9 12-133	27.3% 39.1% 33.6%	13.1	18.6	128	8
Number of countries exported to	0-102 countries	0-4 5-24 25-102	32.8% 40.6% 26.6%	16.4	20.0	128	8
% of turnover from export	0-100%	0-10.99% 11-49.99% 50-100%	35.1% 26.6% 38.3%	39	35.3	128	8

Table 4A.4 Sample Internet-Usage Characteristics

	Distribution of ranges			Data distribution		No. of responses	Missing
	Range	Category ranges	% of firms	Mean	Std Dev.		
Age of Web site (months)	1-120 mos.	1-12	38.8	20.4	14.1	134	2
		13-23	39.6				
		Over 24	21,6				
% of staff that use the Internet regularly	0-100%	1-20	36.4	45.3	34.6	132	4
		20.01-60	34.1				
		60.01-100	29.5				
Hours/week a staff member spends on the Internet	0-30 hours per week	0-2	39.2	5.8	6.6	125	11
		3-5	34.4				
		6-30	26.4				
Internet use applications	Extent of use		% of firms	Mean score on 5-point scale	Std Dev.	No. of responses	Missing
Use the Internet for market information gathering	'Not at all' (1)		17.0	2.9	1.2	135	1
	'To a minor extent ' (2) – 'moderately' (3)		48.9				
	'Somewhat significantly' (4) – 'significantly' (5)		34.1				
Use the Internet for marketing and sales activities	'Not at all' (1)		16.3	2.8	1.3	135	1
	'To a minor extent ' (2) – 'moderately' (3)		51.9				
	'Somewhat significantly' (4) – 'significantly' (5)		31.8				
Use the Internet for communication purposes	'Not at all' (1)		8.1	3.4	1.3	135	1
	'To a minor extent ' (2) – 'moderately' (3)		43.0				
	'Somewhat significantly' (4) – 'significantly' (5)		48.9				

5. Australian Wineries: Factors Perceived to Enhance or Inhibit Export Market Expansion

Rumintha Wickramasekera and Geoff Bamberry

INTRODUCTION

Exporting has a stimulating effect on both the national economy and on the firms involved. For the country, exports represent additional jobs, a positive trade balance on goods and services as well as a multitude of other benefits through the multiplier effect. Exports are also important to individual firms as they represent additional opportunities for expanded markets, profits and future growth.

During the past decade, Australia's trade balance on goods and services has been very volatile, but overall a deficit has been recorded. The current account has been constantly running at a deficit and stood at $23,266 million in 1997–98 (Australian Bureau of Statistics, 1999a). A contributing factor has been the rapid increase in imports. However, there are encouraging signs with an increase in Australia's total exports of goods and services.

TRENDS IN AUSTRALIAN EXPORTS

Australia's exports of some its agricultural and mineral products constitute a significant portion of world trade in those products. Such commodities have an impact on world prices, and in some cases the quantity of exports can only be increased at the cost of reduced prices. The number of primary producers has also been increasing worldwide, leading to greater competition, reductions in profit margins and volatility of prices (Hughes et al.,

1989: 15). Future development in exports will have to be centred around value-added exports and in tapping into niche markets.

Fortunately, this appears to be the case in Australia where there have been increases in value-added exports rather than primary produce. For example, the processed food and beverage sector has shown a steady increase over recent years (Agriculture, Fisheries and Forestry Australia, 1999). However, there are several problems facing the economy. Rural exports as a proportion of total exports have fallen over that past decade. This has been one of the factors contributing to a stagnant rural sector (Australian Bureau of Statistics, 1999a).

Another problem that could have serious repercussions on the Australian economy is the decline of the Asian economies. These include some of Australia's largest export markets with which Australia currently have significant merchandise trade surpluses. Australia may need to diversify into other export markets such as Europe and the United States where Australia experience a significant trade deficit (Hartcher, 1997).

THE AUSTRALIAN WINE INDUSTRY

One industry which has defied the trends in regional Australia has been the wine industry. It has shown dynamism lacking in some of the other regional industries. Over the past decade it has experienced unprecedented growth in exports (Figure 5.1), especially to Europe and the United States (Australian Bureau of Statistics, 1999b), despite there being an oversupply of wine in the world market (Lages, 1999). Overseas demand for Australian wines appears to be continuing to grow. However, Australia remains one of the world's small wine producers, constituting only 2 per cent of global production. With a relatively low domestic consumption rate (18.3 litres per head) there are also opportunities for future domestic expansion. The aim of the industry is to achieve sales of $2.5 billion by the year 2025 (Australian Wine Foundation, 1996).

Value-added exports are important to regional economies and, as in the case of the wine industry, expanded exports result in greater demand for supplies from other industries. If the additional inputs come from within the region, then there will be a flow-on throughout the economy through the multiplier effect, stimulating the economic vigour of the region (Jansen and West, 1996). Additional employment opportunities generated through increased exports would help to reverse negative trends that have been identified in some rural areas such as a decline in the number of manufacturing firms (Bamberry and Wickramasekera, 1999). It would also add to the nation's current account receipts, thus helping to ease the current account deficit.

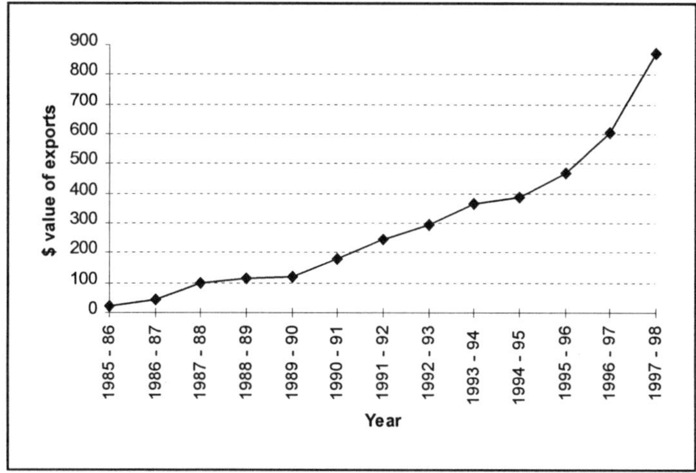

Source: Australian Bureau of Statistics (1999a)

Figure 5.1 Export of Australian wine

This study uses data from an extensive survey into the internationalisation of Australian wineries and is aimed at gaining insights into factors perceived to inhibit or enhance export market expansion of the Australian wine industry.

EXPORT BEHAVIOUR STUDIES

There is an extensive body of literature pertaining to the export behaviour of firms, very wide in its scope with findings sometimes contradictory. Currently, there is no single agreed model to explain how firms move from supplying domestic markets to overseas ones (referred to in the literature as the internationalisation process). However, there is substantial evidence for a stage model (see Bilkey and Tesar, 1977; Cavusgil, 1980; Czinkota, 1982; Andersen, 1993; Crick and Katsikeas, 1995; and Leonidou and Katsikeas, 1996). This study uses a four-stage model (see Wickramasekera, 1998 for a fuller discussion) to provide a profile of wineries at different stages in their export development.

Stage 1: Awareness. During the first stage of the export adoption process the firm (adoption unit) becomes aware of exporting but management is not sufficiently interested in searching for additional information about it. These firms are still domestic-market oriented.

Stage 2: Export Interest. The firms in this stage have a management team that is interested in the innovation of exporting.

Stage 3: Export Trial. Based on the available information, management draws conclusions about exporting. During this stage some firms undertake a 'mental trial' (or desk evaluation) of exporting, whereas other firms will be willing to export on a limited basis. The experience gained during this stage will provide management with the information to adopt or reject the option of exporting (Schiffman and Kanuk, 1994).

Stage 4: Adoption (Established Exporters). Favourable management perceptions of export trials, or a favourable evaluation of them, will usually result in a firm deciding to proceed with exporting on a permanent basis. In this model, the post-adoption evaluation, which can lead to a strengthened commitment and expansion into additional international markets, is also considered to be part of this stage.

STUDIES ON THE DETERMINANTS OF EXPORT ORIENTATION

A vast array of international research has been aimed at understanding the factors that inhibit or aid firms in developing international markets. Fortunately, there are a number of papers that have attempted to integrate or review this vast array of literature. This review is primarily based on these papers in order to build on the findings of others. Because the attitudes of management have been identified as crucial for international success, this review focuses on factors perceived by management to enhance or inhibit export market development (Calof and Beamish, 1995).

Bilkey (1978) reviewed forty-three studies undertaken before 1978. Miesenbock (1988) concentrated his review on studies associated with the export behaviour of small businesses while a year later Aaby and Slater (1989) reviewed fifty-five studies conducted during the decade 1978–1988. Ford and Leonidou (1991) and Leonidou (1995) reviewed the export behaviour literature from a European perspective. Chetty and Hamilton (1993) conducted a meta-analysis on the firm-level determinants of export performance, concentrating on studies published between 1978 and 1991, as well as including a number of studies not included by Aaby and Slater (1989). Sullivan and Bauerschmidt (1989) and Sharkey et al. (1989) considered barriers to exports. Katsikeas and Morgan (1994) provided a synopsis of studies that identified barriers to exports. Based on these reviews a number of variables can be identified.

Some of the important managerial factors identified as influencing the decision to export are managerial perceptions of profit and costs (Simpson and Kujawa, 1974) and knowledge in export matters (Cavusgil and Zou, 1994). Simmonds and Smith (1968) used international outlook versus national outlook to classify managers, while Roux (1987) considers this difference to be based on perceptions of risk; domestically oriented managers being more risk averse than internationally oriented managers.

Firm attributes have been considered as influencing the decision to export, including the quality image of the firm, contractual linkages, promotion of a unique product, terms of sale such as credit offering and competitive pricing (Chetty and Hamilton, 1993) and staff time (Cavusgil and Nevin, 1981). However, there is some debate over the importance of price. Researchers such as Michelle (1979) found there was little importance given to pricing factors by successful exporters in the UK, but Koh (1991) found that pricing was associated with success in exporting.

Other studies have questioned whether management initiates exports because of the confidence it has in the firm's competitive advantage. Tesar (1975) looked at management's perceptions of whether or not the firm had technological, marketing, financial or price advantages in entering export markets.

Environmental factors also have a bearing on the firm's decision to export, such as the rules and regulations of governments (Pavord and Bogart, 1975; Bilkey and Tesar, 1977), size of the domestic market (Kaynak and Kothari, 1984), exchange rate variations, infrastructure factors (Bilkey, 1978), cultural factors, availability of export services, reliable suppliers and the degree of competition in the domestic market (Ford and Leonidou, 1991).

Several studies have found that non-exporters perceive greater barriers to exporting than exporters (Tesar, 1975; Bilkey and Tesar, 1977). In studies conducted in the USA, the serious barriers to exporting were found to be insufficient export finance, foreign government restrictions, insufficient knowledge about market opportunities, inadequate product distribution services abroad and a lack of foreign market connections (Bilkey, 1978).

In Australian studies the following impediments were identified: difficulties in competing on price, variability of exchange rates, the cost of labour and other production costs. (The Bureau of Industry Economics, 1990). Similar findings were made by Daly et al. (1993) with regard to cost of labour, raw materials, freight costs, strong competition and lack of market information. Dwyer (1992) found export licence fees, the cost of raw materials and the cost of shipping to be inhibitors for the wine industry. Other inhibitors identified included the cost of acquiring skilled labour and the lack of support industries for regionally based industries (Owen, 1993).

METHODOLOGY

The population for this study included all the wineries in Australia (ANZSIC code 2183 (Australian Bureau of Statistics, 1994)), estimated at around 853 in 1996. The survey instrument was a questionnaire, its content, design and structure based on an item analysis of theoretical and empirical research published over the previous four decades. Five-point Likert-type questions were developed from the literature. The questionnaire was tested and after some modifications, was administered by post. The sections of the questionnaire relevant to this study were designed to collect information on the following areas:

- managerial perceptions/experiences regarding general benefits/advantages associated with exporting;
- managerial perceptions/experiences regarding general costs/disadvantages associated with exporting;
- managerial perceptions/experiences regarding risks associated with exporting;
- perceived firm-specific advantages/limitations associated with exporting (e.g. product price, product quality, managerial/marketing expertise, innovative production processes, innovative nature of product; and
- actual or perceived barriers and impediments to exporting.

The questionnaires were targeted at the marketing manager of each winery (the key informant), either to fill out personally or to be directed to the person regarded as being responsible for the firm's decision whether or not to export. In total, 302 valid responses were received, 10 being removed due to missing data. For this survey the eligible sample was 292 (out of 853) giving a response rate of over 32 per cent. Based on the definitions established earlier, 71 firms were classified as being in stage 1 (awareness), 115 firms in stage 2 (interested in exports), 60 firms in stage 3 (trialing exports) and 46 firms in stage 4 (established exporters).

Mail surveys have been criticised for possible nonresponse bias. In this study methods proposed by Armstrong and Overton (1977) were used to test for sample bias, including comparing the values derived for the sample with known values for the population and the extrapolation method. It was found that the sample is representative of the population based on these tests.

The aim of this analysis is to gain a better understanding of the factors perceived to inhibit or aid the market expansion of the wine industry. The results are presented on the basis of frequency counts, means and One-Way Analysis of Variance (ANOVA) using SPSS software. The ANOVA procedure requires the assumptions that each of the groups is an independent random sample from a normal population and that in the population, the variances of the groups are equal. Tests were carried out to ensure that these assumptions were met, including the Levene test for homogeneity of variances (Norusis, 1993). The tests confirmed that the sample met these requirements.

In ANOVA analysis the significant *F* value is only an indication that the population means are probably not all equal. However there is no indication which pairs of groups appear to have different means. It is not possible to compare all possible pairs of means using a *t* test as the likelihood of statistical significance increases as comparisons involving the same means are made, though the population means are the same. In order to determine which means are significantly different from each other, multiple comparison procedures need to be adopted (see Winer et al., 1991 for a fuller discussion). These methods protect the researcher from identifying too many differences as significant. The techniques differ in how they adjust the observed significance levels. For this study one of the commonly used techniques and one of the simplest, the Bonforroni test was adopted (Norusis, 1993).

FINDINGS AND DISCUSSION

Perceptions on Factors Enhancing Product Competitiveness

The respondents to the survey were requested to indicate the importance of thirteen 'firm-specific' factors that enhanced their firm's product competitiveness in the market place. In Table 5.1 these items are listed in the order of importance based on the cumulative frequency of 'agree' or 'strongly agree' to the questions. 'The perceived high quality of the wines' and 'the uniqueness of our wines' were deemed to be the most important factors enhancing market competitiveness by more than 80 per cent of the respondents. Other significant factors were 'quality packaging', 'control costs by controlling the entire process', 'the product's price', 'well-established cellar door sales' and 'innovative production skills'. More than 50 per cent of the respondents indicated these as being important in enhancing competitiveness. Out of these six factors only three showed significant difference (at the 95 per cent confidence level) between one or more of the stages. For the factors 'perceived high quality of wines', 'the uniqueness of our wines' and 'product's price' there were no significant differences between the stages. However, the fact that the wineries in all stages consider these factors contributed to the firm's competitiveness in the marketplace (defined as having a mean value greater than 3.0) is likely to reflect on the highly competitive nature of the wine industry.

Table 5.1 Firm-specific factors enhancing competitiveness

	Mean – response					
Firm-specific factors enhancing competitiveness	Stage 1	Stage 2	Stage 3	Stage 4	S p<	%[+]
The perceived high quality of wines	4.42	4.47	4.57	4.61	NS	93.8
The uniqueness of our wines	4.25	4.11	4.42	3.98	NS	81.4
Quality packaging	3.47	3.94[1]	4.02[1]	4.17[1]	.0001	68.8
Control costs by controlling the entire process	3.63	3.55	4.05[2]	3.98	.0165	63.7
The product's price	3.61	3.49	3.77	3.74	NS	60.6
Well-established cellar door sales	3.86	3.39	3.70	3.09[1]	.0089	60
Innovative production skills	3.49	3.50	3.81	3.96	NS	59.6
Well-established network of distributors	2.38	3.30[1]	3.35[1]	4.09[1,2&3]	.0000	49
Well developed marketing skills	2.94	3.37[1]	3.44[1]	3.85[1&2]	.0000	44.2
Reliable suppliers of raw materials	3.07	3.23	3.29	3.75[1]	.0206	42.8
Extensive range of wines produced	2.85	3.04	3.16	3.48[1]	.0501	39.4
Firm's good labour relations	2.84	2.98	3.27	3.41	NS	34.2
Dominant position held by our firm within the industry	1.91	2.25	2.34	3.22[1,2,3]	.000	15.7

Means > than 3 indicates greater importance
S = Significance, NS = Not significant at the 95% confidence level,
1 = Significantly different from stage 1 at the 95% confidence level
2 = Significantly different from stage 2 at the 95% confidence level
3 = Significantly different from stage 3 at the 95% confidence level
+ = Percentage of firms agreeing or strongly agreeing with the question

Overall, out of the thirteen factors listed, seven of the firm-specific attributes showed a significant difference between one or more of the stages. Firms in stages 2 to 4 considered they employed better packaging than firms did in stage 1, with the highest rating being for the established exporters in stage 4. Firms in stage 1 did not consider themselves to possess high level marketing skills (mean < 3.0), while stage 4 firms considered theirs to be well developed. Firms in stage 4 also indicated that they had 'reliable suppliers of raw materials' indicating a significant difference from their counterparts in stage 1 who did not consider this factor to be important (mean value approximately = 3.0)

The 'well-established network of distributors' seems to be the most important factor in terms of differentiating between the stages. Firms in stage 1 clearly indicate that they do not have a good network of distributors.

However, as the wineries develop, their network of distributors becomes better established as indicated by the firms in stage 4, which have significant differences compared with other stages. A similar trend was exhibited for the 'dominant position held by the firm', though indications are that this is not a constraint on smaller firms. With regard to the 'well-established cellar door sales' it is the wineries in stage 1 that agree the most with this factor, decreasing in importance as the winery expands its markets. However, this trend is reversed for the 'range of wines produced' with the wineries in stage 4 indicating that they produce an extensive range of wines

Perceived Advantages of Exporting

As indicated in the review of literature, empirical research found that favourable expectations of exporting on the part of management is an important discriminator in explaining the export behaviour of firms (Cavusgil and Nevin, 1981; and Bilkey and Tesar, 1977). The questionnaire contained seven statements relating to the benefits of exporting and all respondents were asked to indicate their perceptions regarding these statements irrespective of their current status as an exporter or a non-exporter (see Table 5.2).

Table 5.2 Perceived advantages of exporting

	Mean – response					
Perceived advantages of exporting	Stage 1	Stage 2	Stage 3	Stage 4	S p<	%[+]
Exporting allows diversification of markets	4.16	4.45	4.42	4.57[1]	0.0252	88
Exporting reduces the impact of a domestic economic downturn	4.13	4.25	4.25	4.08	NS	82.9
Exporting enables the exploitation of economies of scale	3.69	3.97	4.13[1]	4.15[1]	0.0116	71.3
Exporting enables utilisation of excess capacity	3.99	3.75	3.80	4.07	NS	70.2
Exporting helps overcome a limited home market	3.82	4.02	3.69	4.02	NS	69.2
Exporting adds to the firm's overall profitability	3.27	4.04[1]	4.00[1]	4.21[1]	0.000	63.3
Exporting gives a prestigious image to the firm	3.41	3.77	3.81	3.63	NS	57.2

Means > than 3 indicates greater importance
S = Significance, NS = Not significant at the 95% confidence level
1 = Significantly different from stage 1 at the 95% confidence level
2 = Significantly different from stage 2 at the 95% confidence level
3 = Significantly different from stage 3 at the 95% confidence level
+ = Percentage of firms agreeing or strongly agreeing with the question

The study found only three statistically significant factors: 'exports allow diversification of markets', 'exports add to the firm's overall profitability' and 'exporting enables the exploitation of economies of scale'. However, irrespective of the export behaviour of the firm, the majority of the managers believed that exporting was beneficial. Therefore, it appears that some managers of wineries in stage 1 may have made a deliberate decision not to export, whereas those in stages 2, 3 or 4 are working towards establishing or expanding exports. This study showed that 115 wineries were interested in exporting.

Factors Inhibiting Export Activity

In responses to questions on possible inhibiting factors to exporting, the majority of firms identified 'the limited quantities of stocks for market expansion' as the major barrier. Other potential barriers where more than 50 percent of the firms 'agreed' or 'strongly agreed' included 'lack of financial resources', 'possible risks involved in selling abroad', 'exchange rate variability' and 'low prices required to gain sales in major markets'.

Out of the 15 items listed (see Table 5.3) there were 12 items which showed significant differences between one or more of the stages (the significant differences being most pronounced between stage 1 and 4), exceptions being 'exchange rate variability', 'inability to obtain equipment and other secondary supplies in Australia' and 'anti-alcohol movements in some overseas markets' which did not show any significant differences between the stages. The latter two factors were not seen as serious barriers to export market expansion, whereas all firms considered 'exchange rate variability' a potential problem.

Though all firms indicated 'limited quantities of stocks for market expansion' as the main inhibiting factor, firms in stage 1 found it more so than firms in other stages. 'Lack of financial resources' was a major constraint for firms in stages 1 to 3, showing a significant difference with stage 4 firms. Similar trends were exhibited for 'risks involved in selling abroad', 'legal and regulatory barriers in export markets', 'difficulty in collecting payment from foreign markets', 'problems in selecting a reliable foreign distributor' and 'management's lack of knowledge and experience in export matters'. Firms in stage 3 see these factors as a greater problem than do firms in stage 2, possibly reacting to the discovery that once they start exporting they experience greater difficulties than anticipated. However, once they become established in their export endeavours, these factors are no longer seen as a problem (mean value < 3.0). Similar trends are exhibited for 'inadequate/incorrect market information' and 'unfamiliar foreign business practices'.

All firms agree that there is limited government support to encourage exporting, stage 2 and 3 firms claiming this to be an impediment more than firms in stage 1 and 4. Firms in stage 1 claimed that there is 'low priority

Table 5.3 Factors inhibiting export activity

	Mean – response					
Factors perceived to inhibit export activity	Stage 1	Stage 2	Stage 3	Stage 4	S p<	%$^{+}$
The limited quantities of stocks for market expansion	4.61	4.03^{1}	4.22	4.08^{1}	0.0003	83.5
The lack of financial resources	3.98	3.56	3.78	3.02^{1,2}	0.0004	57.9
Risks involved in selling abroad	3.74	3.36	3.67	2.72^{1,2,3}	0.0000	56.5
Legal and regulatory barriers in export markets	3.79	3.43	3.55	2.91^{1,2,3}	0.0002	52.8
Exchange variability	3.31	3.19	3.30	3.46	NS	52.1
Extremely low prices required to gain sales in major markets	3.91	3.41	3.47	2.87^{1}	0.0003	51
Inadequate/incorrect market information	3.14	3.20	3.34	2.81^{3}	0.0558	49.3
Difficulties in collecting payment from foreign markets	3.62	3.32	3.54	2.74^{1,2,3}	0.0001	48.3
Limited government support to encourage exports	3.27	3.73^{1}	3.67	3.13^{2}	0.0013	46.6
Problems in selecting a reliable foreign distributor	3.72	3.60	3.82	2.74^{1,2,3}	0.0000	45.5
Management's lack of knowledge and experience in export matters	3.51	3.04^{1}	2.88	2.13^{1,2,3}	0.0000	39.4
Unfamiliar foreign business practices	3.64	3.35	3.57	3.00^{1,3}	0.0081	38.4
The inability to obtain equipment and other secondary supplies in Australia	2.54	2.43	2.51	2.07	NS	36.6
The low priority afforded to export market development within the company	3.69	2.67	2.43^{1}	2.04^{1,2}	0.0000	30.5
Anti-alcohol movements in some overseas markets	2.60	2.62	2.76	2.57	NS	12.3

Means > than 3 indicates greater importance
S = Significance, NS = Not significant at the 95% confidence level
1 = Significantly different from stage 1 at the 95% confidence level
2 = Significantly different from stage 2 at the 95% confidence level
3 = Significantly different from stage 3 at the 95% confidence level
+ = Percentage of firms agreeing or strongly agreeing with the question

afforded to export market development within the company', with firms in the other stages generally disagreeing with this notion. 'Management's lack of knowledge and experience in export matters' is considered to be important for firms in stage 1 and marginally so for firms in stage 2, whereas firms in stage 3 and 4 did not consider this to be a serious impediment.

Costs Perceived to Inhibit Export Activity

In order to gauge possible costs that could inhibit exporting, responses were sought for eleven questions relating to this (see Table 5.4). Only two of these factors showed a significant difference between the stages, namely 'cost of international shipping/airfreight' and 'employing managers with export skills and experience'. The latter factor is considered to be marginally important for firms in stages 1 to 3. For 'international shipping/airfreight' it is apparent that established exporters do not find this a constraint. However, firms who are new to exporting (stage 3 firms) do perceive this to be an impediment, possibly due to lack of economies of

Table 5.4 Costs perceived to inhibit export activity

	Mean – response					
Costs perceived to inhibit export activity	Stage 1	Stage 2	Stage 3	Stage 4	S p<	%+
Compliance with export regulations	3.32	3.41	3.50	3.47	NS	50
Financing new plant capacity	3.32	3.41	3.63	3.28	NS	49.3
Domestic government charges	2.85	3.21	3.28	2.96	NS	47.3
Export documentation and procedures	3.35	3.40	3.30	3.00	NS	44.1
Labour in Australia	3.05	3.23	3.23	3.15	NS	40.8
International shipping/airfreight	3.10	3.19	3.52	2.76[3]	0.0085	37.7
Domestic transport	3.08	3.43	3.54	3.17	NS	37
Raw materials	2.73	2.99	2.98	3.22	NS	32.6
Employing managers with export skills/experience	3.06	3.09	3.08	2.39[1,2,3]	0.0038	29.8
Public utilities	2.71	2.91	2.88	2.80	NS	25.7
Insurance associated with exports	2.98	2.96	3.11	2.72	NS	25.7

Means > than 3 indicates greater importance
S = Significance, NS = Not significant at the 95% confidence level
1 = Significantly different from stage 1 at the 95% confidence level
2 = Significantly different from stage 2 at the 95% confidence level
3 = Significantly different from stage 3 at the 95% confidence level
+ = Percentage of firms agreeing or strongly agreeing with the question

scale. Overall only one cost factor, 'compliance with export regulations' was identified as being an important factor by 50 per cent of the respondents, most specifically commenting on the cost of chemical testing for exports as a serious cost factor. Unlike some of the earlier Australian studies (e.g. Dwyer, 1992) which identified cost of labour, transport, raw materials and other inputs as inhibiting factors, this study did not identify them as serious cost-based inhibitors.

CONCLUSION

In this study an attempt was made to identify the key factors which respondents perceived as enhancing or inhibiting the export activities of wineries. In addition, the various factors differentiating the stages of export market development were identified.

The major findings of this analysis point to a very positive outlook with regard to export market expansion based on positive managerial perceptions of exporting. There appear to be very few external constraints preventing export market expansion. The major constraints appear to be the limited quantities of stock available and possibly the lack of financial resources for some wineries. Inhibiting factors such as the cost of labour, transport and other inputs are diminishing in importance, possibly due to a more competitive economic environment in Australia.

It also appears that firms not interested in exporting have made a deliberate decision not to do so for reasons such as insufficient stocks, lack of financial resources, insufficient market knowledge, the lack of a network of distributors and some misgivings about risks involved in selling abroad. These firms also rely more on cellar door sales and on specialising in certain types of wines. This is in stark contrast to wineries that are established exporters who cited lack of stocks and compliance with export regulations, namely chemical testing, as possible inhibiting factors. It was also interesting to note, (though not statistically significant) that there appears to be a 'reality check' for actual new exporters who perceived the external factors to be more inhibiting than firms only interested in exporting.

With a better understanding of the factors perceived to inhibit or enhance export expansion in the wine industry, the next step is to develop a suitable model of export behaviour for the industry, taking into consideration other important variables such as management commitment, management attributes and other firm-specific variables. In order to achieve this objective, a suitable multivariate technique needs to be employed to examine a series of dependent relationships simultaneously and possibly a technique that can recognise measurement errors, a serious limitation in this and other similar studies (Sullivan, 1994). This would help establish the key factors which differentiate wineries at different stages of export development and would add to our understanding of this important and dynamic regional industry.

REFERENCES

Aaby, N.E. and S.F. Slater (1989), 'Management Influences on Export Performance: A Review of the Empirical Literature 1978–88', *International Marketing Review*, **6** (4), 7–26.

Agriculture, Fisheries and Forestry Australia (1999), 'Processed Food and Beverage Industry Performance', *Food News Bulletin*.

Andersen, O. (1993), 'On the Internationalization Process of Firms: A Critical Analysis', *Journal of International Business Studies*, **24** (2), 209–31.

Armstrong, J.C. and T. S. Overton (1977), 'Estimating Nonresponse Bias in Mail Surveys', *Journal of Marketing Research,* **XIV** (August), 396–402.

Australian Bureau of Statistics (1994), *Australian and New Zealand Standard Industrial Classification: Alphabetic Coding Index, Cat. No. 1293.0*, AGPS: Canberra.

Australian Bureau of Statistics (1999a), *Australian Economic Indicators, Cat. No. 1350.0*, AGPS: Canberra.

Australian Bureau of Statistics (1999b), *Sales of Australian Wine and Brandy by Winemakers, Cat. No. 8504.0*, AGPS: Canberra.

Australian Wine Foundation (1996), *Five Year Plan 1997 to 2001: Strategy 2025, The Australian Wine Industry*.

Bamberry, G. and R. Wickramasekera (1999), 'Manufacturing in the Riverina Region', A Report for the Riverina Regional Development Board.

Bilkey, W.J. (1978), 'An Attempted Integration of the Literature on the Export Behavior of Firms', *Journal of International Business Studies,* **9** (Spring–Summer), 33–46.

Bilkey, W.J. and G. Tesar (1977), 'The Export Behavior of Smaller-sized Wisconsin Manufacturing Firms', *Journal of International Business Studies,* **8** (Spring–Summer), 93–98.

Bureau of Industry Economics (1990), 'Impediments to Manufactured Exports', *Discussion Paper*, No.12, AGPS: Canberra.

Calof, J.L. and P.W. Beamish (1995), 'Adapting to Foreign Markets: Explaining Internationalization', *International Business Review*, **4** (2), 115–31.

Cavusgil, S.T. (1980), 'On the Internationalization Process of Firms', *European Research,* **8** (November), 273–81.

Cavusgil, S.T. and J.R. Nevin (1981), 'Internal Determinants of Export Marketing Behavior: An Empirical Investigation', *Journal of Marketing Research,* **18** (February), 114–19.

Cavusgil, S.T. and S. Zou (1994), 'Marketing Strategy–Performance Relationship: An Investigation of the Empirical Link in Export Market Ventures', *Journal of Marketing*, **58** (1), 1–21.

Chetty, S.K. and R.T. Hamilton (1993), 'Firm-level Determinants of Export Performance: A Meta-analysis', *International Marketing Review*, **10** (3), 26–34.

Crick, D. and C.S. Katsikeas (1995), 'Export Practices in the UK Clothing and Knitwear Industry', *Marketing Intelligence and Planning*, **13** (7), 13–22.

Czinkota, M.R. (1982), *Export Development Strategies: US Promotion Policy,* New York: Praeger.

Daly, K., F. Evangelista and C. Kearney (1993), 'Exporting Manufactures from Western Sydney', *Economic Papers,* **12** (4), 73–85.

Dwyer, W. (1992), 'An Analysis of the Australian Wine Exporter', *Discussion Paper Series,* E9208, University of Western Sydney, Sydney.

Ford, D. and L. Leonidou (1991), 'Research Developments in International Marketing', in S.J. Paliwoda (ed.) *New Perspectives on International Marketing,* London: Routledge, pp. 3–32.

Hartcher, H. (1997), 'Australia Swims Against the Tide of Popular Perceptions', *Australian Financial Review (Weekend Edn)*, (November 29–30), 10.

Hughes, H. et al. (1989), *Australian Exports: Performance Obstacles and Issues of Assistance,* AGPS: Canberra.

Jansen, R.C. and G.R. West (1996), 'Input-Output for Practitioners: Theory and Applications', *Australian Regional Developments,* AGPS: Canberra.

Katsikeas, C.S. and R.E. Morgan (1994), 'Differences in Perceptions of Exporting Problems based on Firm Size and Export Market Experience', *European Journal of Marketing*, **28** (5), 17–35.

Kaynak, E. and V. Kothari (1984), 'Export Behaviour of Small and Medium-sized Manufacturers: Some Policy Guidelines for International Marketers', *Management International Review,* **24** (2), 61–9.

Koh, A.C. (1991), 'Relationships Among Organisational Characteristics, Marketing Strategy and Export Performance', *International Marketing Review*, **8** (3), 46–60.

Lages, L.F. (1999), 'Marketing Lessons from Portuguese Wine Exporters: The Development and Application of a Conceptual Framework', *Journal of Wine Research*, **10** (2), 123–32.

Leonidou, L.C. (1995), 'Export Barriers: Non-exporters' Perceptions', *International Marketing Review*, **12** (1), 4–25.

Leonidou, L.C. and C.S. Katsikeas (1996), 'The Export Development Process: An Integrative Review of Empirical Models', *Journal of International Business Studies*, **27** (3), 517–51.

Michelle, P. (1979), 'Infrastructure and International Marketing Effectiveness', *Columbia Journal of World Business,* (Spring), 91–101.

Miesenbock, K.J. (1988), 'Small Business and Internationalisation: A Literature Review', *International Small Business Journal,* **6** (1), 42–61.

Norusis, M.J. and SPSS (1993), *SPSS for Windows, Base System User's Guide Release 6.0*, SPSS, USA.

Owen, K. (1993), *Business Growth and Export Development: Issues for Firms in Rural Areas,* The Rural Development Centre, University of New England, Armidale.

Pavord, W.C. and R.G. Bogart (1975), 'The Dynamics of Decision to Export', *Akron Business and Economic Review,* **6** (Spring), 6–11.

Roux, E. (1987), 'Manager's Attitude towards Risk among Determinants of Export Entry of Small and Medium-sized Firms', in P.J. Rosson and S.D. Reid (eds), *Managing Export Entry Expansion,* New York: Praeger.

Schiffman, L.G. and L.L. Kanuk (1994), *Consumer Behavior,* 4th edn, New Jersey: Prentice Hall.

Sharkey, T.W., J.-S. Lim and K.I. Kim (1989), 'Export Development and Perceived Export Barriers: An Empirical Analysis of Small Firms', *Management International Review,* **29** (2), 33–40.

Simmonds, K. and H. Smith (1968), 'The First Export Order: A Marketing Innovation', *British Journal of Marketing,* **2** (Summer), 93–100.

Simpson, C.L. and D. Kujawa (1974), 'The Export Decision Process: An Empirical Enquiry', *Journal of International Business Studies,* **5** (Spring-Summer), 107–17.

Sullivan, D. (1994), 'Measuring the Degree of Internationalisation of a Firm', *Journal of International Business Studies,* (second quarter), 325–42.

Sullivan, D. and A. Bauerschmidt (1989), 'Common Factors Underlying Barriers to Export: A Comparative Study in the European and US Paper Industry', *Management International Review,* **29** (2), 17–32.

Tesar, G. (1975), *Empirical Study of Export Operations Among Small and Medium-sized Manufacturing Firms*, PhD dissertation, University of Wisconsin-Madison, Madison.

Wickramasekera, R. (1998), 'A Measure of the Stage of Internationalisation of a Firm', in S.J. Gray and S. Nicholas (eds), *Proceedings for the Inaugural Conference of the Australia-New Zealand International Business Academy*, Australian Centre of International Business, Department of Management, University of Melbourne, Victoria, pp. 467–78.

Winer, B.J., D.R. Brown and K.M. Michels (1991), *Statistical Principles in Experimental Design,* 3rd edn, New York: McGraw-Hill.

6. Measuring Export Performance: A Study of New Zealand Manufacturing Exporters

Val Lindsay

INTRODUCTION

The study was part of a larger project concerned with investigating export strategies and performance of New Zealand small and medium-sized enterprise (SME) manufacturers (Lindsay, 1999). The purpose of this chapter is twofold. First, the literature on export performance measurement is reviewed, in order to determine current perspectives on the subject and to highlight the issues still confronting researchers in this field. Second, the chapter aims to explore the relationships between domestic and export sales-related performance measures, moving beyond those generally explored in export performance research. The intention was to try to cast light on the role of the whole firm and its environment in export performance. This contrasts with the view of export performance as an outcome isolated from the rest of the firm's activities and broader strategies. While firm-level strategy has been included as a factor in some export performance models (for example, Aaby and Slater, 1989; Cavusgil and Zou, 1994), few studies include firm-level performance as part of their export performance assessment. This seems to be an important area to explore further, given, in reality, the obvious and complex interplay of activities between domestic and export business within a firm and in the context of its external environment.

Measuring export performance, even with multifaceted measures, as recommended in the contemporary export literature (for example, Matthyssens and Pauwels, 1996) may still not fully represent a firm's engagement with, and performance in, exporting, since overall business performance outcomes may reveal different export dynamics than are evidenced by export-related measures alone. It could also be argued that, over the longer term, the changing dynamics of export performance may reflect performance trends, again not evidenced from static measures taken at single time points in a firm's development – a common method employed in export performance research.

That parallels and lessons in understanding export performance may be drawn from the strategic management literature has been noted by Axinn et al. (1996), in the context of product/market strategies. Similarly, the importance of the whole firm in the performance of business subunits, and the need for subunit strategies to align with whole firm's strategy is well documented in the strategic management literature, particularly that relating to the resource-based view of strategy (for example, Hamel and Prahalad, 1994). If exporting is viewed as a business subunit of a firm, then the interplay between exporting and the rest of the firm's activities is an important consideration, given the strategic perspective just outlined. In other words, as this chapter argues, export performance cannot be viewed in isolation from the rest of the firm and the firm's whole performance.

This has implications for policy-makers who assess exporting as an isolated event, and for researchers debating the appropriate measures to determine export performance. For example, a firm may perform well along many dimensions of export performance, including quantitative and qualitative measures. However, if the firm as a whole shows static or deteriorating performance, the question must be asked as to whether or not the export performance indicators utilised actually reflect a high performing company. This is of crucial importance to policy-makers, who expect some measure of sustainability in performance of the firms that they might be assisting. Following this argument, the contrary situation holds for firms that may be strong overall performers, while showing weak export results. With a sound performance at the level of the whole firm, it could be argued that this is more likely to offer higher potential for successful export business and growth than the former. When potential contingency factors that might influence a firm's overall performance are also considered, it is evident that the scenarios outlined above might just represent the performance dynamics in a longer-term strategy for export growth.

Thus, the issue of how to measure export performance, especially for longer-term sustainability and growth, becomes complex and potentially problematic. It appears that export performance measures need to consider domestic and whole firm performance, longer-term time horizons, and the firm's situational context, in order to reflect the reality of firms' export performance outcomes. Using sales-related indicators, this study aims to provide some preliminary empirical evidence to support the need for these aspects to be included in the determination of export performance measures.

EXPORT PERFORMANCE AND PERFORMANCE MEASUREMENT

Export performance has formed a major strand of research into exporting over the last three decades, along with the internationalisation process. The study of export performance is important from a number of perspectives. General models, which explain export performance more fully, are seen as an important contribution to future research in international marketing research (Axinn et al., 1996). The determinants of export marketing must also be viewed from the perspective of performance, and this should offer valid, reliable measures (Matthyssens and Pauwels, 1996). Knowledge of the determinants of export performance is beneficial to firms initiating and developing export business, particularly those firms becoming increasingly reliant on export business for survival and growth. In addition, government decision-makers strive to assist exporters in the improvement of their export business, and knowledge of export performance determinants is critical to these agencies. It is widely acknowledged that if the correlates of export performance or success can be identified, then government agencies may be able to target potential, or potentially high performing, exporters, as well as focus their assistance programmes more effectively (for example, Crick, 1995).

While one of the main challenges of export research over the last two decades has been the identification and understanding of the antecedents of export performance and the role of exogenous variables, one of the key issues is the measurement of export performance and identification of the particular indicators concerned. This is highlighted by Cavusgil and Zou (1994), who claim that there is no uniform definition of export performance in the export marketing literature. Diamantopoulos and Schlegelmilch (1994) state that: 'As a result of the lack of uniformity and comprehensiveness in the definition of export performance, it is often difficult to obtain a clear picture of the factors impinging on performance' (p. 162). Souchon and Diamantopoulos (1996) raise an important issue in their study of information use in suggesting that 'the absence of a relationship between information use and performance simply may reflect a poorly chosen performance criterion rather than a lack of influence of information use on export success' (p. 65). The performance measurement problem is not unique to export business; it has been researched and debated for many years in the general management and strategy literature (for example, Venkatraman and Ramanujam, 1986). It is also important to recognise that an organisation's performance is situation-specific, and export performance, therefore, must be considered in the context of the objectives of the firm (Shoham, 1991) and the external environment (Aaby and Slater, 1989).

There is little agreement in the literature on how performance and success in exporting should be defined and measured (for example, Cavusgil and Zou, 1994). This is one of the reasons suggested for the large variation in design and analysis of export studies and the inconsistencies in results, and is thus a major contributor to the lack of an underlying theoretical framework of export performance (Aaby and Slater, 1989; Lee and Yang, 1991). Furthermore, there has been little attempt by researchers to identify difficulties in measurement, sampling, validity or particular techniques (Madsen, 1989; Aaby and Slater, 1989). Thach and Axinn (1994) point out that no systematic research has been conducted on the performance measures themselves. It is not unusual, in studies using more than one export performance measure, to find disagreement between the results. For example, in Das's (1994) study of Indian exporters, export intensity yielded more significant and relevant discriminate functions than export growth measures. Rather than attempt to ascertain why these differences occurred, most of the studies that have experienced this outcome merely report separate results for each dependent variable.

Comprehensive reviews of export performance measures are provided by Kirpalani and Balcombe (1989) and Matthyssens and Pauwels (1996). Other authors also provide detailed discussion of the problems associated with determining export performance or success measures (for example, Baker and Abou-Zeid, 1982; Hooley and Lynch, 1985; Buckley et al., 1988, 1990; Ughanwa and Baker, 1989; Diamantopoulos and Schlegelmilch, 1994). Three main problems are associated with the conceptualisation and operationalisation of export performance measures. First, there is a large variety of different approaches to measuring export performance (Diamantopoulos and Schlegelmilch, 1994); second, there is a need to use multidimensional measures; and third, there is a need for export performance indicators to be assessed in a dynamic way, that is, long-term and with a future performance emphasis (Matthyssens and Pauwels, 1996).

In relation to the first issue, export performance measures can be broadly defined as either quantitative or qualitative. Typically, quantitative measures are used, and these include: profitability (sometimes relative to domestic sales, for example, Bilkey, 1982), export intensity (exports as a percentage of total sales), for example, Tookey, 1964), trends in export intensity (Dichtl et al., 1990), export sales and/or export sales growth (Madsen, 1987), changes in export market share (Gomez-Mejia, 1988) and number of export countries (Samiee and Walters, 1991). The most widely used export performance indicator is export intensity, either alone or in combination with other measurements (Diamantopoulos and Schlegelmilch, 1994). However, the use of this measure, especially when used alone, has been increasingly criticised (Cooper and Kleinschmidt, 1985) for a number of reasons. Export intensity may change as domestic business levels change, and a declining domestic business may result in an increased export intensity – the overall business result, however, would be questionable. Furthermore, the export intensity measure gives no indication of export profitability.

Also, export intensity cannot be used as a measure for individual export ventures, as it represents the performance of the entire export business. In some situations, exporters may self-impose a limit on the volume of business that they commit to exporting because of domestic demand (Das, 1994); their export business may, in other respects be deemed successful. Similar issues may arise with export growth, which may not consider other dimensions (for example, meeting strategic goals); exporters may also self-impose a limit to overall or export growth. Caughey and Chetty (1994) suggest that the decision-maker's conception of an ideal size limits the firm's commitment to exporting; in their study, a number of firms felt that they did not want to grow their business beyond a certain point, for reasons largely associated with lifestyle.

More recently, attention has been given to the use of both qualitative and subjective measures of export performance, in order to capture the perspectives of both researchers and practitioners (Matthyssens and Pauwels, 1996), as well as to provide a more contextual understanding of the construct. Qualitative and subjective measures include comparisons with company objectives and competitors' performance (for example, Louter et al., 1991; Cavusgil and Zou, 1994), degree of strategic goal achievement (Cavusgil and Zou, 1994), subjective responder assessment (Evangelista, 1994; Katsikeas et al., 1996), judgemental classification of case material by the researchers and use of a scoring system (Cavusgil and Zou, 1994). Chetty and Hamilton (1996) found that exporters' self-evaluation of export performance was less than objective. In their study, exporters increased their commitment to their exporting ventures, while, at the same time, the financial returns from exporting were diminishing – a situation which suggests that these exporters' perceptions of export performance were different from the reality.

Qualitative measures have been criticised for their weakness associated with measuring perceptions of performance, rather than actual performance itself. Subjective measures have, however, been supported by the view that perceived performance is more important than actual performance (Matthyssens and Pauwels, 1996; Katsikeas et al., 1996). Regardless of these issues, it is generally accepted that such studies offer greater insights into the exporting process, including export performance, than purely quantitative studies using only quantitative measures. Use of both quantitative and qualitative measures in a research study has been agreed as providing the best research outcome, both generally (Miles and Huberman,

1994) and in export research (Matthyssens and Pauwels, 1996; Souchon and Diamantopoulos, 1996).

In their review of the export literature, Aaby and Slater (1989) suggest that export performance studies can also be grouped on the basis of exporter categories, particularly exporters and non-exporters (for example, Cavusgil and Nevin, 1981; Keng and Jiuan, 1989), where the implication is that exporting per se is sufficient to ascribe success to a firm. Some researchers have suggested using different measures for firms of different size, in order to take account of size-related performance measurement difficulties. For example, Diamantopoulos and Schlegelmilch (1994) use indicators in relative, rather than absolute terms. In addition, export market share is very difficult to measure, especially for smaller exporters (Caughey and Chetty, 1994).

The second issue concerns the use of multiple, composite measures of export performance. Use of single performance measures as the sole indicators of export performance has been substantially criticised (for example, Fenwick and Amine, 1979; Rosson and Ford, 1982; Cooper and Kleinschmidt, 1985), as it is argued that the complexity of export success justifies the use of a set of variables (for example, Madsen, 1989; Bijmolt and Zwart, 1994). Nevertheless, Aaby and Slater (1989) suggested that the use of single variable measures is an improvement over the use of the categorical approach, which simply separates firms into exporters and non-exporters. However, multi-indicator measures tend to be more reliable and have less measurement error than single indicator measures (Churchill, 1979).

Notwithstanding these arguments, many studies have taken the single-variable approach (for example, Tookey, 1964; Christensen et al., 1987). Many others which have taken a composite approach have focused on combining export sales-related variables, such as sales growth, export sales and export intensity (for example, Kirpalani and MacIntosh, 1980; Madsen, 1989), which limits the measurement of performance to economic indicators and provides a relatively narrow view of the construct. In utilising a multivariable approach to performance measurement, it has been stressed that financial or economic measures should be complemented by strategic measures, which are more future oriented (Matthyssens and Pauwels, 1996). A number of studies have utilised such an approach (for example, Cavusgil and Zou, 1994; Diamantopoulos and Schlegelmilch, 1994; Souchon and Diamantopoulos 1997). In studying the relationship between a firm's strategy and its export performance, Cavusgil and Zou (1994) stated: 'Previous studies have viewed exporting simply as a means of realising the economic goals of the firm. Performance has been measured in terms of sales or profits, with no deliberate attempt to relate it to a firm's strategic and competitive goals, such as gaining a foothold in foreign markets or neutralising competitive pressure the firm faces in the domestic market' (p. 2). These authors suggest that a proactive marketing strategy has a central role in determining export performance. Export performance measures used in their study of individual product market export ventures incorporated economic and strategic dimensions involving both objective and subjective measures. These measures were: the extent to which the initial strategic goals of management were achieved; the average annual growth rate of export sales over five years of the venture; the overall profitability of exporting over five years of the venture; and management's perceived success of the venture.

According to Matthyssens and Pauwels (1996), two, largely unresolved, problems in using multiple measures have been identified from the new product development and strategy literature. First, it is difficult to differentiate effectively between success and failure, and second, it is difficult to obtain one overall index from combined multiple measures. On the other hand, some researchers (for example, Madsen, 1989; Lee and Yang, 1991) suggest that performance measures should not be combined into one overall measure, but rather, they choose to 'respect the multidimensionality of export performance' (Matthyssens and Pauwels, 1996: 106). This is particularly relevant for the issue of inter-variable relationships and influences, mentioned earlier. Venkatraman and Ramanujam (1986: 807) state: 'A unidimensional composite of a multi-dimensional concept such as business performance tends to mask the underlying relationships among different subdimensions'. (quoted in Matthyssens and Pauwels, 1996: 106).

The third issue concerns the need for export performance measures to be assessed in a dynamic way. This requires measures to represent the long term, rather than, or as well as, the short term (Axinn et al., 1996) and to consider the future expected performance of the firm (Matthyssens and Pauwels, 1996), particularly in the context of the firm's external environment (Axinn et al., 1996). Examples of the few studies which have incorporated these elements are Cavusgil and Zou (1994), Diamantopoulos and Schlegelmilch (1994) and Axinn et al. (1996).

There are also issues in the literature concerned with distinguishing between export success and export performance. Buckley et al. (1988, 1990) point out that problems in measuring 'success' still exist. They suggest that the potential of firms and the process by which the success was achieved should be taken into account with the performance itself. It is also difficult to differentiate effectively between export success and failure when performance involves multiple indicators. For example, Diamantopoulos and Schlegelmilch (1994) found that different subvariables of the manpower variable impacted differently on different performance indicators. Matthyssens and Pauwels (1996) argue that there may be a false dichotomy between success and failure in terms of export performance. They question whether or not success and failure are the extremes of a unidimensional performance scale and suggest that they may not have the same dimensions. This is an important question, with significant implications for theory relating to export performance.

RESEARCH METHOD

The process of case study research developed by Eisenhardt (1989: 533), and similar to that of Yin (1994), was used in a modified format. The research involved a six-year longitudinal study of export performance of 60 SME manufacturing exporting firms in New Zealand, representing varying levels of export performance. While essentially qualitative in design, both qualitative and quantitative methods were used to research and analyse the data, the latter involving non-parametric analysis.

Firms were visited on site and the managing director (MD), and/or export manager were interviewed. Firms were selected to represent a cross-section of export performance, enabling both literal and theoretical replication (Yin, 1994: 46) within a longitudinal context. The study was longitudinal, involving three time points over a six-year period, with approximately equal intervals (mid-1989, end of 1991 and beginning of 1995). Not all 60 firms were present in the latter two phases for reasons that included company failure, unavailability of the MD at the time of the study and relocation of the firm overseas. The numbers of firms for each time period were: 1989: 60; 1991: 50; 1995: 38).

A semi-structured questionnaire was developed, guided by findings from the literature. The focus of the questions was on export performance, but the questionnaire was open-ended to allow exploration of additional aspects of exporting as they arose in the interviews. The cases yielded both qualitative and quantitative data, and the data of most relevance to this study concerned performance-related firm characteristics: trends in total sales, trends in New Zealand market share and trends in New Zealand market sales. Trend figures were used in preference to absolute figures for these characteristics for two main reasons. First, the managing directors of some firms were reluctant to provide absolute figures, and second, the use of relative measures helps to overcome firm differences in aspects such as size and industry type (Diamantopoulos and Schlegelmilch, 1994). It also provides a more dynamic view of the characteristics concerned than is possible with absolute measures taken at any given time point.

Dependent Variables

Notwithstanding the aforementioned concerns in the literature over the use of single measures of export performance, the study utilised only three single measures of export performance, which were all sales-related. These were: export sales trend, export intensity and trend in export intensity (a measure seldom used in other studies, although an exception is Dichtl et al., 1990). Various reasons were associated with this: first, at the time of commencement of the study (1989), there was little debate in the literature on the use of single measures of export performance. Only more recently have the issues surrounding this been prominent. Second, and as noted elsewhere in the literature, absolute financial performance figures are difficult to obtain for small and medium-sized firms, either because of confidentiality, or because of the varied ways in which these results are calculated. Similarly, with respect to more strategic qualitative measures, many of the smaller firms did not have defined strategic export goals, or were too young for these to have been realised at the time of the study. The limited approach to the adoption of more multidimensional measures of export performance is recognised as a limitation of this study. Nevertheless, the use of these three measures and assessments of their relative involvement in export sale performance provided some interesting perspectives on the dynamics of export performance over time and within the export–domestic business relationship of a firm.

Export sales trend is a useful performance measure in providing information about the revenue earned from export over a firm's recent history. Growth in export sales suggests an increase in export business over the time period measured, usually 3 or 5 years. However, increased export sales revenue could arise from static or declining volumes of export product, if, for example, currency or price fluctuations occurred over that time. The export intensity measure seeks to provide information on the ratio of export:domestic business, and, therefore, on the implied degree of export commitment. The main criticism of this measure, however, is that it does not necessarily reflect changes in export earnings or volume. For example, export intensity may increase simply by virtue of a decline in domestic business. Trend in export intensity helps to provide a more stable perspective of the export:domestic business ratios over time, but it is also vulnerable to the same criticisms as absolute export intensity.

By considering all three export sales-based performance measures alongside the other measures of overall and domestic performance (the firm characteristics, or independent variables), it is possible to examine the complex interplay between all three aspects of the firms' sales-based performance, that is, export, domestic and overall. The firm characteristics were analysed as independent variables for two reasons. First, these are widely used indicators in studies assessing the determinants of export performance (for example, Aaby and Slater, 1989) and are thus invariably analysed as independent variables. Second, since the firm characteristics are themselves indicators of performance, the question arose of their specific relationships with export performance. The study aimed to assess their particular role in export performance, particularly from a longitudinal aspect; few studies have analysed these firm characteristics in relation to export performance in terms of trend data.

Data Analysis

All variables involved categorical data, relating to trends, relative market share position or export intensity. While absolute figures were available for the latter variable, categories were used to allow for chi-square analysis of the data. Table 6.1 shows the categories used.

Table 6.1 Categories for independent and dependent variables

Firm characteristic (independent variables)		Categories	
Trend (total sales)	1 Increased	2 Static	3 Decreased
Trend (NZ sales)*	1 Increased	2 Static	3 Decreased
NZ market share	1 Leader/major player	2 Average	3 Low
Dependent Variables		**Categories**	
Trend (export sales)	1 Increased (growth)	2 Static & decreased (no-growth)	
Trend (export intensity)*	1 Increased	2 Decreased	
Export intensity	1 >60%	2 20%–60%	3 <20%

*data available for Phases 2 and 3 only

Interview data were analysed using qualitative data analysis techniques involving within- and between-case analysis, pattern coding and theme building (Miles and Huberman, 1994). The analysis was assisted by the use of the Computer-Assisted Qualitative Data Analysis Software (CAQDAS) package, NUD*IST, which enabled a higher level of data organisation and analysis than would be likely using manual methods (Richards, 1995). The key data relevant to this study from the qualitative analysis involved managing directors' perceptions about the external environment. The categorical data, also obtained in the interview process, was analysed using Pearson chi-square, and Spearman correlation analyses. Data is presented only for 1991 and 1995, since the trend data relating to the firm characteristics were gathered only at those time points. However, the earlier time point (1989) was important because of the managerial perceptions about the external environment at that time, and the fact that this was the base line for the 1991 trend data.

RESULTS AND DISCUSSION

Table 6.2 shows the results of the chi-square analysis of the firm characteristics, using the three dependent variables indicated above, for firms in the 1991 phase of the study.

Table 6.2 Firm characteristics and export performance (categorical data) (1991)

N = 50

	Trend(ES)		ExIntCat		Trend(EI)	
Crosstabs	Pearson chi-square	Spearman correlation	Pearson chi-square	Spearman correlation	Pearson chi-square	Spearman correlation
	(df=2)		(df=4)		(df=2)	
NZMktSh	4.865	0.284*	10.454*	0.338*	3.285	0.140
NZMkTr	7.825*	0.394**	4.844	-0.130	2.108	0.045
Trend(TS)	29.032**	0.762**	7.728	0.260	6.481*	0.346*
Trend(EI)	11.286**	0.475**	13.631**	0.523**	NA	NA
ExIntCat	12.96**	0.444**	NA	NA	NA	NA

Significance: ** 0.01, * 0.05
NA = not applicable
Key: NZMktSh: New Zealand Market Share
NZMktTr: New Zealand Market Trend
Trend(TS): Trend In Total Sales
Trend In Export Intensity
ExIntCat : Export Intensity – Categorised

The significant association and high correlation between Trend(ES) and New Zealand Market Trend (NZMktTr) suggest that domestic and export sales increased together over the previous three years. This is supported by the strong positive relationship between Trend(ES) and Trend(TS). Trend(E1) also increased for export growth firms over this period, suggesting that export sales growth was greater relative to NZ sales growth in these firms. These relationships demonstrate the important interplay between domestic and export sales and their combined impact on export performance. ExIntCat was not related to New Zealand Market Trend (NZMktTr) or Trend in Total Sales (Trend(TS)), but was related to Trend(E1) and Trend(ES), again suggesting that growth was predominantly export led. Trend(EI) was significantly related to Trend(TS) highlighting the interdependence of the domestic, export and total sales situation in exporting firms. The significant results for ExIntCat and New Zealand Market Share (NZMktSh) at the 0.05 level, and with Trend(ES), adds weight to this argument.

The 1995 Pearson chi-square and Spearman correlation analyses of the firm characteristics produced significant results only for Trend(ES), as shown in Table 6.3.

Table 6.3 Firm characteristics and export performance (categorical data) (1995)

N = 38

		Trend(ES)	
Crosstabs	Crosstabs (codes)	Pearson chi-square (df=2)	Spearman correlation
New Zealand Market Share	NZMktSh	8.379*	0.440**
New Zealand Market Trend	NZMkTr	5.188	0.371*
Trend in Total Sales	Trend(TS)	22.679**	0.766**
Trend in Export Intensity	Trend(EI)	5.735	0.276
Export Intensity-Categorised	ExIntCat	3.227	0.294

Significance: **0.01, *0.05

The results suggest that total sales growth was again export driven, because the relationship between Trend(ES) and Trend(TS) was considerably stronger than between NZMkTr and Trend(TS). The apparent lack of sensitivity of the other export performance measures suggest that they should only be used in conjunction with Trend(ES) and interpreted within the context of both domestic and export business. It appears that, in terms of the firm characteristics measured, the distinction between high and low performing exporters, as determined by Trend(ES), depends on the interplay between measures of both export and domestic performance.

Longitudinal Analysis

Differences in various aspects relating to the firm characteristics were observed over the three Stage 2 phases, 1989, 1991 and 1995. The longitudinal part of the study was incorporated mainly in order to investigate changes in variables over time, using time as the dependent variable. Rather than use a time series analysis, such as a repeated measures analysis, the longitudinal analysis focused on changes in the individual independent variables at each time point, in order to assess which variables changed, in terms of performance, over time. From this, it was possible to determine the firms' responses to time-related external environmental changes, noted from economic data and managerial perceptions. For the longitudinal analysis, both the firm characteristics variables and the export performance variables were treated as independent variables. The analysis utilised Pearson chi-square, Spearman correlation and Mann–Whitney analysis since the data were category data. The dependent time variables were represented as 1 (time 1: 1989), 2 (time 2: 1991) and 3 (time 3: 1995).

Table 6.4 shows that the firm characteristics changed over the three time periods, New Zealand Market Share (NZMktSh) and New Zealand Market Trend (NZMktTr) strongly and, Trend in Total Sales (Trend(TS)) weakly.

Table 6.4 Firm characteristics and export performance (categorical data)

N=148

	Time		
Crosstabs	Pearson chi-square (df = 4)	Spearman Correlation	Explanation
NZMktSh	16.488**	0.256**	NZMktSh declined over time
NZMkTr	9.884**	-0.332**	NZMkTr increased over time
Trend(TS)	9.213	-0.185*	Trend(TS) increased over time
Trend(EI)	1.975	-0.057	
Trend(ES)	7.578	0.008	
ExIntCat	2.367	-0.091	

Significance: **0.01 *0.05

Because the time categories ran from 1 (1989) to 3 (1995), and the characteristics were categorised from 1 (increases) to 2 or 3 (decrease), the direction of the relationships was reversed in the table output. The right-hand column in the table explains the nature of the significant relationships. There was no change in any of the export sales-related performance measures (Trend(ES), ExpIntCat and Trend(E1), indicating that the proportion firms in each category associated with these variables remained approximately the same.

These results indicate only that change over time took place; they do not determine the time periods between which the changes occurred. A Mann-Whitney test compared each time period for the variables with significant results in Table 6.4. The results are shown below in Table 6.5.

Table 6.5 Mann–Whitney analysis: firm characteristics (categorical data) (Group Variable = Time); N = 148

Charac-teristic	Variable Code	Periods 1-2	Period 2-3	Period 1-3	Explanation (periods across which differences occurred)
		Z value	Z value	Z value	
NZMktSh	New Zealand Market Share	-2.856**	-0.068	-2.884**	1-2, 1-3
NZMkTr	New Zealand Market Trend	ND	-0.3082**	ND	2-3
Trend(TS)	Trend in Total Sales	-0.157	-2.629**	-2.624**	2-3, 1-3

Significance: **0.01
ND = no data

Combining results from Tables 6.4 and 6.5, the following indications are apparent. New Zealand market share for the firms decreased over the period 1989 to 1991. This is consistent with economic changes over that period, when many study firms rated declining NZ market opportunity through import deregulation as a key issue. Even though firms tended to focus on increasing domestic sales and market share between 1991 and 1995, as evidenced by the significant result for New Zealand Market Trend (NZMkTr) between these periods, they had not recovered market share to original 1989 levels, since there was still a significant difference between periods 1 and 3. Crick and Katsikeas (1995) suggest that low profit exporters tend to focus on the domestic market, but the study results indicate that other, more complex, reasons associated with overall firm growth, may be the key drivers for the domestic focus.

Trend in Total Sales (Trend(TS)) follows the same argument as that for NZMkTr, with many firms focusing on overall (domestic and export) sales growth over the period 1991–95. Other results described earlier suggest that the increase in total sales was predominantly export led, although domestic sales growth also occurred. Since the trend towards overall growth occurred in the latter stages of the study, it may relate to the finding by Ogbuehi and Longfellow (1994) that firms with more experience tend to focus more on firm-level growth strategy. The absence of change in Trend(TS) over the period 1989–91, suggested that, on balance, firms managed to retain overall sales performance over that time, even though there was a decline in New Zealand Market Share (NZMktSh). Some of the differences noted in Table 6.5 are likely to have arisen solely because of the removal of failed firms from the study, and this needs to be considered in the interpretation of the results. Conclusions and implications of these results are discussed in the following section.

CONCLUSIONS AND IMPLICATIONS

The study has provided a preliminary perspective on the relationships between domestic, export and total sales performance in determining export performance. It highlights the fact that these variables have a complex interrelationship, which is influenced by the firm's situational context, and managerial perceptions relating to the external environment. In this respect, the findings support the co-alignment and contingency view of exporting noted by, respectively, Cavusgil and Zou (1994) and Yeoh and Jeong (1995). The study highlighted the key involvement of overall firm-level, rather than export-level, sales-based objectives and performance in determining export sales performance. These objectives appear to be influenced by the firm's situational context, and are underpinned by firm-level, rather than export-level strategy.

The variable, Trend in Export Sales (Trend(ES)) tended to have the most significant relationships with the independent variables (firm characteristics), and thus provided the greatest insights into the export sales performance phenomenon. However, the apparent lack of, or limited, significant relationships between the independent variables and the export intensity variables (the other dependent variables) raises some concerns about their use as export performance measures. This echoes and extends the concerns already noted in the literature. For example, the data suggested that export growth occurred across firms with a range of export intensities, not just those with high intensities. When the export intensity variables are used as sole export performance measures, the lack of relationship with the independent variables implies their lack of involvement in export performance. When the strong positive relationships with the export sales trend variable (Trend(ES)), found in this study, are considered, it is clear that the independent variables, which are focused on the firm's domestic and overall business, are involved in export performance.

Since the export intensity variables are the main measures used in export research to incorporate perspectives on a firm's domestic business involvement, it is not surprising, given these results, that the involvement of the domestic and overall performance of firms in exporting has been largely overlooked. Examination of these performance components independently in this study has indicated important involvements with export sales performance (measured as Trend(ES)). These results suggest, therefore, that, while inappropriate as sole export performance measures, important insights about domestic and overall sales performance can be gained by using the export intensity measures. These, and other measures of domestic and overall firm sales performance should, therefore, be considered as part of any multifaceted approach to measuring export performance.

This conclusion is supported by the other main finding from the study. This shows that a firm may adjust the balance of export and domestic business in response to its situational context, in particular its external environment, and managerial perceptions about its influence. In other words, while still following an export growth strategy, a firm may focus on its overall growth opportunity, which may involve, at times, a focus on its domestic business, in response to external influences. In this respect, all three aspects of the firm's sales performance (domestic, export and total) may thus be important. The longer-term performance outcomes are, therefore, also a key component of measuring export performance. This has been noted by other researchers (for example, Axinn et al., 1996; Matthyssens and Pauwels, 1996; Diamantopoulos and Schlegelmilch, 1994), indicating the importance of measuring managerial perceptions of future export performance as part of the export performance measurement process.

Implications

Since the emphasis of this chapter is on the challenges of measuring export performance for policy-makers, the implications are discussed mainly from that perspective. It is acknowledged that the preliminary findings and suggestions discussed in this chapter also have wider implications for managers and researchers.

Policy-makers have traditionally used export performance and success models to guide them in directing export assistance in a prescriptive way, but research results have shown that outcomes are mixed and inconsistent

(Aaby and Slater, 1989). Ongoing assessment and in-depth understanding of the firm's external environment, and its impacts on exporting, are critical. Policy-makers must be able to work with managers in developing the firm's overall and export strategy in accordance with changes in external drivers.

The importance and influence of overall firm-level performance and strategy on export performance must be understood, particularly as these relate to the firm's situational context. These also impact on the interpretation of export performance measures. Policy-makers must recognise that there is no 'universal' measure of export, or export sales, performance, as different measures are likely to give different results, depending on the firm's overall strategy and its situational context. The impact of environmental and organisational change must be considered in the interpretation of results from various export performance measures.

All of these dimensions suggest that there is a need for government policy-makers to acquire a holistic understanding of exporting, where all the variables and contingencies are recognised, both internally and externally. This requires more inclusive measures of export performance in order to reflect wider strategic, as well as financial, export performance outcomes of firms. This means that policy-makers have to work closely with exporting firms on an ongoing basis. Such a perspective of export performance would then enable policy-makers to develop and direct appropriate assistance programmes, as well as measure their impact, qualitatively and quantitatively.

Finally, because the political/economic environment provides such an important contextual element to the export performance process, government has a responsibility to communicate policies that will impact on exporting firms, and to be aware of their effects on individual exporters. A contingency-based model of export performance can be helpful in this regard.

Limitations of the Research

The study outlines a preliminary investigation of the relationships between a firm's domestic, export and total sales performance in export sales performance. The use of only three single measures of export performance in this study represents an important limitation, as discussed earlier in the chapter. It is therefore important that future research on the performance-related dynamics of firm-level and export-level strategy incorporates the multidimensional measures of export performance discussed in this chapter.

Research needs to be conducted to explore these issues in more depth and to develop ways of incorporating the wider firm-level variables into multi-faceted export performance measures. Analysis of the time-related changes in the study should be extended, perhaps using time series analysis, thereby enabling more detailed changes to be determined. Finally, while the use of only sales-based export performance measures was helpful in examining other sales-based variables, the incorporation of wider measures of export performance would assist in providing a better understanding of the relationships identified in the study and a broader perspective of the export performance phenomenon called for in the research literature.

REFERENCES

Aaby, N.E. and S.E. Slater (1989), 'Managerial Influences on Export Performance: A Review of the Empirical Literature 1978–88', *International Marketing Review,* **6** (4), 53–68.

Axinn, C.N., T. Noordewier and J.M.J. Sinkula (1996), 'Export Strategies and Export Performance: An Empirical Investigation of a Products/ Markets Typology', *Advances in International Marketing,* **8** (2), 7–58.

Baker, M.J. and E. Abou-Zeid (1982), *Successful Exporting: A Survey of Marketing Practice in Winners of the Queen's Award for Export Achievement,* Glasgow: Westfield.

Bijmolt, T.H.A. and P.S. Zwart (1994), 'The Impact of Internal Factors on the Export Success of Dutch Small and Medium-sized Firms', *Journal of Small Business Management,* **32** (2), 69–83.

Bilkey, Warren J. (1982), 'Variables Associated with Export Profitability', *Journal of International Business Studies,* **13**, 39–55.

Buckley, P.J., C.L. Pass and K. Prescott (1988), 'Measures of International Competitiveness: A Critical Survey', *Journal of Marketing Management,* **4** (2), 175–200.

Buckley, J., C.L. Pass and K. Prescott (1990), 'Measures of International Competitiveness: Empirical Findings from British Manufacturing Companies', *Journal of Marketing Management,* **6** (l), 1–13.

Caughey, M. and S. Chetty (1994), 'Pre-export Behaviour of Small Manufacturing Firms in New Zealand', *International Small Business Journal,* **12** (3), 62–8.

Cavusgil, S.T. and J.R. Nevin (1981), 'Internal Determinants of Export Marketing Behaviour: An Empirical Investigation', *Journal of Marketing Research,* **8** (February), 114–19.

Cavusgil, S.T. and S. Zou (1994), 'Marketing Strategy–Performance Relationship: An Investigation of the Empirical Link in Export Market Ventures', *Journal of Marketing,* **58** (January), 1–21.

Chetty, S.K. and Hamilton, R.T. (1996), 'The Process of Exporting in Owner-controlled Firms', *International Small Business Journal*, **14** (2): 12–25.

Christensen, C.H., A. da Rocha and R.K. Gertner (1987), 'An Empirical Investigation of the Factors Influencing Exporting Success of Brazilian Firms', *Journal of International Business Studies,* **18** (Fall), 61–77.

Churchill, G.A. (1979), 'A Paradigm for Developing Better Measures of Market Constructs', *Journal of Marketing Research,* **16** (February), 64–73.

Cooper, R.G. and E.J. Kleinschmidt (1985), 'The Impact of Export Strategy on Export Sales Performance', *Journal of International Business Studies,* (Spring), 37–55.

Crick, D. (1995), 'An Investigation into the Targeting of U.K. Export Assistance', *European Journal of Marketing,* **29** (8), 76–94.

Crick, D. and Katsikeas, C.S. (1995), 'Export practices in the UK clothing and knitwear industry', *Marketing Intelligence & Planning,* **13** (7): 13–22.

Das, M. (1994), 'Successful and Unsuccessful Exporters from Developing Countries', *European Journal of Marketing,* **28** (12), 19–33.

Diamantopoulos, A. and B.B. Schlegelmilch (1994), 'Linking Export Manpower to Export Performance: A Canonical Regression Analysis of European and U.S. Data', *Advances in International Marketing,* (6), 161–81.

Dichtl, E., H. Koglmayer and S. Mueller (1990), 'The Export Decision of Small and Medium-sized Firms: A Review', *Management International Review,* **24** (2), 49–60.

Eisenhardt, K. M. (1989), 'Building Theories for Case Study Research', *Academy of Management Review,* **14** (4), 523–50.

Evangelista, F.U. (1994), 'Export Performance and its Determinants: Some Empirical Evidence from Australian Manufacturing Firms', *Advances in International Marketing,* (6), 207–29.

Fenwick, I. and L. Amine (1979), 'Export Performance and Export Policy: Evidence from the U.K. Clothing Industry', *Journal of Operational Research Society,* **30** (8), 747–54.

Gomez-Mejia, L.R. (1988), 'The Role of Human Resources Strategy in Export Performance: A Longitudinal Study', *Strategic Management Journal,* **9** (5), 493–505.

Hamel, G. and C.K. Prahalad (1994), *Competing for the Future,* Boston, MA: Harvard Business Press.

Hooley, G. and J. Lynch (1985), 'Marketing Lessons from the UK's High-flying Companies', *Journal of Marketing Management,* **1** (l), 65–74.

Katsikeas, C.S., N.F. Piercy and C. Ioannidis (1996), 'Determinants of Export Performance in a European Context', *European Journal of Marketing,* **30** (6), 6–35.

Keng, K.A. and T.S. Jiuan (1989), 'Differences between Small and Medium-sized Exporting and Non-exporting Firms: Nature or Nurture', *International Marketing Review,* **6** (4), 27–40.

Kirpalani, V.H. and D. Balcombe (1989), 'International Marketing Success: On Conducting More Relevant Research', in P.J. Rosson and S.D. Reid (eds), *Managing Export Entry and Expansion: Concepts and Practice,* New York: Praegar, pp. 387–97.

Kirpalani, V.H. and N.B. MacIntosh (1980), 'International Marketing Effectiveness of Technology Oriented Small Firms', *Journal of International Business Studies,* **10** (Winter), 81–90.

Lee, C.S. and Y.S. Yang (1991), 'Impact of Export Market Expansion Strategy on Export Performance', *International Marketing Review,* **7** (4), 41–50.

Lindsay, V.J. (1999), *A Strategic View of Export Performance: A New Zealand Perspective,* Ph.D. Thesis, University of Warwick, UK.

Louter, P.J., C. Ouwerkerk and B.A. Bakker (1991), 'An Inquiry into Successful Exporting', *European Journal of Marketing,* **25** (6), 7–23.

Madsen, T.K. (1989), 'Successful Export Marketing Management: Some Empirical Evidence', *International Marketing Review,* **6** (4), 41–57.

Matthyssens, P. and P. Pauwels (1996), 'Assessing Export Performance Measurement', *Advances in International Marketing*, (8), 85–114.

Miles, M.B. and A.M. Huberman (1994), *Qualitative Data Analysis: An Expanded Sourcebook*, London: Sage.

Ogbuehi, A.O. and T.A. Longfellow (1994), 'Perceptions of US Manufacturing SMEs Concerning Exporting: A Comparison Based on Export Experience', *Journal of Small Business Management,* **32** (4), 37–47.

Richards, L. (1995), 'Transition Work! Reflections on a Three-year NUD*IST Project', *Studies in Qualitative Methodology: Computing and Qualitative Research*, (5), 105-40.

Rosson, P.J. and L.D. Ford (1982), 'Manufacturer–Overseas Distributor Relations and Export Performance', *Journal of International Business Studies,* **13** (Fall), 57–72.

Samiee, S. and P.G.P. Walters (1991), 'Segmenting Corporate Exporting Activities: Sporadic versus Regular Exporters', *Journal of the Academy of Marketing Science,* **19** (2), 93–104.

Shoham, A. (1991), 'Performance in Exporting: State-of-the-art Literature Review and Synthesis and Directions for Future Research', paper presented at the Conference of the Academy of International Business, Miami, Florida.

Souchon, A.L. and A. Diamantopoulos (1996), 'A Conceptual Framework of Export Marketing Information Use: Key Issues and Research Propositions', *Journal of International Marketing,* **4** (3), 49–71.

Souchon, A.L. and A. Diamantopoulos (1997), 'Use and Non-use of Export Information: Some Preliminary Insights into Antecedents and Impact on Export Performance', *Journal of Marketing Management,* **13** (1-3), 135–51.

Thach, S.V. and C.N. Axinn (1994), 'Redefining Export Success: Not Which Measures, but Why Measure', Paper Presented at the Second Annual CIMAR Conference, COPPEAD, UFRJ, Brazil.

Tookey, D. (1964), 'Factors Associated with Success in Exporting', *Journal of Management Studies*, **1** (2): 48–66.

Ughanwa, D.O. and M.J. Baker (1989), *The Role of Design in International Competitiveness,* London: Routledge.

Venkatraman, N. and V. Ramanujam (1986), 'Measurement of Business Performance in Strategic Research: A Comparison of Approaches', *Academy of Management Review,* **1** (4), 801–14.

Yeoh, P.-L. and I. Jeong (1995), 'Contingency Relationships between Entrepreneurship, Export Channel Structure and Environment: A Proposed Conceptual Model of Export Performance', *European Journal of Marketing,* **29** (8), 95–115.

Yin, R.K. (1994), *Case Study Research: Design and Methods*, London: Sage.

PART III

Foreign Direct Investment Issues

7. Do Incentives Attract Japanese FDI to Singapore and the Region?

Stephen Nicholas, Sidney J. Gray and William R. Purcell

INTRODUCTION

Since the 1980s, the empirical work on foreign direct investment has focused on the institution making the foreign investment rather than the act of FDI per se. Dunning (1998) has labelled this lacuna the 'neglected factor'. The firm's FDI decision involves two simultaneous and interdependent decisions: the choice of location for an overseas investment and the choice of the multinational form. The location decision lacks well-articulated theory. In contrast, internalisation theory, modified by resource-based and agency approaches, provides a comprehensive paradigm for explaining why ownership of assets is selected as the cross-border form of transacting in goods and services. The multinational form is selected to internalise transactions that occur in imperfect intermediate product markets and imperfect markets for the sale of firm-specific capabilities (Hymer, 1976; Dunning, 1973; Buckley and Casson, 1976; Hennart, 1982; Williamson, 1979; Wernerfelt, 1984; Nicholas, 1983; Peteraf, 1993; Markusen, 1995).

Intermediate product markets are characterised by uncertainty and asymmetric information that allows sellers/buyers, who have better and different information than the MNE, to act opportunistically in supplying inputs/buying outputs from the MNE. Opportunistic hold-up by suppliers/buyers poses special risks when the MNE makes investments in specialised physical and human capital assets and transactions are frequent (Klein et al., 1978; Williamson, 1979). Secure of the high costs of contracting through markets or other long-term contracts (licences and franchises), MNEs vertically integrate to secure inputs and source outputs. The sale of capabilities (know-how) in international markets is further subject to uncertainty and the presence of imperfect information.

As a result, arm's-length markets and intermediate contracts (licensing and subcontracting) fail to secure the full value of the MNE's ownership advantages, related to technology, work and managerial practices, marketing and distribution skills. The MNE is an institution for appropriating the rents from firm-specific ownership advantages in foreign markets (Johnson, 1970; Teece, 1980; Buckley and Casson, 1976).

Of course, the use of the firm as an alternative to the market or intermediate contracts for transferring know-how to overseas markets or sourcing inputs and outputs is not costless. Parents design complex hierarchical control structures to monitor, supervise and detect opportunistic behaviour by subsidiary managers (Carlos and Nicholas, 1993). Information flows, the structuring of lateral decision processes, horizontal networks and shared decision premises reduce potential opportunism, aligning head quarter–subsidiary goals (Birkinshaw, 1994). In contrast to the well–developed theory of the form of overseas involvement, the theory of the location decision has been neglected.

LOCATION DECISIONS AND INCENTIVES

The location decision is usually treated as a secondary factor, grouped into an undifferentiated list, including market characteristics (size and growth), socio-political factors (stability and risk), cultural distance, tariffs and trade barriers and government incentive policies. Recently, there has been a convergence between trade theory and the theory of the MNE. The new trade theory allows for gains from trade to arise from imperfect competition, transport costs, increasing returns and trade policy regimes independent of comparative advantage. (Markusen, 1995; Horstmann and Markusen, 1996; Krugman, 1993). The MNE takes centre stage since industries characterised by imperfect competition and scale economies are often dominated by MNEs (Markusen, 1995). The focus of the new trade theory is not only on the institutional form of overseas involvement, but also on the decision of the MNE to locate in a particular country.

States compete for MNEs. David (1984) termed 'location tournaments' the policy adjustments, promotional programmes and incentive regimes used by states to attract MNEs. State policy creates a path-dependent location process, where incentives lay down layer after layer of new firms upon inherited location formations (Arthur, 1994). The result is industry agglomeration economies, where both history and incentives regimes matter (Wheeler and Mody, 1992). Equally, non-policy variables, such as market characteristics, transport costs and cultural distance, attract MNEs, creating industry agglomerations.

Net benefits from firms locating together include sharing of information, infrastructure, supply networks, labour markets and ancillary services (legal and financial), up to congestion. Such agglomerations are 'sticky', with countries or regions attracting further new investment quickly or shedding firms only reluctantly. The eastern US 'rust belt' is an example of 'sticky' agglomerations only slowly shedding firms while the Silicon Valley (California) and M4 (UK) corridors might be modelled as regions quickly attracting firms. Some authors have found that such regional clusters of economic interdependent production within the global economy provide an early start or first-mover advantage.

Incentives provide one mechanism for states to attract MNEs, building agglomeration economies that attract further investment. Endowments, or non-policy variables, such as the country's resources, rate of economic growth or economic and political stability, provide an alternative route for the creation of agglomeration economies (Krugman, 1991; Scott, 1996; Arthur, 1994). When incentives attract MNEs, they are 'historical accidents' that 'lock-in' regions as an attractive investment destination due to agglomeration economies. Incentives are important because states can alter these quickly, while it takes years to alter non-policy factors such as labour force skills, infrastructure and market size (Loree and Guisinger, 1995).

Scott (1996) argued that in the battle for regional clusters, states enter into predatory poaching wars, with MNEs playing regions off against each other. The outcomes of international tournaments depended on the trade-off MNEs made between the benefits of agglomeration and classical location factors. For a developing economy to get started, Wheeler and Mody (1992) recommended states focus on infrastructure development, stability and rapid economic and market growth, rather than incentives. For US MNEs, Loree and Guisinger (1995) found that both policy and non-policy variables played a role in the location decision, but warned that incentives might provoke the prisoner's dilemma trap, where all countries increase their incentives simultaneously but no country increases its relative share. Following David (1984) and Arthur (1994), Loree and Guisinger (1995) also argued that the incentives that attract MNEs to a region may be the historical accident that 'lock-in' firms to a sub-optimal regional cluster. There are also likely to be significant differences across time and between developing and developed economies. In a review article, Blair and Premus (1987) found a time dimension, with incentives more important after the 1980s than before, as markets became more integrated and transport and communication systems improved.

Broadening the perspective, there is a substantial traditional literature on the role of incentives in FDI. Aharoni's (1966) interviews with executives revealed that investors looked to incentives after some other factors made them investigate the possibility of investing. Studying tax incentives by developing countries, Usher (1977) found that the rate of redundancy, or the difference between the dollar value of the subsidised investment and the net increase in total investment as a proportion of the dollar value of the subsidised investment, was unknown and there was no way to discovering what it is. In short, the impact of incentives on FDI cannot be measured. The most important concessions reduced the risk of investment (such as tariffs or embargoes on imports), followed by incentives that reduced the costs of production (such as tax policies). Lim (1983) claimed that natural resources and a proven record of economic growth (measured by rate of economic growth and level of economic development), not incentives, mattered for developing countries seeking FDI. For Commonwealth developing countries, Cable and Persaud (1987) emphasised the importance of 'fundamentals', including political stability and natural resources, although project-specific investment was modestly sensitive to tax incentives. Trade policy and special zones were relatively unimportant in the investment decision, although 'red tape' and government restrictions discouraged investment. Hughes and Dorrance (1987) found incentives, such as tax holidays, were expensive and did little to encourage foreign investment in East Asian Commonwealth countries, where good reasons for investment existed in the form of natural resources, protected markets or an export base.

Rolfe et al. (1993) found the incentives were specific to market location (local market penetration or export platform), nationality, first or re-investment and time. Countries need to determine the type of industry they prefer, then match the incentives to the needs of the targeted industries. This is consistent with Woodward and Rolfe (1993) who found that export-oriented investment in the Caribbean Basin was influenced by profit repatriation restrictions and free trade zones (including tax holidays and no foreign exchange restrictions). Based on a small sample of OECD small and large MNEs, Fong (1987) argued that incentives in Singapore were directed toward export-oriented industries and skill and capital intensive firms, but that political and economic stability were more important than policy factors. Singapore's emphasis on economic efficiency and growth, rather than national ownership, created a climate favourable to foreign firms, smoothing the way for the Economic Development Board to attract investors (Fong, 1987).

Nationality may matter for understanding the choice of investment location. Wheeler and Mody (1992) found non-policy variables, especially labour costs and market size had large positive impacts on US investment, while policy factors, such as corporate tax, risk and openness of the economy had no impact. Comparing Japanese and US MNEs, Mody and Srinivasan (1998) reported that Japanese MNEs displayed great fluidity (although persistence rose in the later 1980s), placing no importance on market size and corporate tax rates and attaching great value to labour quality and low wage inflation compared to US investors. In a study covering 59 Japanese MNEs in the USA, Nakabaysahi (quoted in Donahue, 1997: 173) found that incentives were of minor importance in the location decision, although incentives provided a sign of 'goodwill'. For Japanese MNEs in the UK between 1984 and 1991, Taylor (1993) reported that Japanese firms favoured assisted areas, with only 24 per cent of establishments outside non-assisted areas. However, the choice of the UK as an investment country was dominated by production costs, reliable labour and good labour relations. Incentives, such as tax rates and financial assistance, determined where Japanese firms invested within a country, but only after the choice of host country was made.

This study investigates the Japanese MNE location decision in Singapore and the Asia-Pacific region. It provides comparative data holding nationality constant, but allowing the destination countries to vary. The chapter seeks to understand how Japanese MNEs differentiate between policy and non-policy variables in country-specific location decisions and how Japanese MNEs differentiate between policy variables. The data includes observations both on both initial investments and re-investments.

THE SURVEY AND DATA

A list of Japanese MNEs that invested in the region (Singapore, Australia, Indonesia, Malaysia, Thailand, Philippines) was collected from *Who Owns Whom* (1997). A questionnaire in Japanese was designed to uncover the policy and non-policy factors in the investment decision by Japanese MNEs in Singapore, Australia, Thailand, Malaysia, Indonesia and the Philippines. The survey was translated from English into Japanese, back translated, then independently reviewed and revised[1].

The survey was conducted through the Centre for Economic Research at Nagoya University, with endorsement through the 'brand name' of the Centre[2]. A reminder was sent to all non-responding firms four weeks after the first mail-out. The return rate was 34 per cent, 134 firms from the total sample of 390 firms. The sample was stratified in two ways. First, manufacturing (63 per cent) and non-manufacturing (31 per cent) firms and, second, those with investments in Singapore and the region (61 per cent) and those with no investments in Singapore (39 per cent).

Three statistical tests were used to analyse the data. Kruskal–Wallis one-way analysis of variance by ranks test were used. This is a non-parametric test that determines whether the means from different samples are from the same population (Siegel and Castellan, 1988). However, the test does not reveal where actual differences lie. To determine which variables account for the differences in means, we also employed a Kruskal–Wallis post-hoc pair-wise test in the differences of mean ranks. Finally, Mann–Whitney U tests were employed as a non-parametric version of an independent sample *t* test (Bryman and Craner, 1997; Siegel and Castellan, 1988).

THE FDI LOCATION DECISION

Types of Technology Transferred

States encourage MNEs to invest since MNEs transfer a bundle of technology and know-how to host countries. Distribution and marketing skills (3.6) and management skills (3.6) were the most important technology transferred into Singapore, followed by product technology (3.3) and brand names (3.3). According to Kruskal–Wallis tests in Table 7.1, there were significant differences across countries in the types of technology and know-how transferred by Japanese MNEs to their subsidiaries. Kruskal–Wallis *post hoc* tests revealed that Japanese MNEs displayed few differences between know-how transferred to Singapore and the other countries in the region. Thailand received more product technology than Singapore; Indonesia and Thailand more process technology than Singapore; Indonesia more distribution and marketing know-how than Singapore; and Australia less management skill know-how than Singapore. While there were significant differences across countries, Table 7.1 shows that Singapore received the same types of know-how as its regional competitors. This suggests that Singapore's incentive and non-policy factors did not shape a different profile of technology transfer by Japanese MNEs to Singapore as compared with Japanese technology transfer to Singapore's regional competitors.

Choice of Country

Compared with nine countries (both regional competitors and China, North America and Europe), Japanese MNEs rated Singapore (3.0) the same as all other regional countries as an investment location with the exceptions of China (4.0), which was more important, and Australia (2.2), which was less important (see Table 7.2). Kruskal–Wallis tests also showed that North America (3.6) was a significantly more important (re-) investment location than Singapore. Singapore was simply another country competing for Japanese investment, without the special status of China or North America. Competing with regional neighbours for Japanese FDI, Singapore faced the

Table 7.1 Country differences in Japanese MNEs' transfer of technologies and know-how

	Kruskal–Wallace test[1]	Mean Rating[2,3]					
		Singapore	Australia	Indonesia	Malaysia	Philippines	Thailand
Product technology	0.000	3.33	2.77	3.97	3.62	3.79	**4.04**[a]
Process technology	0.000	3.01	2.45	**3.80**[b]	3.41	3.21	**3.74**[b]
Brand names/trade marks	0.795	3.34	3.08	3.22	3.26	3.27	3.45
Distribution & marketing skills	0.031	3.56	2.90	**2.93**[a]	3.08	2.90	3.17
Management skills	0.034	3.59	**2.85**[b]	3.38	3.27	3.38	3.47
HRM practice	0.098	3.15	2.60	2.92	3.02	2.94	3.12

Notes: [1]Tests for overall difference between the means for the six countries

[2]Means are on a scale 1 (no importance) to 5 (high importance)

[3]Values in bold denote significant difference to Singapore (Kruskal–Wallis Test, at [a]alpha = 0.10, [b]alpha = 0.05)

Table 7.2 Rank importance of countries as Japanese MNEs' investment locations[1,2,3]

	Mean	1	2	3	4	5	6	7	8	9
1. China	4.0			3.3	3.3	3.1	3.0	2.8	2.8	2.2
2. North America	3.6						3.0	2.8	2.8	2.2
3. Europe	3.3	4.0							2.8	2.2
4. Thailand	3.3	4.0								2.2
5. Indonesia	3.1	4.0								2.2
6. Singapore	3.0	4.0	3.6							2.2
7. Malaysia	2.8	4.0	3.6							2.2
8. Philippines	2.8	4.0	3.6	3.3						
9. Australia	2.2	4.0	3.6	3.3	3.3	3.1	3.0	2.8		

Notes: [1]Blank cells indicate no significant difference (Kruskal–Wallis Test, alpha = 0.05)
[2]Cells with means indicate a significant difference (Kruskal–Wallis Test, alpha = 0.05)
[3]Means are on a scale 1 (no importance) to 5 (high importance)

choice of selecting a mix of policy and non-policy instruments to differentiate Singapore as an investment location for other equally attractive countries. If non-policy variables were driving Japanese MNE investment in Singapore, then it would be difficult for Singapore to change in the short run its attractiveness relative to other regional economies. On the other hand, if policy variables were important factors in enticing Japanese MNEs to Singapore, then Singapore could be caught in a zero-sum bargaining game with its neighbours.

Japanese MNEs treated Singapore as an exception in one important way. Dividing the data into manufacturing and non-manufacturing firms, Mann–Whitney tests show that Japanese non-manufacturing firms (3.4) ranked Singapore significantly higher as an investment location than manufacturing firms (2.8). Japanese manufacturing and non-manufacturing firms did not rate any other market (including North America, Europe and the five regional countries) differently, except for China. Japanese manufacturing MNEs preferred China compared to non-manufacturing MNEs. In contrast, Japanese non-manufacturing MNEs preferred Singapore over manufacturing MNEs.

POLICY AND NON-POLICY VARIABLES

Table 7.3 considers incentives, tariffs and 17 non-policy variables as location incentive factors. The seven most important factors attracting Japanese MNEs were non-policy variables including, size of local market (4.3), political (4.1) and economic stability (4.1), low production (3.9) and labour costs (3.8), infrastructure quality (3.7) and raw material availability (3.5). Ranking eighth, incentives (3.4) were of second order importance, and significantly different according to Kruskal–Wallis tests from the three most important non-policy factors and the six least important factors in Table 7.3. Tariffs and quota restrictions were rated only 2.8, and were significantly less important than the seven most important non-policy variables and incentives. Non-policy variables in Table 7.3 dominated the reasons Japanese MNEs invested in the Asian region.

There were significant differences in how Japanese non-manufacturing and manufacturing MNEs treated the Asian region. Manufacturing firms rated raw material supply (3.7) and low production costs (4.0) higher, but political (4.0) and economic stability (3.9) lower than non-manufacturing firms. Similarly, firms investing in Singapore rated raw material supply (3.7) and low production costs (4.0) lower than firms that did not invest in Singapore. What is surprising is that only a handful of the 19 variables differentiated manufacturing and non-manufacturing firms and investors and non-investors in Singapore. Incentives were not among the factors

Table 7.3 Policy and non-policy[1] factors in Japanese MNEs' location decision[2,3,4]

		Mean	1	2	3	4	5	6	7	8	9	10	11	12	13	14	15	16	17	18	19
1.	Size of local market	4.3					3.8	3.7	3.5	3.4	3.1	3.1	3.1	3.0	3.0	2.8	2.8	2.8	2.8	2.7	2.4
2.	Political stability	4.1							3.5	3.4	3.1	3.1	3.1	3.0	3.0	2.8	2.8	2.8	2.8	2.7	2.4
3.	Economic stability	4.0							3.5	3.4	3.1	3.1	3.1	3.0	3.0	2.8	2.8	2.8	2.8	2.7	2.4
4.	Low production costs	3.9	4.3								3.1	3.1	3.1	3.0	3.0	2.8	2.8	2.8	2.8	2.7	2.4
5.	Low labour costs	3.8	4.3								3.1	3.1	3.1	3.0	3.0	2.8	2.8	2.8	2.8	2.7	2.4
6.	Infrastructure quality	3.7	4.3									3.1	3.1	3.0	3.0	2.8	2.8	2.8	2.8	2.7	2.4
7.	Raw material availability	3.5	4.3	4.1	4.0										3.0	2.8	2.8	2.8	2.8	2.7	2.4
8.	*Incentives (tax advantages)*	3.4	4.3	4.1	4.0											2.8	2.8	2.8	2.8	2.7	2.4
9.	Size of export market	3.1	4.3	4.1	4.0	3.9	3.8														2.4
10.	Establishment costs	3.1	4.3	4.1	4.0	3.9	3.8	3.7													2.4
11.	Labour skills	3.1	4.3	4.1	4.0	3.9	3.8	3.7													2.4
12.	Business ethic	3.0	4.3	4.1	4.0	3.9	3.8	3.7													2.4
13.	Country/region experience	3.0	4.3	4.1	4.0	3.9	3.8	3.7	3.5												
14.	Local suppliers	2.8	4.3	4.1	4.0	3.9	3.8	3.7	3.5	3.4											
15.	*Tariffs/quota on imports*	2.8	4.3	4.1	4.0	3.9	3.8	3.7	3.5	3.4											
16.	Favourable exchange rates	2.8	4.3	4.1	4.0	3.9	3.8	3.7	3.5	3.4											
17.	Sources of finance	2.8	4.3	4.1	4.0	3.9	3.8	3.7	3.5	3.4											
18.	Cultural proximity	2.7	4.3	4.1	4.0	3.9	3.8	3.7	3.5	3.4											
19.	Competitive rivalry	2.4	4.3	4.1	4.0	3.9	3.8	3.7	3.5	3.4	3.1	3.1	3.1	3.0							

Notes: [1]Policy factors are in italics
[2]Blank cells indicate no significant difference (Kruskal–Wallis Test, at alpha = 0.05)
[3]Cells with means indicate a significant difference (Kruskal–Wallis Test, at alpha = 0.05)
[4]Means are on a scale 1 (no importance) to 5 (high importance)

separating the behaviour of manufacturing and non-manufacturing firms or Singapore investors and non-investors.

Raw material availability and raw material supply reflect the underlying comparative advantage of Singapore relative to other countries in the region. Competition for Japanese MNEs depended on slow changing non-policy factors. It is unlikely that a set of policy variables could be implemented to influence these factors, or the underlying political regime, that dominated the investment location decision by Japanese MNEs. Tax-related incentives and other policy incentives did not give Singapore a competitive advantage as an investment location over other economies in the region.

POLICY AND NON-POLICY IMPACT ON FUTURE INVESTMENTS

The impact of the Asian economic and financial crises on Japanese MNEs' location decisions is assessed in Table 7.4. Comparing Table 7.3 and Table 7.4, the same non-policy variables that dominated the pre-Asian crisis investment/location decision by Japanese MNEs also dominate the post-Asian economic crisis location decisions. Size of the local market (4.4) and political and economic stability (4.4) dominated both pre and post-crisis investment decisions, and labour costs and raw material availability were more important variables than policy factors. Market size and political and economic stability were significantly different from all other factors in Table 7.4. Policy variables were of medium importance, clustered in the bottom half of Table 7.4.

Policy Variables

Policy variables did not drive the location decision for Japanese MNEs. But policy variables played a second order role in the location decision as indicated in both Tables 7.3 and 7.4. To better understand the second order impact of policy factors, Table 7.5 ranks the policy variables by importance. Tax-related incentives dominated the location decision by Japanese MNEs, ranking as the most important policy variables except for input duty exemptions (3.6) and unrestricted repatriation of dividends (3.5) and profits (3.4). Corporate tax concessions ranked medium–high, but all the other incentive variables were of medium or low importance. Table 7.5 shows that the top four policy variables (corporate tax concessions, import duty exemptions, tax holidays and unrestricted repatriation of dividends) were significantly different from the last seven policy variables. There were no significant differences in the ranking of policy variables by manufacturing

Table 7.4 Policy and non-policy factors[1] in Japanese MNEs' future location decision[2,3,4]

	Mean	1	2	3	4	5	6	7	8	9	10	11	12	13	14
1. Scale of local market	4.4			3.7	3.6	3.2	3.2	3.2	3.1	3.0	3.0	3.0	2.9	2.6	2.4
2. Political & economic stability	4.4			3.7	3.6	3.2	3.2	3.2	3.1	3.0	3.0	3.0	2.9	2.6	2.4
3. Lower labour cost	3.7	4.4	4.4						3.1	3.0	3.0	3.0	2.9	2.6	2.4
4. Raw materials/input availability	3.6	4.4	4.4							3.0	3.0	3.0	2.9	2.6	2.4
5. Import & tariff barriers	3.2	4.4	4.4											2.6	2.4
6. Exemption of import taxes	3.2	4.4	4.4											2.6	2.4
7. Country knowledge	3.2	4.4	4.4												2.4
8. Establishment of export base	3.1	4.4	4.4	3.7											2.4
9. State & local government incentives	3.0	4.4	4.4	3.7	3.6										2.4
10. Tax holiday	3.0	4.4	4.4	3.7	3.6										2.4
11. Exemption of local content	3.0	4.4	4.4	3.7	3.6										
12. Free trade zone	2.9	4.4	4.4	3.7	3.6										
13. Government subsidies	2.6	4.4	4.4	3.7	3.6	3.2	3.2								
14. Follow competitors	2.4	4.4	4.4	3.7	3.6	3.2	3.2	3.2	3.1	3.0	3.0				

Notes: [1]Policy factors are in italics
[2]Blank cells indicate no significant difference (Kruskal–Wallis Test, at alpha = 0.05)
[3]Cells with means indicate a significant difference (Kruskal–Wallis Test, at alpha = 0.05)
[4]Means are on a scale 1 (no importance) to 5 (high importance)

Table 7.5 Ranking of policy variables in Japanese MNEs' location decision[1,2,3]

		Mean	1	2	3	4	5	6	7	8	9	10	11	12	13	14	15	16
1.	Corporation tax concessions	3.8								3.1	3.0	2.9	2.9	2.9	2.8	2.7	2.7	2.5
2.	Import duties exemptions	3.6									3.0	2.9	2.9	2.9	2.8	2.7	2.7	2.5
3.	Tax holidays	3.5										2.9	2.9	2.9	2.8	2.7	2.7	2.5
4.	Unrestricted repatriation of dividends	3.5										2.9	2.9	2.9	2.8	2.7	2.7	2.5
5.	Unrestricted repatriation of profits	3.3															2.7	2.5
6.	Withholding tax exemption	3.2															2.7	2.5
7.	Sales tax exemptions	3.2															2.7	2.5
8.	Land tax exemptions	3.1	3.8															2.5
9.	Payroll tax exemptions	3.0	3.8	3.6														
10.	Local content requirements exemption	2.9	3.8	3.6	3.5	3.5												
11.	Free trade zones	2.9	3.8	3.6	3.5	3.5												
12.	Infrastructure grants	2.9	3.8	3.6	3.5	3.5												
13.	Tax relief for infrastructure	2.8	3.8	3.6	3.5	3.5												
14.	Employment grants	2.7	3.8	3.6	3.5	3.5												
15.	Loans at discount rates	2.7	3.8	3.6	3.5	3.5	3.3	3.2	3.2									
16.	Land donations	2.5	3.8	3.6	3.5	3.5	3.3	3.2	3.2	3.1								

Notes: [1]Blank cells indicate no significant difference (Kruskal–Wallis Test, alpha = 0.05)

[2]Cells with means indicate a significant difference (Kruskal–Wallis Test, alpha = 0.05)

[3]Means are on a scale 1 (no importance) to 5 (high importance)

and non-manufacturing firms, and the rating by manufacturing and non-manufacturing firms was the same as that in Table 7.5. Nor did MNEs that invested in Singapore rank or rate incentives differently from non-Singapore investors. The ranking and significant differences between policy variables suggest that the range of incentives available to countries to attract Japanese MNEs is very small. It is unlikely that Singapore can develop alternative policy variables that will provide a competitive edge over other countries in the region.

COUNTRY DIFFERENCES: SINGAPORE AND THE REGION

Policy and non-policy investment location factors are likely to vary by country. For first investments made by Japanese MNEs in each of the six countries, we investigated the importance of seven policy and seven non-policy factors in Table 7.6. Non-policy variables again dominated Japanese MNEs' decision to invest in Singapore. Policy variables were all of medium to low importance, ranking lower in importance than all non-policy variables except for labour costs and 'follow competitors'. In Table 7.6 Kruskal–Wallis tests in bold show that there were significant differences across countries for establishment as an export base, size of the local market, raw material/input availability, free trade zone, labour costs and local content exemption.

The means highlighted in bold in Table 7.6 show where Singapore differs significantly from the other 5 countries, using a Kruskal–Wallis *post hoc* test. Considering the non-policy variables, Singapore as an export platform ranked ahead of all other countries, but was only significantly different from Australia (2.4) and Malaysia (2.9). Although Japanese MNEs rated Singapore's local market size (3.6) as of less importance than all other countries, Singapore was only significantly different from Indonesia (4.2). Given the variances in market characteristics between Singapore and the Philippines, Thailand and Malaysia, Japanese MNEs were interpreting market size both in terms of population size and per capita income. Singapore's local market was viewed as a rich market, sharing similarities with Australia rather than Malaysia or the Philippines. Raw material supply did not differentiate Singapore from any other country. Labour costs were not rated as an important factor attracting Japanese MNEs to Singapore (2.7), but labour costs differentiated Singapore from all her Asian competitors, except Australia (2.3).

Policy variables in Table 7.6 were either not significantly different across countries, or did not differentiate Singapore from other countries in the region. Only two variables, free trade zones and local content, were significantly different across the region, but Singapore did not differ

Table 7.6 Country differences in Japanese MNEs' first investment location decision[1]

	Kruskal–Wallace test[2]	Mean Rating[3,4]					
		Singapore	Australia	Indonesia	Malaysia	Philippines	Thailand
Political & economic stability	0.094	4.0	4.0	3.7	3.9	3.7	4.0
Establishment of export base	0.003	3.6	**2.4**[b]	3.1	**2.9**[a]	3.0	3.1
Size of local market	0.017	3.6	4.1	4.2[a]	3.8	4.0	4.2
Country knowledge	0.466	3.6	3.3	3.4	3.5	3.2	3.5
Raw materials/input availability	0.009	3.2	2.7	3.3	3.4	3.0	3.5
Import tariffs & barriers	0.287	3.1	2.6	2.9	2.8	2.7	2.8
Free trade zone	0.006	2.9	**1.9**[b]	2.4	2.4	2.4	2.4
Import tax exemption	0.106	2.8	2.2	2.8	2.8	2.5	2.8
Labour costs	0.000	2.7	2.3	**3.9**[b]	**3.6**[b]	**3.6**[b]	**3.7**[b]
Tax reductions	0.093	2.7	2.0	2.6	2.6	2.3	2.7
State & local govt. incentives	0.535	2.5	2.3	2.5	2.5	2.3	2.6
Local content exemption	0.038	2.5	1.9	2.6	2.6	2.5	2.7
Government subsidies	0.268	2.3	2.1	2.3	2.4	2.1	2.5
Follow competitors	0.965	2.2	2.1	2.1	2.2	2.0	2.3

Notes: [1]Policy factors are in italics
[2]Tests for overall difference between the means for the six countries
[3]Means are on a scale 1 (no importance) to 5 (high importance)
[4]Values in bold denote significant difference to Singapore (Kruskal–Wallis Test, at [a] alpha = 0.10, [b] alpha = 0.01)

significantly on either of these policy variables from her neighbours, except for Australia (1.9) in relation to free trade zones. The only significant difference for Japanese non-manufacturing firms across countries was labour costs, with Singapore significantly different from Indonesia and Thailand. For manufacturing firms, the significant regional differences related to the size of local market (significantly different from Malaysia, Indonesia and Thailand), export base (significantly different from Australia) and labour rates (significantly different from Indonesia, Malaysia, Philippines and Thailand). None of these differences were related to incentives. For firms with no investment in Singapore, there were no regional differences. For Singapore investors, no policy variables were significant, although non-policy regional differences comprised export base (significantly different from Australia and Malaysia), labour costs (significantly different from Indonesia, Malaysia, Philippines and Thailand) and free trade zones (significantly different from Australia).

Japanese MNEs did not differentiate between Singapore and other Asian countries on the basis of incentives. From the perspective of Singapore's policy-makers, incentives may have been a zero sum game, with incentive bargaining by each country leading to a prisoners' dilemma outcome. Singapore also did not have significant non-policy advantages over her neighbours according to Japanese MNEs, although Singapore led the region for political and economic stability (4.0) and as an export base (3.6).

Reinvestment in a country may involve a different set of location variables than the first investment in a country. There is a sequential investment literature, but little recognition of the role of policy variables in attracting subsequent investment by existing MNEs, as opposed to first time investment. Kogut (1990) identified the difference between initial investments and the sequential advantages of the coordinated multinational system for subsequent investments. Scale economies and aggregation advantages interacted with economies of scope to drive both a different set of location decision factors and a different structure and organisational design for sequential investing firms. Japanese MNEs built capabilities through initial investments, with sequential investments allowing these capabilities to be used for diversification into non-core businesses (Chang, 1995).

Japanese MNEs' ratings of the factors influencing their re-investment decision are reported in Table 7.7. Comparing Table 7.6 (first investments) with Table 7.7 (reinvestments), there is no significant change in the way that Japanese MNEs ranked and rated the location variables. Non-policy factors, especially political and economic stability (3.9), country knowledge (3.7), size of local market (3.5) and export base (3.5) dominate as medium–high influences. Only the size of local market (3.5) and labour costs (2.7) differed significantly across countries, and only labour costs differentiated

Table 7.7 Country differences in Japanese MNEs' re-investment location decision[1]

	Kruskal–Wallace test[2]	Mean Rating[3,4]					
		Singapore	Australia	Indonesia	Malaysia	Philippines	Thailand
Political & economic stability	0.933	3.9	3.7	3.9	3.7	3.7	3.8
Country knowledge	0.914	3.7	3.3	3.3	3.4	3.4	3.4
Size of local market	0.024	3.5	3.6	**4.3**[a]	3.8	4.0	4.3
Establishment of export base	0.414	3.5	2.9	3.7	3.1	3.6	3.6
Raw materials/input availability	0.693	3.3	3.1	3.6	3.3	3.6	3.6
Import tariffs & barriers	0.878	2.9	2.8	2.9	2.8	3.2	3.1
Free trade zone	0.230	2.9	1.8	2.6	2.5	3.0	2.7
Labour costs	0.000	2.7	2.4	**4.0**[b]	**3.6**[b]	**3.7**[b]	**3.8**[b]
Tax reductions	0.782	2.7	2.5	2.4	2.5	2.4	2.7
Import tax exemption	0.924	2.7	2.6	2.7	2.7	2.8	2.8
Follow competitors	0.646	2.5	2.0	2.2	2.2	2.2	2.5
Local content exemption	0.194	2.5	1.8	2.5	2.6	2.8	2.8
Government subsidies	0.924	2.4	2.4	2.2	2.3	2.2	2.4
State & local govt. incentives	0.755	2.4	2.3	2.3	2.2	2.3	2.6

Notes: [1]Policy factors are in italics
[2]Tests for overall difference between the means for the six countries
[3]Means are on a scale 1 (no importance) to 5 (high importance)
[4]Values in bold denote significant difference to Singapore (Kruskal–Wallis Test, at [a] alpha = 0.10, [b] alpha = 0.01)

Singapore as a less attractive investment location from other countries in the region (except Australia (2.4)).

Policy variables did not vary significantly across countries for the re-investment decision. Japanese MNEs did not see incentive policies as variables influencing the decision to re-invest in one country in preference to another, making the rapid building of agglomeration economies through policy variables difficult. Not only did policy variables have a second order effect, but Japanese MNEs did not differentiate between incentive policies by different countries.

CONCLUSION

This paper analysed the role of policy (incentives) and non-policy factors in the Japanese investment/location decision in Singapore and the region (Australia, Thailand, Malaysia, Indonesia and Philippines). Singapore received the same bundle of Japanese technology and know-how as the other five countries in the region. Location factors did not favour significantly different bundles of transferred know-how, with Japanese MNEs providing subsidiaries with a generic set of parent know-how.

Similarly, Japanese MNEs did not differentiate between Singapore and other countries in the region as an investment location. Japanese non-manufacturing MNEs preferred Singapore compared to manufacturing firms. This split between manufacturing and non-manufacturing firms' preferences only occurred for Singapore and China. For all other countries and regions, manufacturing and non-manufacturing Japanese MNEs treated investment locations the same.

Non-policy factors dominated the reasons Japanese MNEs selected investment locations. This applied to past investments (before the Asian economic crisis) and to future investment intentions. Policy variables were second-order factors in the investment decision by Japanese MNEs in the region. In terms of policy variables, tax incentives dominated, and there were no differences between manufacturing and non-manufacturing firms in their preferences for investment incentives.

The survey was able to differentiate between the impact of location variables across countries. For Singapore, non-policy variables dominated the location decision for Japanese MNEs; policy variables were of second order importance. There were differences across countries. Labour costs differentiated Singapore from the other five countries in the region, with local market size and export base less important factors. There was no difference between the initial investment decision and re-investments by Japanese MNEs.

These results suggest that policy factors were not important in the location decision process by Japanese MNEs. Japanese MNEs did not see the use of investment incentives by Singapore as different from the incentives offered by all other countries in the region. The economic fundamentals (growth and the size of the market) and political stability dominated the investment location calculations by Japanese MNEs. The evidence suggests that regional countries have entered into a zero-sum prisoners' dilemma game, where each country offers the same types of incentives.

Notes

1. The survey was translated and back translated by Masako Ogawa and William Purcell in the School of International Business, UNSW and reviewed and revised by the Japanese staff at the Economics Research Centre, Nagoya University.
2. The authors acknowledge the valuable assistance provided by staff at the Economics Research Centre, Nagoya University, for their assistance in the processing of the survey.

REFERENCES

Aharoni, Yair (1966), 'The Foreign Investment Decision Process', Boston: Division of Research, Graduate School of Business Administration, Harvard University.

Arthur, W. Brian (1994), *Increasing Returns and Path Dependence in the Economy,* Ann Arbor: University of Michigan Press.

Birkinshaw, Julian M. (1994), 'Approaching Heterarchy: A Review of the Literature on Multinational Enterprise Strategy and Structure', *Advances in International Comparative Management*, **9**, 111–44.

Blair, John P. and Robert Premus (1987), 'Major Factors in Industrial Production: A Review', *Economic Development Quarterly,* **1** (1).

Bryman, Alan and Duncan Cramer (1997), *Quantitative Data Analysis with SPSS for Windows: A Guide for Social Scientists*, London and New York: Routledge.

Buckley, P.J. and M. Casson (1976), *The Future of Multinational Enterprise*, London: Macmillan.

Cable, Vincent and Bishnodat Persaud (eds) (1987), *Developing with Foreign Investment,* New York: Croom Helm.

Carlos, Ann M. and Stephen J. Nicholas (1993), 'Managing the Manager: An Application of the Principal Agent Model to the Hudson's Bay Company', *Oxford Economic Papers*, (45), 243–56.

Chang, Sea Jin (1995), 'International Expansion Strategy of Japanese Firms: Capability Building through Sequential Entry', *Academy of Management Journal,* **38** (2), 383–407.

David, Paul (1984), *High Technology Centres and the Economics of Locational Tournaments,* (mimeo) Stanford University.

David, Paul (1985), 'Clio and the Economics of QWERTY', *American Economic Review, Proceedings,* (75), 332–7.

Donahue, John D. (1997), *Disunited State,* New York: Basic Books.

Dunning, John H. (1973), 'The Determinants of International Production', *Oxford Economic Papers*, **25** (3): 289–336.

Dunning, John H. (1998), 'Location and the Multinational Enterprise: A Neglected Factor?', *Journal of International Business Studies,* **29** (1), 45–66.

Fong, Pang Eng (1987), 'Foreign Investment and the State of Singapore', in Vincent Cable and Bishnodat Persaud (eds), *Developing with Foreign Investment*, New York: Croom Helm.

Hennart, Jean-Francois (1982), *A Theory of Multinational Enterprise,* Ann Arbor: University of Michigan Press.

Horstmann, Ignatius J. and James R. Markusen (1996), 'Exploring New Markets: Direct Investment, Contractual Relations and the Multinational Enterprise', *International Economic Review,* **37** (1), 1–19.

Hughes, H. and G. Dorrance (1984), *Economic Policies and Foreign Direct Investment with Particular Reference to the Developing Countries of East Asia*. Paper prepared for the Commonwealth Secretariat, London.

Hymer, Stephen (1976), 'The International Operations of National Firms: A Survey of Direct Foreign Investment', Cambridge: MIT Press.

Johnson, H.G. (1970), 'The Efficiency and Welfare Implications of the Multinational Corporation', in C.P. Kindleberger (ed.), *The International Corporation: A Symposium*, Cambridge, MA: MIT Press.

Klein, Benjamin, Robert G. Crawford and Armen A. Alchian (1978), 'Vertical Integration, Appropriable Rents, and the Competitive Contracting Process', *Journal of Law and Economics,* **21** (2), 297–326.

Kogut, Bruce (1990), 'International Sequential Advantages and Network Flexibility', in Christopher A. Bartlett, Yves Doz and Gunnar Hedland (eds), *Managing the Global Firm,* London: Routledge.

Krugman, Paul R. (1991), 'History and Industry Location: The Case of the Manufacturing Belt', in Ronald L. Oaxaca and Wilma St John (eds), *American Economic Association*, *Papers and Proceedings*, **81** (2), 80–83.

Krugman, Paul R (1993), 'On the Relationship between Trade Theory and Location Theory', *Review of International Economics,* **1** (2), 110–22.

Lim, David (1983), 'Fiscal Incentives and Direct Foreign Investment in Less Developed Countries', *The Journal of Development Studies* January, 207–12.

Loree, David W. and Stephen E. Guisinger (1995), 'Policy and Non-policy Determinants of U.S. Equity Foreign Direct Investment', *Journal of International Business Studies,* (2nd quarter), 281–99.

Markusen, James R. (1995), 'The Boundaries of Multinational Enterprises and the Theory of International Trade', *The Journal of Economic Perspectives,* **9** (2), 169–89.

Mody, Ashoka and Krishna Srinivasan (1998), 'Japanese and U.S. Firms as Foreign Investors: Do They March to the Same Tune?', *Canadian Journal of Economics*, **31** (4), 778–99.

Nicholas, Stephen (1983), 'Agency Contracts, Institutional Modes and the Transition to Foreign Direct Investment by British Multinationals Before 1939', *The Journal of Economic History*, **43**, 675–86.

Nicholas, Stephen, David Merrett, Greg Whitwell, William Purcell and Sue Kimberley (1996), 'Japanese Foreign Direct Investment in Australia in the 1990s', *Pacific Economic Papers*, (256), 1–18.

Peteraf, Margaret A. (1993), 'The Cornerstones of Competitive Advantage: A Resource-based View', *Strategic Management Journal,* (14), 179–91.

Rolfe, Robert J., David A. Ricks, Martha M. Pointer and Mark McCarthy (1993), 'Determinants of FDI Incentive Preferences of MNEs', *Journal of International Business*, **24** (2), 335–55.

Scott, Allen J. (1996), 'Regional Motors of the Global Economy', *Futures,* **28** (5), 391–411.

Siegal, S. and J. Castellan (1998), *Nonparametric Statistics for the Behavioural Sciences*, New York: McGraw Hill.

Taylor, Jim (1993), 'An Analysis of the Factors Determining the Geographical Distribution of Japanese Manufacturing in the UK, 1984–2001', *Urban Studies*, **30** (7), 1209–24.

Teece, David J. (1980), 'Economies of Scope and the Scope of the Enterprise', *Journal of Economic Behaviour and Organisation,* **1** (3), 223–47.

Usher, Dan (1977), 'The Economics of Tax Incentives to Encourage Investment in Less Developed Countries', *Journal of Development Economics,* (4), 119–48.

Wernerfelt, B. (1984), 'A Resource Based Theory of the Firm', *Strategic Management Journal*, **5**, 171–80.

Wheeler, David and Ashoka Mody (1992), 'International Investment Location Decisions: the Case of U.S. Firms', *Journal of International Economics,* (33), 57–76.

Who Owns Whom, Volume 1 Australasia & the Far East (1997), Buckingham, UK: Dun & Bradstreet Ltd.

Williamson, Oliver (1979), 'Transaction Cost Economics: The Governance of Contractual Relations', *Journal of Law and Economics*, (22), 233–61.

Woodward, Douglas and Robert Rolfe (1993), 'The Location of Export-oriented Foreign Direct Investment in the Caribbean Basin', *Journal of International Business Studies,* **24** (1), 121–44.

Woodward, Douglas P., 'Locational Determinants of Japanese Manufacturing Start-ups in the United States', *Southern Economic Journal*, **58** (3), 690–708.

8. Australian Manufacturers' Perceptions of Indonesia as a Host for Direct Investment

Anna Zarkada-Fraser and Campbell Fraser

INTRODUCTION

The aim of this chapter is to examine Australian manufacturers' perceptions of Indonesia as a host for direct investment and explore variations in the decision-making mechanisms produced by different levels of experience of firms currently making or considering such investment.

There is a significant rhetoric in the popular press, as well as part of the policy formulation process, concerning Australian firms' lack of competitiveness in the international arena. Based mainly on trade figures, it reflects the fact that Australia does not have the 'normal' mix of exporting multinational enterprises (MNEs) and multidomestic firms like the ones typically found in industrialised economies (Johansen and Valhne, 1990). As Yetton et al. (1991) succinctly pointed out, the rhetoric is largely unfounded since Australia boasts a number of firms that are particularly successful in establishing overseas manufacturing bases.

Statistical as well as qualitative data clearly indicate that the conventional pattern of firm development from import substituting to opportunistic exporting, to strategic exporting to finally becoming a multinational is not really followed by Australian firms (Craig and Yetton, 1994). Especially in Australia's manufacturing sector, overseas production was found to contribute substantially more than trade to total revenue (Yetton et al., 1991). Since the late 1980s, foreign direct investment has been growing at consistently higher rates than trade and this trend is expected to be sustained (Craig and Yetton, 1994).

This chapter focuses on Australian manufacturing firms investing in Indonesia. The importance of Indonesia to Australia cannot be overstated.

Former Prime Minister Keating stated that no country is more important to Australia than Indonesia (Ng, 1996). The promotion of Australian investment in Indonesia, especially in the form of joint ventures, is high on the nation's list of strategic priorities (DFAT, 1994: 82). In the period 1967 to 1994, Australian firms contributed 1.7 per cent of all foreign investment in Indonesia, making Australia the 8th largest investor in the country (Ng, 1996).

The preference for FDI over exporting has been attributed to the fact that despite recent attempts at liberalisation, Indonesia is largely a protected market. Forest products such as plywood and particle board or paper that are important to Australia's export future attract a 20–30 per cent tariff in Indonesia compared to no tariff in Australia and only 10 per cent in Europe or Japan (Carter, 1994). The combination of low rupiah-based costs and relatively high dollar income (or replacement of costly dollar imports) acts as a further incentive for investment (AIDB, 1998). Moreover, Indonesia is endowed with vast natural resources, a strategic location along the equator, liberal foreign currency rules and a very large labour force that is less costly than that of Australia. As a market, Indonesia has 190 million people with a rapidly growing middle class (Bociurkiw, 1996). Its industrial basis is fairly sophisticated (Aswicahyono et al., 1996). Especially for the production of labour-intensive manufactures where limited skills are needed, Australian investment through joint ventures or strategic partnerships is most welcome in Indonesia since it provides opportunities for employment and quality improvements as well as the transfer of technology and management expertise (Ng, 1996; AIDB, 1998). However, even in high-technology industries the cross-fertilisation of engineering and organisational practices is seen as a means to improve productivity (Soedarsono, et al., 1998).

Important as Indonesia might be, however, it is also a country in political turmoil, under intense economic pressures and with a future that is difficult to predict. After over three decades of continuous growth, Indonesia has accumulated basic skills and technology. However, it is presently facing difficult economic times as well as a long and complex process of adjustment to new political regimes. Long-established institutions, as well as the 'rules of the game' (including the deregulation of several important commodity markets and measures to decentralise government functions) are undergoing significant changes (AIDB, 1998). During this transitional period, the key economic players are also likely to change. All these factors, coupled with the language and culture barriers that naturally exist between Indonesia and Australia, create a relatively high level of business risk that firms need actively to manage. If the concept of risk is taken to be any risk associated with investments by firms in specific operating assets, then Australian firms are working towards the generation of a high return by making maximal use of their distinctive competence, at the same time as limiting the threats to that return by selecting investments that reduce the range or variance of projected returns (Craig and Yetton, 1994).

From a theory development perspective, the interest in Indonesia as an investment target for Australian firms lies with the identification and evaluation of the relative impact of those variables that are seen by the managers as determinants of risk. Moreover, their relationship to sources of information that the managers utilise in procuring businesses or developing new partnerships is also important in mapping the investment decision-making process.

Despite the theoretically expected increased risk, Australian businesses not only remain in Indonesia, but a number of currently domestic firms are considering it as the first stepping stone to internationalisation. The question then arises of how these prospective entrants assess the risks involved. The aim of this chapter is to explore variations in the decision-making mechanisms produced by different levels of experience.

The pioneering Australian manufacturing firms have cleared a path through a jungle of regulation, bureaucracy and socio-cultural mismatches and are now willing to share their experiences and expertise. This chapter presents an analysis of experiences that can serve as a basis for the development of a prospective investor's toolbox to assist in the identification and management of the multifaceted risks, as well as the exploration of the many opportunities Indonesia presents.

DIMENSIONS OF THE RISK AUSTRALIAN MANUFACTURERS FACE IN INDONESIA

In deciding to invest in a foreign market, firms consider a large number of variables that can be grouped under six general headings, reflecting the micro and macro environments of the firm (Zarkada, 1993; Cavusgil, 1980; Chisnall, 1977; Ford, 1990). These are:

1. *Clients and business partners.* The idea of internally initiated exporting activity, has been repeatedly challenged, and the findings of numerous research projects lead to the conclusion that internationalisation is often an unplanned and intuitive reaction to external stimuli including unsolicited orders (Simpson and Kujawaa, 1974; Bilkey, 1978; Kaynak and Erol, 1989; Diamantopoulos et al., 1990). Firms are often invited to expand in international markets by existing or potential clients (Phillips et al., 1994: 268), suppliers and business partners. Even following investment banks has

been cited as a reason for investing in a foreign market (*Financial Times*, 1994). In the case of Indonesia, it has been reported that, although there is little evidence of Australian firms successfully identifying a local joint venture partner (Craig and Yetton, 1994: 64), there is substantial evidence that a number of them have been sought out for their technology or management expertise (AIDB, 1998).

2. *Project.* The decision to expand in international markets is not one based solely on environmental factors. The particular project that the firm is contemplating is logically expected to be an issue of paramount importance. A specific market could be extremely attractive, but the proposed project might be fraught with contractual or technical difficulties. Similarly, even in the riskiest of markets there can be a solid business opportunity that is irresistible in itself, almost irrespective of the external circumstances. Overall, what is sought is to minimise the potential mismatch between firms' area of expertise and local consumption needs (Craig and Yetton, 1994; Cutler, 1994).

3. *Firm.* The internal capabilities (Cutler, 1994) as well as the strategic directions of the firm are a factor in any expansion decision, including that of the establishment of an overseas manufacturing base (Heizer and Render, 1999; Cavusgil and Naor, 1989). Moreover, personal vision, the thrill of winning international work (Lucas, 1986) and the commitment of the top management towards a specific course of action determine the choice of markets to invest in (Thomas, 1977).

4. *Marketing implications.* Every expansion decision is expected to impact on the long-term marketing and competitive advantage positioning of the firm (Heizer and Render, 1999: chapter 2). Competition is found to have 'an extra bite' in international marketing (Phillips et al., 1994: 117) and moves of manufacturing capability and subsequent sales to new markets are likely to influence the balance of competitive forces in the new as well as the existing markets. Marketing implications can also be related to the firm's product that needs to be adapted for overseas manufacturing and consumption, or the product's life cycle, image and positioning that could be negatively or positively affected (Phillips et al., 1994; Cundiff and Hilger, 1988).

5. *Technological environment.* Even though technology is becoming increasingly less subject to country boundaries (Phillips et al., 1994), in the case of manufacturing, the level of technological expertise in the workforce,

as well as the general infrastructure and cost of technology transfer are still major concerns (Heizer and Render, 1999).

6. *Country*. Environmental analysis of markets, their dimensions and the way they apply to Indonesia as a host for Australian direct investment are examined in the following section.

COUNTRY-RELATED RISK FACTORS: INDONESIA AS A BUSINESS ENVIRONMENT

There is extensive literature on the impact of country-related factors on the decision to invest, as well as the risk assessment process of executives. It has been argued that, when asked, business executives appear to attach a highly negative significance to risk, but empirical research on the relationship between political risk and foreign direct investment has produced weak or inconclusive results (Akhter and Lusch, 1987). There is general agreement, however, on the component variables of the construct of risk. These are presented in this section. The analysis is based on an extensive literature review of problems faced by Western investors in transitional economies (Zarkada, 1993) updated to reflect the particularities of Australian investment in neighbouring countries (Craig and Yetton, 1994: 62–4).

The Political Environment

It has been argued that in cases of socio-political systems failure entropy is experienced and through it society restructures itself (Akhter and Lusch, 1987). In the case of Indonesia, however, there is a demonstrated basic conservatism, as well as a set of major faultlines in the relationships between civilians and the military and among races and religions that inhibit the natural process of restructuring (Bird, 1999). The recent elections, the first free elections in 44 years, have yet to resolve the instability problem, improve the human rights record of the nation (Bird, 1999) and address the separatist movements in different provinces that are threatening the country's unity (*Economist*, 1999).

Government Attitude towards Foreign Investment

The State Minister for Investment in the Suharto government indicated a desire to make Indonesia as attractive as possible for foreign investors (Bociurkiw, 1996) and there do not seem to be any indications that this attitude has changed. Since 1994, foreign concerns have been allowed up to

95 per cent ownership of Indonesian firms (up from the previous 49 per cent) (Goodfellow, 1997: 110–11), and 70 per cent of the volume of trade in the Jakarta stock exchange, where state-owned businesses are also listed, is carried out by foreign investors (Bociurkiw, 1996).

Public utilities, such as ports, power stations, water supply, road, railway and telecommunications networks have been singled out by the government to be increasingly opened up to foreign capital, as is the mass media (Goodfellow, 1997).

The positive, business-as-usual attitude of government might explain why, despite bouts of domestic political turbulence in Indonesia, the market has continued and business concerns are still attracted to the country (Bociurkiw, 1996).

The General State of the Economy

Despite all efforts, the economy shrank by over 13 per cent last year (Bird, 1999). The shrinking economy is accompanied by galloping external debt, which currently stands at 75 per cent of the gross domestic product, high interest rates and a collapsed Rupiah (*World Trade*, 1999).

The International Monetary Fund bailout package carries with it the obligation to overhaul the banking sector and control corruption. The issue of ownership of those of Indonesia's vast natural resources that used to belong to Mr Suharto's cronies and children also needs to be resolved (*Economist*, 1999).

Indonesia's dismal economic situation is not a phenomenon in isolation. The problems hit many countries simultaneously and affected the region's economies in many different ways. It has been argued that they need to be addressed simultaneously in all countries with effective policies and structural reform (Johnson, 1998).

The Legislative Framework for International Business

Political and economic reforms need to be accompanied by legal reform if they are to succeed. It has been suggested that foreign experts are at work trying to invigorate the legal system (Bird, 1999). Aspects of Indonesia's legal system that have been identified as in need of urgent attention are: competition policy, something Indonesia has never had (*Economist*, 1999); fairer trade policies (*Business Asia*, 1996); and the introduction of appropriate legislation to cover the new labour unions (Bird, 1999). Businesses are also faced with taxes, charges and fines that are imposed without warning, thus adding to the insecurity produced by often unclear property rights (AIDB, 1998).

Regulatory reform is underway in a number of problem areas such as commodities markets, inter-island trade, export restrictions on unprocessed raw materials (as part of a 'value-adding' strategy) and taxes on commodities which are exported. Non-transparent regulation has also been cited as the reason for marketing through particular channels that results in lower prices to producers and loss of export markets (AIDB, 1998).

In summary, as in any other country undergoing reforms, a legal code that is efficient, flexible and at the same time reliable enough is a prerequisite for success of the restructuring process (Zarkada, 1993). Further to the creation of formal legal and contractual structures, however, it is the function of institutions – durable, routinised patterns and regularities of entrepreneurial and social behaviour (Yamin and Batstone, 1992) – that will create the trust in the legal system which will, in turn, inspire the confidence in foreign business circles necessary for investment and expansion of business activities in Indonesia.

Business Infrastructure

Indonesia has a relatively underdeveloped physical infrastructure for business. There is a lack of secondary roads, low penetration of electricity (AIDB, 1998) and inefficient production (Noland, 1990) and the second lowest ratio of telephone lines to inhabitants in the South-East Asia region (Cutler, 1994). Moreover, the existing networks of roads, harbours and bridges is in need of repair (Noland, 1990), which is currently sought through privatisation rather than public investment.

Vital to business activity is access to up-to-date, reliable market information such as basic demographic data which is needed to estimate market sizes and growth rates and business finance. Both are scarce in Indonesia (AIDB, 1998).

Underdevelopment itself, especially in essential quality of life indicators such as clean water (the water in the capital is undrinkable and boiling is strongly recommended since enteric infections are widespread (da Gama Pinto, 1997)) and health facilities (1,560 persons per hospital bed compared to 250 in Australia (SBS, 1999)), is a constraint to development (AIDB, 1998) and a concern for any prospective investor.

Bureaucratic Attitudes and Identification and Access to Decision-Makers

Power is defined by Indonesians as adherence to an established pattern of order, so history is interpreted as the oscillation between concentration of power or loss of control by the ruling dynasty (Goodfellow, 1997). With such an understanding of life as a foundation, it may be the case that Indonesian business and governmental structures are inherently bureaucratic and unavoidably hierarchical. The practical implications are a complex multi-tier state bureaucracy (Goodfellow, 1997: 30-31) and overly complex processes at the sub-national government levels that are especially manifest in cumbersome and centralised investment approval procedures mostly administered in Jakarta (AIDB, 1998).

Bureaucracies often go hand in hand with corruption, especially when there is concentrated power at the top, unchecked by political processes, and when the lower members of a bureaucracy are underpaid. Both conditions exist in Indonesia, and no serious signs of change have been reported, despite the change in the political structure.

The ever-present and omnipotent patrimonial networks of Indonesian society and business life are difficult for foreigners to understand (AIDB, 1998) and near impossible to penetrate. 'Few contracts were awarded without the "help" of one of Suharto's relatives' (Dobbs-Higginson, 1994: 310–11) but foreign business people had learnt to call on these sources of help and utilise them as needed. The collapse of the regime has brought about the partial demise of the economic base of the former ruling family thus adding confusion to the problem of managing the foreign business and state relationship.

Decisions are mostly taken at the top (Dobbs-Higginson, 1994) but identifying the precise member of the hierarchy that is authorised to make a decision is not always easy. Even when the person is identified, there still are bureaucratic procedures to be tackled and modes of prescribed behaviour to be learnt before an agreement that saves everybody's face can be reached (Goodfellow, 1997).

Interestingly, nepotism, and the closely related widespread political favouritism (Abegglen, 1994) was defended by a segment of the business community who did not want to see the power of the Chinese community increased (Dobbs-Higginson, 1994; Abegglen, 1994). This, previously quiet, resentment was made shockingly public last year when mob violence in the Chinese and commercial sections cost over a thousand lives and vast damages to businesses and houses of ethnic Chinese (Bird, 1999). In a similar manner of reasoning, bribes to officials, even at the lowest levels, are widespread and morally justified on the basis of very low salaries paid to civil servants (Dobbs-Higginson, 1994).

Cultural Differences

Dobbs-Higginson (1994) considers the Indonesians to be gently spoken, very polite and largely to view their world as self-sufficient. Mysticism and harmony, smoothness of spirit, self control and a knowledge of order are the essential qualities of Javanese culture, one that dominates the modern Indonesian state (Goodfellow, 1997; Dobbs-Higginson, 1994). These qualities are not at all alien to Muslim and Chinese Indonesians, thus producing a society that is both hierarchical and communal.

While significant differences can be found in the Australian and Indonesian cultures, they have in common the fact that a variety of cultural and ethnic backgrounds are brought together into a single political unit, widespread over a vast area. The managers and employees of large Indonesian companies are highly exposed to Western corporate culture and they believe themselves to be modern, but their efforts, thoughts and activities continue to exist within certain, almost immovable cultural terms of reference (Yudianti and Goodfellow, 1997).

EMPIRICAL RESEARCH METHOD

The empirical data presented in this chapter were collected using highly structured interviews with the international business development and marketing executives of manufacturing firms attending a business development workshop on Indonesia. The participants formed two distinct groups: (a) firms currently involved in manufacturing operations in Indonesia and (b) firms interested in setting up a manufacturing base in the country but not as yet involved in it.

The interview schedule was an adaptation of the instrument used by Zarkada (1993). Out of the 38 participants to the seminar, 33 (13 currently involved in Indonesia and 20 prospective investors) voluntarily participated in the research. Complete anonymity was promised to all respondents and no incentives for participation were offered. The interviews lasted between 10 and 15 minutes and covered the profile of the businesses, their international and Indonesian experiences as well as sources of business development information and the respondents' opinions about aspects of risk present in the target market. The responses were coded and entered on the response sheets by the researcher in the presence of the respondents.

DATA ANALYSIS

Demographic Profile of the Respondent Firms

None of the firms interested in investing in Indonesia had any international experience. The ones that are active in the market, however, are mostly fairly experienced, with four of them having a high degree of internationalisation and business interests in most of the world (especially Latin America, Europe and Asia). The firms with overseas experience had started their internationalisation process as early as 1951, with most of them expanding overseas in the 1970s and 1980s. The earliest presence in Indonesia was 1983 but the majority of the firms first got involved in the 1990s.

It has been reported (Craig and Yetton, 1994) that a lot of the Australian firms' apparent insularity can be attributed to negative previous experience: those that invested in South-East Asia in the 1970s have exited these markets. This claim, however, cannot be substantiated through the present data set, as a number of firms in the sample had started their Asian operations in the 1970s and are still operating and expanding in these markets. The sample of firms, however, cannot be taken as representative of the whole of the Australian economy.

The majority (60 per cent) of the firms was medium-sized in relation to the domestic market, and 23 per cent were large firms but only 6 per cent were large by international standards as well.

Marketing Development

The marketing development of the firms was measured using an 8-item scale (Zarkada, 1993). The reliability of the scale was reassessed and found to be a satisfactory Cronbach's alpha of 0.83. A composite index score of marketing development was calculated for each firm by adding the scores of all the items in the scale. The scores were very high indeed with most firms having marketing departments responsible for international business development, formal marketing planning and information systems and in-house domestic and international market research capabilities.

The marketing development scores of the two samples (the firms involved in Indonesia and those interested in expanding there) were compared using t-tests. No significant differences were detected, thus, in terms of their marketing development, both internationalised and domestic firms interested in overseas business development were at comparable stages of marketing development.

The Importance of the Indonesian Market

The respondents were asked to indicate Indonesia's importance as a market today, and its forecasted importance in five years time on a five-point scale, from 'vital' (5) to 'of no value' (1). For the firms that are exploring the possibility of investing in the country, Indonesia is of an overall limited importance (mean = 2.04 but with a large standard deviation = 0.99). As would naturally be expected, it was of more importance to the firms that are currently involved in manufacturing in Indonesia (mean = 3.30, and standard deviation = 0.855, indicating that the importance ranged from important to very important and in some cases vital). The difference of Indonesia's present value was statistically highly significant between the two groups ($p = 0.000$).

Interestingly, Indonesia's forecasted value was very similar for both groups. The respondents expected it to be closer to 'very important' than 'important' (means for the interested and involved groups were 3.63 and 3.92 respectively with smaller standard deviations = 0.658 and 0.862). Overall, the majority of firms expected an increase in the value of Indonesia as a manufacturing base. The firms that are exploring opportunities in the country were much (and at a high level of statistical significance $p = 0.007$) more optimistic. Their mean of forecasted change was 1.6 (on a scale of –4 to +4).

Relative Importance of Issues Influencing the Decision to Invest in Indonesia

The respondents were asked to rank the following issues in order of magnitude of impact on their assessment of the Indonesian market: business partner and client-related issues; the specific project they were investigating; internal capabilities and strategic objectives of their firms; the marketing implications of their decision to invest in Indonesia; the technological environment of the country and other non-technical country-related factors.

Non parametric (Mann–Whitney) tests were used to compare the responses of the experienced firms with those of the firms interested in investing in Indonesia. The differences in the rankings were not statistically significant for any of the issues with the exception of country-related non-technical factors that are presented in detail in the next section. The rankings for each issue, together with the sum of ranks and the values for each quadrille are presented in Table 8.1. The issues are sorted in ascending order of rank in order to illustrate the relative importance assigned to them by the respondents.

The results are very similar to those of previous research (Zarkada, 1993) with the exception of the reaction to chance events and opportunities as an incentive for internationalisation that was found to be very important for the most internationally experienced Australian contracting firms but less so for those with limited experience (Zarkada-Fraser and Woodhall, 1998).

Table 8.1 Issues impacting on the decision to invest in Indonesia

Issue	Mode	Sum*	Percentiles 25th	50th	75th
Country (non-technical)					
Involved in Indonesia	1	19	1	1	2
Interested in Indonesia	3	49	2	3	3
Technological environment	2	69	1	2	3
Firm	1	87	1	3	4
Client	5	127	3	4	5
Project	6	151	4	5	6
Marketing implications	6	158	5	5	6

* The theoretical range of the sum is from 35 to 175. The smaller the sum, the higher the ranking of the issue.

The business environment of Indonesia is the single most important concern for the firms that are already involved in the market and the overall most important concern for all firms, followed very closely by the country's technological environment. Internal capabilities and experiences of the firm were ranked at the top by most firms, but the opinions varied across a large range of possibilities. The client or other exogenous, non-strategic incentive as well as the project particularities were ranked very low. Interestingly, marketing implications were of no concern to the respondents, when ranked against country factors.

Environmental Issues in Indonesia

The list of dimensions of country risk identified through the review of the academic literature as well as the business press presented above was presented to the respondents for evaluation. Experiences and opinions were provided by the respondents and after a brief discussion, summarised into a scale of 1 = irrelevant to 5 = critical by the researcher and the respondents together. The results of the analysis of the quantified impressions are provided in Table 8.2. The variables are sorted in the table by order of the absolute magnitude of difference to illustrate the variations of opinions caused by exposure to the country's environment, as opposed to impressions formed by the market analysis process (based mainly on readings of the popular and business press and discussions with prospective business partners as well as other Australian firms with operations in Indonesia).

Table 8.2 Problems facing foreign businesses in Indonesia

Problems	Mean	SD	Mean difference	2-tail sig
Identifying and contacting key decision makers in organisations				
Interest	2.818	.733	-1.336	.000
Involved	4.154	.987		
Cultural differences				
Interest	3.091	.750	-1.063	.008
Involved	4.154	1.144		
Future government attitude towards foreign investment				
Interest	3.136	.889	-.864	.007
Involved	4.000	.816		
Business infrastructure				
Interest	2.864	.710	.864	.001
Involved	2.000	.603		
Political environment				
Interest	3.318	.839	-.759	.005
Involved	4.077	.641		
Language as a barrier in developing business relationships				
Interest	3.300	.979	.608	.153
Involved	2.692	1.251		
Bureaucratic attitudes				
Interest	2.727	.767	-.427	.196
Involved	3.154	.987		
General state of the economy				
Interest	3.136	.774	-.248	.427
Involved	3.385	1.044		
Legislative framework for property rights and profit repatriation				
Interest	2.682	.646	.182	.603
Involved	2.500	1.087		
Law towards joint ventures with local partners				
Interest	3.273	.550	-.182	.622
Involved	3.455	1.128		

For the firms that are currently involved in Indonesia, three risk factors stand out as particularly important: identifying key decision-makers, cultural differences and future government attitudes towards foreign investment. Interestingly, these appear to be the three areas where the largest (and statistically of high significance) differences between experienced and inexperienced firms were observed. For those firms that are currently researching the market, the political environment, the economy, joint venture law and the language barrier are the most important variables. The political environment is also one of the most important variables for the firms involved in Indonesia, and it is actually much more important to them than to the prospective investors.

The problems posed by the underdeveloped business infrastructure in Indonesia are considered insignificant by the firms that are currently operating there. Language barriers and concerns about the legal framework are also not of significance. The joint venture law, however, is a moderate cause for concern for all respondents. The opinions of the experienced firms on this variable are widely dispersed.

Overall, the opinions of the firms that are currently involved in Indonesia were spread across the range whilst for the firms that are interested in the country but have not yet had any experience the choices were mostly on the line of indifference between the two extremes. The responses of the two groups varied significantly on exactly half the variables, thus strongly indicating that experience has a great role to play in the evaluation of a business environment.

Sources of Information Used in Market Assessment

Part of the interview was focused on the sources of information firms utilise in order to identify and evaluate information about business opportunities in Indonesia. The responses can be grouped under the following general headings:

(a) official publications – a source of little significance to firms involved in Indonesia but quite important for those researching the market;

(b) advertisements in trade and business publications for specific projects and joint ventures – a source of moderate importance for both groups;

(c) headquarters personnel travelling in Indonesia – an important source for both groups, and slightly more so for the firms with a presence in the country, as it would be logically expected; and

(d) personal contacts in official or competitors' organisations – the most important source of information, described as vital by most of the experienced firms but of only moderate importance to prospective investors.

Overall, it was shown that the higher the degree of involvement in the country, the more personalised and informal the sources of information used are. This observation confirms the conceptualisation and concurs with the findings of Zarkada (1993).

CONCLUSIONS AND IMPLICATIONS

The exploratory study of direct investment in the manufacturing sector of Indonesia by Australian firms presented in this chapter has provided a useful set of observations Despite the current adverse socio-political and economic circumstances, or the cultural differences, Indonesia is an attractive environment for Australian businesses. Its value is significant to them, and their forecast is that, regardless of the outcome of the transition the country is currently undergoing, its value will increase.

In evaluating the business opportunities that the country presents, firms mostly concentrate on external environmental and technical factors and the possibility of utilising their competencies in order to exploit these opportunities and overcoming the difficulties presented. The approach of both experienced and prospective investors seems to be strategic rather than an opportunistic reaction to chance events – an attitude that is to be expected in view of the nature and scope, as well as the magnitude, of the resource commitment involved in the projects under investigation.

The way the dimensions of risk that Indonesia presents to investors are evaluated differs according to the firms' international experience and level of exposure to the country itself. The observations made on the basis of the present data set can only be tentative ones, given the relatively small size of the sample used. However, they have provided indications of the direction of the expected relationship that needs to be tested using a larger and representative sample and a quantitative methodological design.

The same applies to the sources of information that firms used. Due to the nature of the sample and the data collection used in this study it is not possible to assess the impact of the sources and the nature of information used in the final evaluation of the impact of specific risk dimensions. It is, however, possible to hypothesise that the higher degree of personal involvement in the market will provide opportunities to access more personalised and thus more specific information which in turn will result in a different evaluation of risk factors than an analysis of secondary data would produce.

Firms want to learn as much as they can where it is as easy as possible, so avoidance of countries that are perceived as very different should not be interpreted as insularity. A willingness to tackle a new language or legal system is developed in parallel with the accumulation of organisational capabilities brought about by increased international experience (Craig and Yetton, 1994: 63). In a very similar manner, as countries' experience of accepting foreign direct investment increases, their capabilities grow and the risks for the investors are reduced (Craig and Yetton, 1994). In the successful alignment of the timing of the two processes lies the possibility of successful interaction between economies and foreign firms, in this case of Indonesia and Australian manufacturers.

REFERENCES

Abegglen, James C. (1994), *SEA Change: Pacific Asia as the New World Industrial Center,* New York: The Free Press.

AIDB (1998), 'The Crisis and Beyond: SME Development in Indonesia–A Background Paper', The Australia–Indonesia Business Council.

Akhter, Humayun. and Robert F. Lusch (1987), 'Political Risk: A Structural Analysis', in Cavusgil, S. Tamer (ed.) *Advances in International Marketing,* Vol. **2**, Greenwich, Conn.: JAI Press.

Aswicahyono, H.H., Kelly Bird and Hal Hill (1996), 'What Happens to Industrial Structure When Countries Liberalise? Indonesia Since the Mid-1980s', *Journal of Development Studies,* **32** (3), 340–64.

Bilkey, W.J. (1978), 'An Attempted Integration of the Literature of the Export Behaviour of Firms', *Journal of International Business Studies,* **9** (1), 33–46.

Bird, Judith (1999), 'Indonesia in 1998: The Pot Boils Over', *Asian Survey,* **39** (1), 27–8.

Bociurkiw, Michael (1996), 'Indonesia: Land of Opportunity', *Forbes,* (2 December), 72–6.

Business Asia (1996), 'Driving into Roadblocks', 16 December, **28** (25), 4–5.

Carter, Colin (1994), 'The Industry Policy Debate: A Business Strategy Perspective', in I. Marsh (ed.) *Australian Business in the Asia Pacific Region: The Case for Strategic Industry Policy,* Melbourne: Longman Professional, pp. 67–102.

Cavusgil, S. Tamer (1980), 'On the Internationalisation Process of Firms', *European Research,* **8** (November), pp. 273–81.

Cavusgil, S. Tamer. and J. Naor (1989), 'Firm and Management Characteristics as Discriminators of Export Marketing Activity', *Journal of Business Research,* **15**(3), pp. 221–36.

Chisnall, Peter M. (1977), *Effective Industrial Marketing,* London: Longman.

Craig, Jane and Phillip Yetton (1994), 'Australia's International Firms: Contributions and Prospects' in I. Marsh (ed.), *Australian Business in the Asia Pacific Region: The Case for Strategic Industry Policy,* Melbourne: Longman Professional, pp. 32–66.

Cundiff, Edward W. and Marye Tharp Hilger (1988), *Marketing in the International Environment,* Englewood Cliffs, NJ: Prentice-Hall International Editions.

Cutler, Terry (1994), 'Telecommunications in the Future Australian Economy: An Electronic Switzerland or an Electronic Backwater', in I. Marsh (ed.), *Australian Business in the Asia Pacific Region: The Case for Strategic Industry Policy,* Melbourne: Longman Professional, pp. 166–81.

da Gama Pinto, Clarence (1997), in R. Goodfellow (ed) *Indonesian Business Culture,* Singapore: Butterworth-Heinemann Asia, pp. 175–207.

Department of Foreign Affairs and Trade (1994), *Australian Trade and Investment Development,* Canberra: Australian Government Publishing Service.

Diamantopoulos, A., B.B. Schlegelmilch and C. Allpress (1990), 'Export Marketing Research in Practice: A Comparison of Users and Non-users', *Journal of Marketing Management,* **6** (3), 257–74.

Dobbs-Higginson, Michael S. (1994), *Asia Pacific: Its Role in the New World Disorder,* Tokyo: The Japan Times.

Economist, 'Asia: Indonesia's Second Chance', 5 June, 37.

Financial Times (1994), 'The Birth of a Business', 25 January.

Ford, David (1990), 'Buyer/Seller Relationships in International Industrial Markets', in D. Ford (ed.), *Understanding Business Markets: Interaction, Relationships and Networks, The Industrial Marketing and Purchasing Group,* London: Academic Press.

Goodfellow, Rob (1997), *Indonesian Business Culture,* Singapore: Butterworth-Heinemann Asia.

Heizer, Jay and Barry Render (1999), *Principles of Operations Management,* Upper Saddle River, NJ: Prentice Hall.

Johansen, J. and J.E. Valhne (1990), 'The Mechanism of Internationalisation', *International Marketing Review,* **7** (4), 11–24.

Johnson, Chalmers (1998), 'Economic Crisis in East Asia: The Clash of Capitalisms', *Cambridge Journal of Economics,* Special Issue on the Asian Crisis (November), 653–9.

Kaynak, E. and C. Erol (1989), 'The Export Propensity of Turkish Manufacturing and Trading House Firms', *Journal of Marketing Management,* **5** (2), 23–47.

Lucas, C.L. (1986), *International Construction Business Management,* New York: McGraw Hill.

Ng, Siang (1996), 'Indonesia', in R. Edwards and M. Skully (eds), *ASEAN Business Trade and Development: An Australian Perspective*, Melbourne: Butterworth Heinemann Australia, pp. 54–80.

Noland, Marcus (1990), *Pacific Basin Developing Countries: Prospects for the Future,* Washington, DC: Institute for International Economics.

Phillips, Chris, Isobel Doole and Robin Lowe (1994), *International Marketing Strategy: Analysis, Development and Implementation,* London and New York: Routledge.

SBS (1999), *The SBS World Guide,* Melbourne: Reed International Books Australia.

Simpson, C.L. and D. Kujawaa (1974), 'The Export Decision Process: An Empirical Inquiry', *Journal of International Business Studies,* **5** (1), 107–17.

Soedarsono, Adik A, Susan L. Murray and Yildirim Omurtag (1998), 'Productivity Improvement at a High-tech State-owned Industry – an Indonesian Case Study of Employee Motivation', IEEE (Institute of Electrical and Electronics Engineers Inc.) *Transactions on Engineering Management,* **45** (4 November), 388–98.

Thomas, R. (1977), *15 Export Case Studies,* London: British Overseas Trade Board.

World Trade, (1999), 'Indonesian Economy Collapsing', **12** (6), 27.

Yamin, M. and S. Batstone (1992), 'Institutional Obstacles to Marketisation in Post-Socialist Economies', Manchester School of Management – University of Manchester Institute of Science and Technology, Manchester.

Yetton, P., J. Davies and P. Swan (1991), *Going International: Export Myths and Strategic Realities,* Melbourne: Australian Manufacturing Council.

Yudianti, Ninik and Rob Goodfellow (1997), in R. Goodfellow (ed.), *Indonesian Business Culture,* Singapore: Butterworth-Heinemann Asia, pp. 175–207.

Zarkada, Anna (1993), 'An Investigation into the Marketing Orientation of UK Construction Contractors into the Russian Market', M.Sc. Thesis, Manchester School of Management, UMIST.

Zarkada-Fraser, Anna and Torstein Woodhall (1998), 'Internationalisation Motives of Australian Contractors', paper presented at the Australia–New Zealand International Business Academy Inaugural Meeting, Melbourne.

PART IV

Managing International Business Relationships

9. Multinational Knowledge Acquisition Modes of the Taiwan Electronics Industry

Cheng-Min Chuang, Shih-Chieh Fang, Julia L. Lin and Luke Y.C. Hsiao

INTRODUCTION

In an era of knowledge-based economies, the acquisition and management of technological knowledge have become crucial for firms to develop and maintain competitive advantages. With the rapid improvement of technology as well as the systemisation and complexity of technological knowledge, individual firms can seldom develop the necessary technological knowledge through internal competence alone. Therefore, gaining necessary technological knowledge by outsourcing has become one of the most important issues facing the management of technologically-based businesses (Hagedoorn and Narula, 1996).

Traditionally, most small to medium-sized enterprises in Taiwan have successfully acquired international technologies thereby improving low-tech production and increasing export competitiveness. In an era of upgrading and changing industrial structure, most firms with which Taiwan enterprises compete are well-known multinationals. Firms need higher levels of technological knowledge in order to survive and develop in such international markets. And it is more difficult to acquire and adapt technological knowledge by patent or machinery purchase (Fang and Hsiao, 1999). In short, as long as enterprises cannot develop all the necessary technological knowledge alone, the effective acquisition and learning of multinational technology is one of the most crucial issues of increasing international competitiveness for all Taiwanese enterprises.

The relevant research literature regarding enterprises' technological acquisition can be divided into three categories:

(1) new product or technological development;
(2) technological collaboration and authority; and
(3) technological transfer or acquisition (Lambe and Spekman, 1997).

The relevant research on new product or technological development mainly addresses internal technological knowledge acquisition. The study of technological collaboration and authority entails external technological knowledge acquisition. And technological transfer or acquisition may involve both internal and external acquisition. More recently, the field of research has seen an increasing interest in the determinants of technological acquisition modes (Tidd and Trewhella, 1997; Poppo and Zenger, 1998; Robertson and Gatignon, 1998). This chapter will systemically review the relevant literature in order to establish an integrated conceptual framework of multinational knowledge acquisition mode for Taiwanese enterprises. In short, this chapter has two major research questions:

(1) What are the multinational knowledge acquisition modes of the Taiwanese electronic industry?
(2) What factors influence the choice of modes and how do they do this?

LITERATURE REVIEW AND THE ESTABLISHMENT OF THEORETICAL FRAMEWORK

Definition and Classification of Knowledge

In this study the term 'technology' denotes any system of knowledge whose purpose is to resolve various problems arising during a firm's operation, which includes manufacturing, marketing, organisational management, and so on (Shariff, 1998). Many recent related researches have pointed out that, under the knowledge-based economy, technology is actually a core knowledge asset of any enterprise (Hamel, 1991; Inkpen, 1998). Thus, this chapter identifies technology and knowledge as synonymous. According to Sharif's (1988) classification, knowledge can be divided into four major categories:

(1) *Technoware*: which denotes object-embodied technology, including manufactured products and infrastructures such as machinery;
(2) *Infoware*, which denotes document-embodied technology, including technological blueprints, procedural flows, formulas, and so on;
(3) *Humanware*: which denotes person-embodied technology, including experience, knowledge, skill, innovative ability, and so on; and

(4) *Orgaware*: which denotes institution-embodied technology, including organisational, managerial, coordination ability, and so on.

Multinational Knowledge Acquisition Modes

Knowledge accessibility and knowledge importance for business competitiveness are primary factors for enterprises' choice of multinational knowledge acquisition modes. Besides input of capital, human resource and 'ownership', the knowledge commitment also involves a collaborative relationship of the knowledge source (Contractor and Kundu, 1998). In terms of ownership and cooperation relationships, multinational knowledge acquisition modes in this chapter can be divided into four categories: contract, alliance, joint venture and merger (see Table 9.1).

Table 9.1 Multinational knowledge acquisition mode

Ownership cooperation	Yes	No
Yes	Joint venture (3)	Alliance (2)
No	Merge (4)	Contract (1)

Theoretical Basis of Multinational Knowledge Acquisition Modes

The research literature of business knowledge acquisition modes depends primarily on transaction cost theory, resource-based theory and knowledge-based theory. Transaction cost theory entails the efficiency of knowledge acquisition and learning processes. Resource-based theory demonstrates the choices of knowledge acquisition modes based on acquisition of organisational core competitive capability and complementary assets (Teece, 1986). And knowledge-based theory addresses knowledge acquisition modes by establishment of dynamic core capability and the effective improvement of organisational learning capability. In addition to decisions about knowledge acquisition modes, knowledge-based theory also implies the importance of learning conditions on knowledge acquisition modes (Steensma, 1996; Moon, 1998).

Transaction Cost Theory

Teece (1977) was the first to apply transaction cost theory to decisions about technological transfer modes. Subsequently, many scholars strongly supported the empirical study of transaction cost theory in applying the research of optimal knowledge acquisition mode over time (Teece, 1986;

Tapon, 1989; Pisano, 1990, 1991; Brockhoff, 1992; Tidd and Trewhella, 1997; Poppo and Zenger, 1998; Robertson and Gatignon, 1998). The logic of transaction cost theory, just like normal commercial products, indicates that most 'technological knowledge' exists within a 'technological market' stemming from supply and demand of technology. Due to specific characteristics of the technology itself (such as uncertainty, complexity, tacitness and appropriability), firms are often unable simply to acquire and learn necessary knowledge via an open market transaction (Barney, 1999). In other words, an enterprise's alternative is to internalise the process of knowledge acquisition when high transaction cost occurs in the market during attempts to acquire knowledge. Of course, a firm can seek a cooperative strategy to reduce the transaction cost so that the modes of joint venture or alliance become the second-best choice (Dyer, 1997; Contractor and Kundu, 1998).

The firm itself also becomes an influential factor because of its own capabilities and experiences. In the process of knowledge acquisition and learning, these organisational capabilities and experiences can respond to the hazards of uncertainty, opportunism, informational asymmetry and so on (Mowery et al., 1996; Tsang, 1997; Poppo and Zenger, 1998). Generally, the variables of the firm's characteristics include technological capability, the CEO's commitment to knowledge acquisition, strategic importance, market direction of the firm and so on (Pisano, 1991; Brockhoff, 1992; Poppo and Zenger, 1998).

Resource-based theory

From the perspective of resource-based theory, business knowledge acquisition mainly addresses the establishment and enhancement of 'core capability' as well as acquisition of complementary assets (Teece, 1986; Combs and Ketchen, 1997; Barney, 1999). And what kind of mode can gain the necessary knowledge of business? This decision is determined by several variables of firm characteristics. There are the advantages and constraints of the firm's internal resources and capability, the necessary resource input of specific knowledge acquisition, strategic importance of specific knowledge for the firm, as well as strategic direction of the firm itself (Tsang, 1997; Tidd and Trewhella, 1997; Mowery et al., 1998; Barney, 1999). Taking into account these variables, an enterprise can make a decision to input the suitable resources and accommodate the accessibility of external resources so that a choice can be made of the 'optimal' knowledge acquisition mode (Tsang, 1997; Combs and Ketchen, 1997; Barney, 1999).

Knowledge-based theory

From the perspective of knowledge-based theory, the functions of a firm are development, application and integration of related technological knowledge to provide the value-added activities of production and/or service (Pisano, 1991; Grant, 1996a,b). A firm can certainly gain the necessary technological knowledge through internal accumulation and development. A firm may, however, more effectively acquire and learn this technological knowledge by outsourcing (Steensma, 1996; Makhija and Ganesh, 1997; Tidd and Trewhella, 1997; Lane and Lubatkin, 1998). From the point of view of multinational knowledge acquisition, the perspective of knowledge-based theory suggests that an unbounded organisational learning pattern can establish and enhance a firm's internal capacity. Furthermore, this capability can improve the competitiveness of the firm. The choice of knowledge acquisition modes is determined by whether the optimal mode can maximise firm learning (Zander and Kogut, 1995; Steensma, 1996; Grant, 1996a; Makhija and Ganesh, 1997; Moon, 1998). Concretely, a firm should carefully conduct an evaluation of organisational internal/external conditions, choose the optimal knowledge acquisition mode and increase the performance of knowledge acquisition through a suitable learning pattern. The external and/or internal conditions above include at least: (1) characteristics of knowledge itself, (2) firm characteristics, and (3) organisational learning condition in the process of knowledge acquisition (Hamel, 1991; Makhija and Ganesh, 1997; Moon, 1998; Barney, 1999).

The Relationship of Knowledge Characteristics, Firm Characteristics, Organisational Learning Condition and Knowledge Acquisition Modes

From this review of transaction cost, resource-based and knowledge-based theories, we conclude that there are three factors influencing multinational knowledge acquisition mode: (1) characteristics of knowledge itself, (2) firm characteristics, and (3) organisational learning condition. The following discussions examine how these three influence multinational knowledge acquisition mode.

Knowledge characteristics

In the process of acquiring knowledge, the nature of the knowledge itself will generate difficulties, thereby resulting in transaction costs (Williamson, 1985). When market transaction cost is too high, the firm's alternatives are to internalise the process of knowledge acquisition (such as by a merger), or to seek inter-organisational collaboration in order to reduce transaction costs or uncertainty. In the literature, knowledge characteristics include four dimensions.

(1) *Uncertainty*: whether the technological knowledge truly matches the firm's needs, and whether the new technological innovation can be rapidly adapted (Teece, 1986; Hippel, 1987; Teece et al., 1997; Robertson and Gatignon, 1998; Poppo and Zenger, 1998; Fang et al., 1999).

(2) *Complexity*: indicates the interdependence and systematisation among the elements of the knowledge (Lambe and Spekman, 1997; Fang and Hsiao, 1999). In other words, the full commercial implementation of technological knowledge depends on a degree of knowledge compatibility.

(3) *Tacitness*: indicates the degree to which the literalisation and formalisation of knowledge is explicit and clear (Hippel, 1987; Teece, 1986,1992; Moon, 1998).

(4) *Appropriability*: refers to the profit the holder of technological knowledge can gain if the knowledge were utilised. Therefore, it also implies some trading characteristics, such as public good and information asymmetry (Teece, 1986; Pisano, 1990; Helfat, 1997; Robertson and Gatignon, 1998).

Firm characteristics

Transaction cost theory addresses firm capabilities that can decrease transaction cost stemming from uncertainty, information asymmetry and so on, in the process of knowledge acquisition. Both resource-based theory and knowledge-based theory focus on an internal analysis of the firm and provide an extremely important avenue for research on knowledge acquisition modes to examine the ways firms attempt to establish and develop core competence as a competitive advantage. Thus, there are several major determinants of firm characteristics that can reduce the costs associated with the transaction and increase strategic competitive competence of firms:

(1) A CEO's commitment to a knowledge acquisition project plays an important role when a firm adopts the internal knowledge acquisition mode (Brockhoff, 1992; Madhok, 1996; Makhija and Ganesh, 1997). If the CEO strongly supports a knowledge acquisition project, then the firm will input more resources, even to the point of 100 per cent ownership (that is, a merger) to acquire the knowledge.
(2) Firm competence includes past accumulated technological and managerial competence. In addition, the related competencies of team management and experience can seriously impact different knowledge

acquisition modes (Lyles and Salk, 1996; Teece et al., 1997; Poppo and Zenger, 1998; Moon, 1998).

(3) Strategic importance of knowledge within a firm: both resource-based theory and knowledge-based theory state that a firm will input more resources to secure and control the usage of particular knowledge when the strategic importance of particular knowledge is high. Thus, firms trend to adopt the knowledge acquisition mode of internalisation (Teece, 1986; Tsang, 1997; Poppo and Zenger, 1998).

(4) Market direction of firm: recently, research in the field of organisational learning and R&D innovation points out that firms with more market direction have more positive impact on the establishment and maintenance of organisational learning competence (Hurley and Hult, 1998; Morgan et al., 1998; Tunisini and Zanfei, 1998). That is, firms with market direction will tend to adopt a knowledge acquisition mode requiring larger resource input so that they can enhance organisational learning, through either a merger or joint venture (Barkema and Vermeulen, 1998).

Organisational learning condition

Knowledge-based theory views multinational knowledge acquisition as a process of organisational learning. Thus, organisational learning is key to the efficiency of increasing learning or multinational knowledge acquisition. Organisational learning can be attributable to the process of multinational knowledge acquisition: (1) whether or not technological suppliers and receivers can create a win–win learning condition, (2) whether technological receivers themselves have strong learning motives and competence, and (3) whether both parties have a good interactive relationship (Hamel, 1991; Steensma, 1996; Makhija and Ganesh, 1997; Tidd and Trewhella, 1997; Teece et al., 1997; Khanna et al., 1998; Lane and Lubatkin, 1998; Moon, 1998; Davenport et al., 1999).

Different acquisition modes imply that both parties have different degrees of interaction and resource commitment. Thus, a better learning condition exists when the firm devotes more resources to knowledge acquisition and has more competence to control the process and outcome. A better learning condition here means that both parties to knowledge acquisition have compatible organisational cultures and goals as well as organisational competence. Therefore, both parties will have less conflict in communication, and the interaction process can enhance the learning effect of knowledge acquisition (Lane and Lubatkink, 1998; Makhija and Ganesh, 1998; Lorenzoni and Lipparini, 1991; Davenport et al., 1999).

From the perspectives of transaction cost theory, resource-based theory, and knowledge-based theory, this chapter categorises several decisive variables of multinational knowledge acquisition mode into (1) knowledge characteristics, (2) firm characteristics, and (3) organisational learning condition. The cause–effect relationship of decisive variables to knowledge acquisition mode is illustrated in Table 9.2.

Table 9.2 The impact of knowledge characteristics, firm characteristics and organisational learning condition to multinational knowledge acquisition modes

Knowledge acquisition modes factors	Merge	Joint venture	Alliance	Contract	Theoretical basis
Knowledge characteristics					
• Uncertainty		+	++		TC
• Complexity		++	++		TC,KB
• Tacitness	++	+			TC,KB
• Appropriability	++	+			TC,KB
Firm characteristics					
• CEO commitment	++	+			KB,RB
• R&D capability	++	+			TC,KB,RB
• Strategic importance	++	+			KB,RB
• Market-oriented	++	+			KB
Organisational learning conditions					
• Organisational learning gap				++	KB
• Organisational culture difference				++	KB
• Organisational goal difference				++	KB
• Organisational structure difference				++	KB

Notes:
'++'represents that mode of adoption of possibility is higher;
'+'represents that the chance of this mode is next to that above.
TC: transaction cost theory; RB: resource-based theory;
KB: knowledge-based theory.

Conceptual framework and research hypotheses

Based on the literature review, this chapter proposes the conceptual framework of multinational knowledge acquisition mode as displayed in Figure 9.1. First, this theoretical framework points out that knowledge and firm characteristics determine the choice of multinational knowledge acquisition modes from several angles, such as efficiency of transaction cost, accessibility of core competence, the impact of organisational dynamic capability and learning conditions and so on. Second, as this chapter also points out, the choice of multinational knowledge acquisition modes is influenced by the learning conditions.

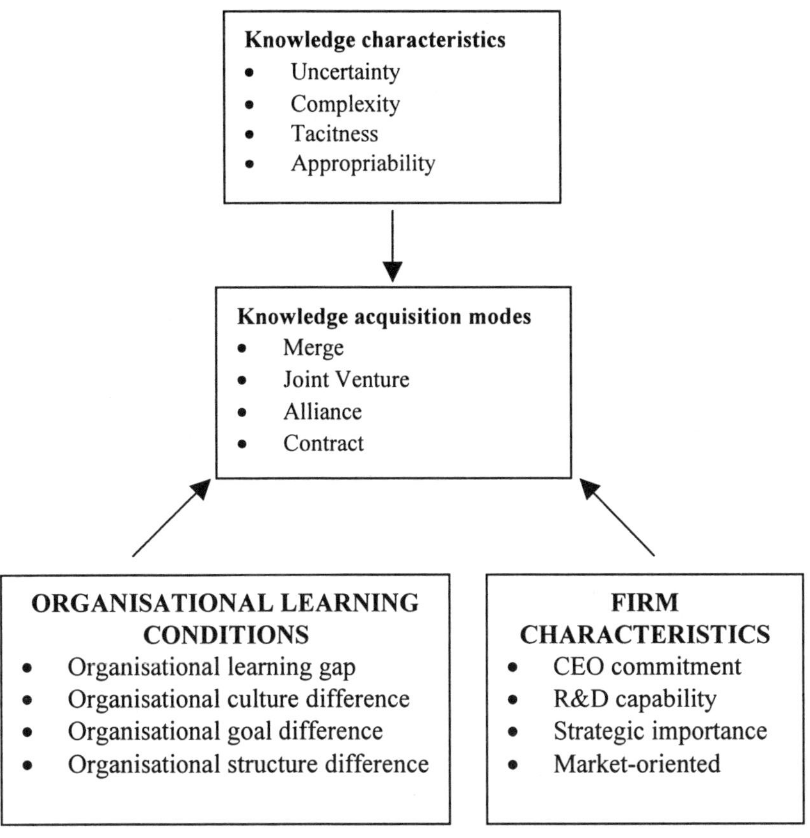

Figure 9.1 The conceptual framework of multinational knowledge acquisition modes

Based on the conceptual framework in Figure 9.1, the purpose of this chapter is to examine empirically the impact of knowledge characteristics, firm characteristics and organisational learning condition on the choice of multinational knowledge acquisition mode. Three hypotheses are offered as explicit statements of the relationships displayed in Table 9.2.

H_1: Characteristics of knowledge itself, such as uncertainty, tacitness and so on, can significantly influence the knowledge acquisition mode.

H_2: Firm characteristics, such as CEO's commitment, firm technological competence and so on, can significantly influence the knowledge acquisition mode.

H_3: With better organisational learning conditions in terms of organisational culture, strategic goal, and technological competence, a firm will tend to adopt the mode with high resource input and control, such as merger or joint venture.

RESEARCH METHOD AND DESIGN

Measurement and Operationalisation of Variables

The main concepts and variables for this study include four knowledge acquisition modes of merger, joint venture, alliance and contract, as well as relevant influencing factors, such as knowledge characteristics, firm characteristics and organisational learning condition. The results of combining the measurement and operationalisation of variables from the previous related literature are displayed in Table 9.3.

Empirical Data Collection and Questionnaire Design

This research used a questionnaire to collect data. There are two major data sources for this study: the first included the top 1000 manufacturers listed in the annual published report of the *Commonwealth* magazine; the second is the manufacturers of Chinchu science-based industrial park. This chapter used each multinational knowledge acquisition project as the unit of analysis. Some key manufacturers, therefore, needed two or more copies of the questionnaire.

Table 9.3 Concepts, variables measurement and operationalisation

Concepts	Variables Measurement	Variables Operationalisation	Related Literature
Knowledge characteristics	• Uncertainty • Complexity • Tacitness • Appropriability	• Standardisation degree of technological knowledge • Crystallisation degree of knowledge • Interdependent degree of knowledge • Production degree of knowledge	Tapon (1989) Pisano (1990) Brockhoff (1992) Robertson & Gatignon (1998) Moon (1998)
Firm characteristics	• R&D capability • CEO commitment • Strategic importance • Market-oriented	• Capital & human investment ratio of R&D • Technological capability of related fields • CEO's supporting degree on specific knowledge acquisition project • Necessity of core capability or not • Important degree of market competition • Commitment degree to customer • Pursuit of customer satisfaction • Understanding of customer need	Cohen & Levinthal (1990) Teece et al. (1997) Robertson & Gatignon (1998) Morgan et al. (1998) Hurley & Hult (1998) Lane & Lubatkin (1998) Grant (1996) Hamel (1991) Teece (1986)
Knowledge acquisition modes	• Internalisation • Cooperation • Market-oriented	• Contractual trading • Ownership degree of joint venture minor or major • Merge	Pisano (1991) Lyles & Salk (1996) Moon (1998) Robertson & Gatignon (1998) Contractor & Kundu (1998)
Organisational learning conditions	• Organisational culture difference • Organisational structure difference • Organisational goal difference • Organisational learning gap	• Similarity of organisational structure • Similarity of enterprise's goal • Similarity of product competition • Similarity of managerial formalisation & centralisation • Similarity of conflict & tolerance • Related capability asymmetry • Gap of informational recondition • Gap of human quality & profession	Lane & Lubatkin (1998) Hurley & Hult (1998) Makhija & Ganesh (1997) Steensma (1996) Hurley & Hult (1998) Lane & Lubatkin (1998)

Aside from the basic background of the sampled firms, the questionnaire used seven-point Likert scales for all of the variables of concern. In addition, personal visits were made to three manufacturers for direct assessment of industrial practices, and to modify and finalise the questionnaire.

Data Analysis Method

In this chapter, the dependent variable is knowledge acquisition mode, which is, of course, nominal data. The relevant influencing factors are independent variables. Therefore, to test the association among all variables as well as between the dependent and independent variables, this chapter adopted logistic regression model.

The following is the logistic regression formula for multinational knowledge acquisition mode:

$$P_i = \alpha_1 K_{1i} + \alpha_2 K_{2i} + \alpha_3 K_{3i} + \alpha_4 K_{4i} + \beta_1 F_{1i} + \beta_2 F_{2i} + \beta_3 F_{3i} + \beta_4 F_{4i}$$

$$+ \gamma_1 L_{1i} + \gamma_2 L_{2i} + \gamma_3 L_{3i} + \gamma_4 L_{4i} \qquad i = 1,2,\ldots..,98$$

K_1: Uncertainty	F_1: CEO commitment	L_1: Organisational learning gap
K_2: Complexity	F_2: R&D capability	L_2: Organisational culture difference
K_3: Tacitness	F_3: Strategic importance	L_3: Organisational goal difference
K_4: Appropriability	F_4: Market-oriented	L_4: Organisational structure difference

K represents Knowledge characteristics, F represents firm characteristics and L represents organisational learning conditions

P_i is the probability that the firm selects a specified mode. For the logistic regression analysis, a particular mode must be selected as a base to compare with the other three modes. The basis mode has zero probability (P_i) in the formula above. And P_i includes the pooled probabilities of the other three modes. The modes of this chapter include: (1) authorised contract, (2) alliance (excluding the cooperation of ownership), (3) joint venture, and (4) merger (100 per cent of ownership). In the following analysis, the dimensions of cooperation and ownership were adopted in this chapter for comparison. Therefore, the modes that may be selected as basis are (a) cooperation vs. non-cooperation, that is, (2) + (3) vs. (1) + (4), or (b) ownership vs. non-ownership, that is, (1) + (2) vs. (3) + (4) (see Table 9.1).

BASIC STATISTICS AND RELIABILITY ANALYSIS OF SAMPLING DATA

Basic Statistics of Sampling Data

Out of the valid 98 respondents, 4 selected purchasing mode to conduct multinational knowledge acquisition projects. Two, 22, and 70, respectively, identified 'joint venture', 'alliance', and 'authorised contract' modes. For analysis, joint venture and alliance were combined as the same knowledge acquisition mode and called the cooperative mode. In other words, multinational knowledge acquisition modes can be divided into three categories: (a) merger, 4 projects, (b) cooperative mode, 24, and (c) authorised contract, 70. The means and standard deviations of three cognitive knowledge characteristics, firm characteristics and organisational

Table 9.4 The basic statistics of multinational knowledge acquisition and the factors–mean and standard deviation

Knowledge acquisition modes factors	(a) Merger N = 4	(b) Joint venture & alliance N = 24	(c) Authorised N = 70
Uncertainty (K_i)	4.26 (0)	3.65 (0.80)	3.06 (1.03)
Complexity (K_2)	5.25 (0.29)	4.87 (0.81)	4.91 (0.92)
Tacitness (K_3)	4.32 (0.48)	4.64 (0.68)	4.02 (0.60)
Appropriability (K_4)	5.00 (0)	4.78 (0.68)	4.82 (0.94)
CEO commitment (F_i)	5.35 (1.08)	5.25 (1.03)	5.02 (0.94)
R&D capability (F_2)	5.25 (0.50)	4.68 (1.06)	4.05 (0.97)
Strategic importance (F_3)	4.95 (1.26)	4.58 (1.15)	4.05 (1.93)
Market-oriented (F_4)	6.06 (0.66)	5.04 (0.83)	5.35 (0.85)
Organisational learning gap (L_i)	3.19 (0.63)	4.15 (0.68)	4.01 (0.89)
Organisational culture difference (L_2)	3.12 (0.50)	3.22 (1.06)	3.95 (1.35)
Organisational goal difference (L_3)	3.67 (0.58)	3.40 (1.46)	3.32 (1.45)
Organisational structure difference (L_4)	3.78 (0.82)	3.54 (1.47)	3.50 (1.40)

Note: Figures in parentheses represent standard deviation.

learning condition appear in Table 9.4. In Table 9.5, the respondents' national identities are given: Japan (40); USA (35); Europe (18, including UK, Holland, Germany); and others (5, including Korea, Singapore and Hong Kong).

Table 9.5 The national resources of multinational knowledge acquisition

Japan	USA	Europe	Other
40	35	18	5

Reliability Test of Sampling Data

The data source for this research was a questionnaire. Some variables were based on responses to only one question. Others were based on multiple items. Table 9.6 displays the reliability coefficients for all variables based on multiple items.

Table 9.6 The reliability of research variables

Research variables	Questions	Cronbach α	Research variables	Questions	Cronbach α
Knowledge characteristics			• Strategic importance	1	-
• Uncertainty	1	-	• Market-oriented	8	0.95
• Complexity	2	0.92	**Learning conditions**		
• Tacitness	2	0.45	• Organisational learning gap	4	0.89
• Appropriability	1	-	• Organisational culture difference	1	-
Firm Characteristics			• Organisational goal difference	1	-
• CEO commitment	2	0.93	• Organisational structure difference	1	-
• R&D capability	2	0.82			

Results' Analysis and Discussion

The following analysis of outcomes is based on the comparisons of the cooperative mode (alliance and joint venture) with the non-cooperative mode (authorised contract). The cooperative mode is (b) mode of Table 9.4. There are 24 cases. The non-cooperative mode is (c) mode of Table 9.4.

The number of cases is 70. The outcome of Logistic regression analysis is displayed in Table 9.7. (The 4 cases categorised as 'merger' mode were excluded from the analysis).

Table 9.7 The logistic regression result of factors

Variables	Knowledge characteristics (K)				Firm characteristics (F)				Learning conditions (L)			
	K_1	K_2	K_3	K_4	F_1	F_2	F_3	F_4	L_1	L_2	L_3	L_4
Estimated coefficient	0.13*	-0.16*	0.17*	-0.79	0.21*	0.10*	-0.14	0.15**	0.26*	-0.92**	0.06	0.20

Notes:

K_i, F_i, L_i, i=1~4 All variables meanings will equal to the meanings in equation of logistic regression above.

$\chi^2_{(12)} = 26.86$; P = 0.02.

* represents p < 0.10; ** represents p < 0.05.

In Table 9.7, the logistic regression model generates a significance level of 95% ($\chi^2_{(12)} = 26.86$; P = 0.02). The 12 influencing variables of transaction cost theory, resource-based theory, and knowledge-based theory can reasonably explain the choice of multinational knowledge acquisition mode for these respondents. The results in Table 9.7 are based on the authorised contract mode as a criterion. If the estimated coefficients were positive, then the firm would be likely to adopt the cooperative mode. If the coefficient were negative, the firm would be likely to adopt the authorised contract mode.

Knowledge Characteristics and Multinational Knowledge Acquisition Mode (H_1)

Among four variables, only K_1(uncertainty) and K_3(tacitness) produce a significant value. Both values (α) are positive. The higher the degree of knowledge uncertainty and tacitness, the more the firm will tend to adopt the cooperative mode of knowledge acquisition. When the uncertainty of knowledge is lower (higher standardisation degree in this chapter), the firm will adopt an authorised contract mode because of the low transaction cost. On the other hand, when the tacitness of knowledge is higher, then firm can effectively acquire particular technological knowledge through the cooperative mode.

Neither complexity (K_2) nor appropriability (K_4) of knowledge reach the .10 significance level. Both coefficients demonstrate an effect opposite to the logic of Table 9.2. Coefficient values(α_2 and α_4) of Table 9.7 suggest that when complexity and appropriability of knowledge are higher, the firm may tend to adopt the authorised contract mode to acquire the technological knowledge. However, they do not reach the level of significance.

Firm Characteristics and Multinational Knowledge Acquisition Mode (H_2)

Except for the strategic importance of particular technological knowledge (F_3), all variables of firm characteristics reach a significance level. The estimated coefficients (β_1, β_2, β_4) are positive, which is consistent with the logic in Table 9.2. When a CEO has more commitment to knowledge acquisition, the R&D capacity of the firm is higher, the firm's goal is more market-oriented and the firm will tend to adopt the cooperative mode to acquire technological knowledge.

The insignificance of strategic importance (F_3) implies that the firms of this study do not consider multinational knowledge acquisition as part of their strategic decisions. In other words, the modes of multinational knowledge acquisition are not important for organisational strategic planning. If particular technological knowledge is of strategic importance, then a firm may rapidly acquire this technological knowledge by the authorised contract mode (β_3 coefficient of F_3 is negative).

Organisational Learning Condition and Multinational Knowledge Acquisition Mode (H_3)

From the organisational point of view, multinational knowledge acquisition may be thought of as a process of multinational learning. The ease of communication between a knowledge acquirer (Taiwan firm) and knowledge supplier (foreign company) can affect the organisational learning condition of the knowledge acquirer. The variables of the learning condition may include differences in competence, culture, goal and so on between two parties. The larger the differences, the larger the barrier to communication which is likely to discourage organisational learning. Under these conditions, firms tend to adopt the authorised contract mode to acquire knowledge because this mode does not depend on interactive learning between organisations.

Table 9.7 also shows that gaps in organisational competence (L_i) and culture (L_2) have a significant impact on firms' knowledge acquisition modes. On the other hand, the estimated coefficient (γ_1) of L_1 indicates that when the gap between two organisation's capabilities is bigger, the firm tends to adopt a cooperative mode of knowledge acquisition, which does not match the logic of knowledge-based theory. This may be common among Taiwanese firms. In the course of interacting with a foreign company, Taiwanese firms usually expect to acquire more technological knowledge from foreign companies with higher technological R&D competence, consistent with a 'catching-up' economic pattern. Therefore, Taiwan firms tend to adopt the cooperative mode to acquire foreign technological knowledge. In addition, the estimated coefficient (γ_2) of L_i is negative, showing that it is very difficult to learn necessary technological knowledge through the cooperative mode, because the gap between organisational cultures is bigger. This leads to a firm's tendency to adopt the simple authorised contract mode to acquire knowledge. The variables of organisational strategic goal (L_3) and organisational structure (L_4) do not reach the level of significance.

In short, the hypotheses that are established from transaction cost theory, resource-based theory and knowledge-based theory are generally supported by the empirical data (the outcome of Logistic regression reaches the significant level of 0.05). Some individual hypotheses, however, receive only partial support; and some influencing variables do not reach significance. In addition, the estimated coefficients of some variables that are significant are consistent with the logic of Table 9.2. The gap in organisational competence L_i is the only empirical finding that is significant and inconsistent with the theoretical logic. The empirical outcomes show that Taiwanese firms tend to adopt the cooperative mode of multinational technological knowledge acquisition to increase their technological competence when the gap between the organisational competencies of Taiwanese and foreign firms is greater.

CONCLUSION AND IMPLICATIONS

With the trend to globalisation, firms' multinational knowledge acquisition is not only workable, but also absolutely necessary for competitive viability. However, different knowledge acquisition modes under the different situations have different implications for firms. Thus, it is important that research addresses the issue of which variables influence multinational knowledge acquisition. From the perspectives of transaction cost theory, resource-based theory and knowledge-based theory, this chapter identifies 12 major influencing variables stemming from knowledge characteristics, firm characteristics and organisational learning conditions of multinational knowledge acquisition modes or decisions. Taiwanese electronics firms that involve multinational knowledge projects were the subjects of this empirical analysis.

The outcome of analysis shows that the conceptual framework developed in this chapter gains support from the empirical data. The outcome for every variable is not exactly as anticipated. In general, with higher knowledge uncertainty as well as lesser organisational culture gap with the technological knowledge supplier, then acquiring firms tend to adopt a cooperative mode of knowledge acquisition. Those variables are all significant and consistent with the theorised direction. Moreover, with a bigger gap in organisational competence, Taiwanese electronics firms tend to adopt the cooperative mode, although this outcome differs from the theoretical deduction.

This chapter reports an exploratory study. It discusses decisions about multinational knowledge acquisition modes from the point of view of the governance structure of an organisation. The theoretical framework of this chapter integrated major contemporary organisational theories. It addressed both the 'efficiency' perspective of economic theory and the 'effectiveness' implication of strategic management.

Every multinational knowledge acquisition mode (such as merger, joint venture, alliance and authorised contract) has its advantages and disadvantages from the perspective of organisational management. The findings reported in this chapter can provide a reference for managers to evaluate the appropriateness of the different multinational knowledge acquisition modes.

REFERENCES

Barkema, H.G. and F. Vermeulen (1998), 'International Expansion through Start-up or Acquisition: A Learning Perspective', *Academy of Management Journal*, **4** (1), 7–26.

Barney, J.B. (1999), 'How a Firm's Capabilities Affect Boundary Decisions', *Sloan Management Review*, (Spring), 137–44.

Brockhoff, K. (1992), 'R&D Cooperation between Firms : A Perceived Transaction Cost Perspective', *Management Science*, **38** (4), 514–24.

Cohen, W.M. and D.A. Levinthal (1990), 'Absorptive Capacity: A New Perspective on Learning and Innovation', *Administrative Science Quarterly*, **35**, 128–52.

Combs, J.G. and D.J. Ketchen (1997), 'Toward a Synthesis of the Resource-based View and Organisational Economics in the Context of Grand Strategies', *Journal of Business Strategies*, **14** (2), 83–195.

Contractor, F.J. and S.K. Kundu (1998), 'Model Choice in a World of Alliances: Analyzing Organisational Firms in the International Hotel Sector', *Journal of International Business Studies*, **29** (2), 325–58.

Davenport, S., J. Davies and C. Grimes (1999), 'Collaborative Research Programs: Building Trust Form Difference', *Technovation*, **19** (1), 31–40.

Dyer, J.H. (1997), 'Effective Interfirm Collaboration: How Firms Minimise Transaction Costs and Maximise Transaction Value', *Strategic Management Journal*, **18** (7), 535–56.

Fang, S.C. and Luke Y.C. Hsiao (1999), 'Internationalisation of Taiwanese Firms: An Empirical Study of Electronic and Textile Industries', Paper presented at the 1999 Annual Conference of the Academy of International Business Southeast Asia Region, Melbourne, Australia.

Fang, S.C., Julia L. Lin and Luke Y.C. Hsiao (1999), 'Enterprise Technology Collaborative Strategies in the Electronic Industry', Paper presented at the Conference on Globalisation, Economic Reforms and Development in Asia Pacific Region, Sydney, Australia.

Grant, R.M. (1996a), 'Toward a Knowledge-based Theory of the Firm', *Strategic Management Journal*, **17**, 109–22.

Grant, R.M. (1996b), 'Prospering in Dynamically-Competitive Environments: Organisational Capability as Knowledge Integration', *Organisation Science*, **7** (4), 375–87.

Hagedoorn, J. and R. Narula (1996), 'Choosing Organisational Modes of Strategic Technology Partnering: International Sectoral Differences', *Journal of International Business Studies*, 265–84.

Hamel, G. (1991), 'Competition for Competence and Inter-partner Learning within International Strategic Alliances', *Strategic Management Journal*, **12**, 83–103.

Helfat, C.E. (1997), 'Know-how and Asset Complementarity and Dynamic Capability Accumulation: The Case of R&D', *Strategic Management Journal*, **18**, 339–60.

Hippel, E. Von (1987), 'Cooperation between Rivals: Informal Know-how Trading', *Research Policy*, **16**, 291–302.

Hurley, R.F. and G.T.M. Hult (1998), 'Innovation, Market Orientation, and Organisational Learning: An Integration and Empirical Examination', *Journal of Marketing*, **62** (3), 42–54.

Inkpen, A. (1998), 'Learning, Knowledge Acquisition, and Strategic Alliances', *European Management Journal*, **16** (2), 223–9.

Khanna, T., R. Gulati and N. Nohira (1998), 'The Dynamics of Learning Alliances: Competition, Cooperation, and Relative Scope', *Strategic Management Journal*, **19**, 193–210.

Lambe, C.J. and R.E. Spekman (1997), 'Alliances, External Technology Acquisition, and Discontinuous Technological Change', *Journal of Production Innovation Management*, **14**, 102–16.

Lane, P.J. and M. Lubatkin (1998), 'Relative Absorptive Capacity and Interorganisational Learning', *Strategic Management Journal*, **19**, 461–77.

Lorenzoni, G. and A. Lipparini (1991), 'The Leveraging of Interfirm Relationships as a Distinctive Organisational Capability: A Longitudinal Study', *Strategic Management Journal*, **20**, 317–38.

Lyles, M.A. and J.E. Salk (1996), 'Knowledge Acquisition from Foreign Parents in International Joint Venture: An Empirical Examination in the Hungarian Context', *Journal of International Business Studies,* 877–903.

Madhok, A. (1996), 'Know-how, Experience and Competitive-related Considerations in Foreign Market Entry: An Exploratory Investigation', *International Business Review*, **5** (4), 339–66.

Makhija, M.V. and U. Ganesh (1997), 'The Relationship between Control and Partner Learning in Learning-related Joint Venture', *Organisation Science*, **8** (5), 508–27.

Moon, C.H. (1998), 'Technological Capacity as a Determinant of Governance Form in International Strategic Combinations', *Journal of Technology Management Research*, **9** (1), 35–53.

Morgan, R.E., C.S. Katsikeas and K. Appian-Adu (1998), 'Market Orientation and Organisational Learning Capabilities', *Journal of Marketing Management*, **14**, 353–81.

Mowery, D.S., J.E. Oxley and B.S. Silverman (1998), 'Technological Overlap and Interfirm Cooperation: Implications for the Resource-based View of the Firm', *Research Policy*, **27** (5), 507–23.

Mowery, D.S., J.E. Oxley and B.S. Silverman (1996), 'Strategic Alliances and Interfirm Knowledge Transfer', *Strategic Management Journal*, **17**, 77–91.

Mowery, D.C. (1983), 'Innovation, Market Structure and Government Policy in the American Semiconductor Electronics Industry: A Survey', *Research Policy*, **12**, 183–97.

Olk, P. (1998), 'A Knowledge-based Perspective on the Transformation of Individual-level Relationships into Interorganisational Structures : The Case of R&D Consortia', *European Management Journal*, **16** (1), 39–49.

Pisano, G.P. (1991), 'The Governance of Innovation: Vertical Integration and Collaborative Arrangements in the Biotechnology Industry', *Research Policy*, **20**, 237–49.

Pisano, G.P. (1990), 'The R&D Boundaries of the Firm: An Empirical Analysis', *Administrative Science Quarterly*, **35** (1), 153–76.

Poppo, L. and T. Zenger (1998), 'Testing Alternative Theories of the Firm: Transaction Cost, Knowledge-based, and Measurement Explanations for

Make-or-Buy Decisions in Information Services', *Strategic Management Journal*, **19**, 853–77.

Robertson, T.S. and H. Gatignon (1998), 'Technology Development Mode: A Transaction Cost Conceptualisation', *Strategic Management Journal*, (19), 515–31.

Sharif, M.N. (1988), 'Basis of Techno-economic Policy Analysis', *Science and Public Policy*, **15** (4), 217–29.

Steensma, H.H. (1996), 'Acquiring Technological Competencies through Inter-organisation Collaboration: An Organisational Learning Perspective', *Journal of Engineering and Technology Management*, **12** (4), 267–86.

Tapon, F. (1989), 'A Transaction Cost Analysis of Innovations in the Organisation of Pharmaceutical R&D', *Journal of Economic Behavior and Organisation*, **12**, 197–213.

Teece, D.J. (1986), 'Profiting from Technology Innovation: Implications for Integration, Collaboration, Licensing and Public Policy', *Research Policy*, **15** (6), 285–305.

Teece, D. (1977), 'Technology Transfer by Multinational Firms: The Resource Cost of Transferring Technological Know-how', *Economic Journal*, **87**, 241–61.

Teece, D.J., G. Pisano and A. Shuen (1997), 'Dynamic Capabilities and Strategic Management', *Strategic Management Journal*, **18**, 281–93.

Tidd, J. and M.J. Trewhella (1997), 'Organisational and Technological Antecedents of Knowledge Acquisition and Learning', *R&D Management*, **27** (4), 359–75.

Tsang, E.W.K. (1997), 'Choice of International Technology Transfer Mode: A Resource-based View', *Management International Review*, **37** (2), 151–68.

Williamson, O.E. (1985), *The Economic Institution of Capitalism,* New York: Free Press.

Zander, U.R. and B. Kogut (1995), 'Knowledge and the Speed of the Transfer and Imitation of Organisational Capabilities: An Empirical Test', *Organisation Science*, **6** (1), 76–92.

10. Beyond Institutional Means of Intellectual Property Protection across Borders: Lessons from an Australian MNE

Sara L. McGaughey

INTRODUCTION

The competitive advantage of firms from more highly industrialised nations is increasingly recognised as deriving from the firms' ability to create and effectively manage knowledge assets (for example, Lyles and Salk, 1996; Kogut and Zander, 1993; Kidd, 1998; *Long Range Planning,* 1997; Teece, 1998). As a corollary, the *protection* of knowledge assets – or intellectual property – through either withholding it from the public domain or securing the rights to control its use has been elevated in importance. For multinational enterprises (MNEs)[1], large and small, the management of intellectual property protection is complicated by vast differences in the coverage and strength of enforcement of legally defined intellectual property rights protection (IPRP) regimes of the nations in which the firm may chose to operate. In particular, the newly emerging markets in which significant opportunities are thought to lie for many MNEs historically have had weak IPRP (de Almeida, 1995). Accordingly, this chapter attempts to address the question: *How can MNEs protect their intellectual property, on which their competitive advantage is based, in nations deemed to have weak IPRP regimes?*

In addressing this question, a diversity of literatures is drawn upon, including those of information economics, knowledge management and learning, strategic management and international business. After a brief overview of the relationship between knowledge assets and IPRP regimes, including the basis of national variations, an understanding of the fundamental characteristics that underpin and maintain the value of any knowledge asset and the knowledge creation process is sought principally through the scholarly works of Boisot, Nonaka, Polanyi and Takeuchi, amongst others. Employing Boisot's (1995, 1998) 'Information-Space' in particular as an entry point from which to garner insights into the nature of knowledge assets and flows, the potential impact of IPRP regimes on the management of knowledge assets is explored. The notion of *strategic interventions* by firms in the transformations and associated flows of information throughout Boisot's conceptual Information-Space is introduced as a means by which firms may internalise IP protection, rather than relying solely on institutionalised means. Two concepts critical to understanding the risks of appropriation of a firm's knowledge assets by a competitor are developed and introduced, namely *transparency* and *replicability*. Together with the notion of strategic interventions, these two concepts are used to explain how some MNEs are able to protect their intellectual property even in countries with weak IPRP regimes. The operations of an Australian manufacturer of high-speed car and passenger carrying catamarans, INCAT, engaged in a joint production arrangement with its former Hong Kong licensee for the construction of its vessels in southern China (McGaughey et al., 2000), provide a practical illustration of the utility of these concepts to understanding novel firm-based strategies for protecting knowledge assets across borders.

KNOWLEDGE ASSETS AND INTELLECTUAL PROPERTY RIGHTS PROTECTION

The firm's knowledge assets are the stocks of knowledge under that firm's ownership or control, from which services (including their embodiment in products) are expected to flow for a period of time. This period of time may be difficult to specify in advance as it is dependent on how fast the broader knowledge base that sustains the specific knowledge asset is changing and on the firm's success in protecting this asset from appropriation by other firms (Sanchez and Heene, 1997; Boisot, 1998). Knowledge assets have their foundation in data, in information and in learning processes that are often organisational-specific. That is, different firms make different uses of commonly available data and information because they learn differently (Baets, 1998). Data can be construed simply as a discernible difference between alternative states in a system: an example of data would be as stream of 0s and 1s in binary code (Baets, 1998). Information is data that modify the expectations of the observer, or the *meaning* embodied in the 0s and 1s. Information is thus data that is interpreted, and not all data are necessarily informative. Knowledge, then, is the set of expectations that an observer holds with respect to an event or phenomenon. These expectations may change through an individual's learning: knowledge is modified by the arrival of new information which, in turn, has been extracted from data (Boisot, 1998; Sanchez and Heene, 1997; Baets, 1998).

While a firm's capturing and securing superior knowledge may provide a source of competitive advantage, this is not always the case. The commercial value of any resource, whether physical or informational, is a function of the utility of the services it yields over time and its scarcity (Stigler, 1965; Penrose, 1959). A critical distinction between knowledge and physical resources is, however, that knowledge derived from data resources is not *naturally* scarce. Physical (private or public) goods are bounded by spatio-temporal locality such that a particular physical object is only in one location at any one time (Boisot, 1995, 1998). If sold, it is no longer available to the original owner (Suchman, 1989). Data resources, and the information that is yielded by their interpretation, may be used concurrently by many people with no erosion in their utility to each individual. Purchasers of information can resell their information to a third party while leaving their own holdings intact. Thus, it is typically argued that new ideas or inventions are costly to develop but inexpensive to imitate, although Lamberton (1998) suggests this point may be exaggerated. Furthermore, an idea is most valuable to the receiver the first time it is received. To the original owner's lament, there is no incentive for a consumer to purchase the same information a second time (Suchman, 1989). Maintenance of the scarcity value of knowledge assets thus becomes a significant challenge for firms and an issue around which intellectual property rights protection (IPRP) regimes have evolved.

REGIMES OF INTELLECTUAL PROPERTY RIGHTS PROTECTION

The World Trade Organisation's Trade Related Aspects of Intellectual Property (TRIPs) Agreement – which came into effect on 1 January 1995 – is to date the most comprehensive multilateral agreement on intellectual property (Drahos, 1998). The IPRP regimes it identifies are reflective of newer growth industries in biotechnology and information technology, and include: copyright and related rights; trademarks including service marks; geographical indications including appellations of origin; industrial designs; patents including the protection of new varieties of plants; the layout-designs of integrated circuits; and undisclosed information including trade secrets and test data. Two additional regimes not included in the TRIPs agreement and often overlooked in the academic considerations of IPRP (see, for example, Correa, 1995; Jain, 1996) are natural intellectual property and secrecy. In natural intellectual property, the IP embodied in a 'unique' product or service is tied to a physical object or persona over which the individual or firm has exclusive control. Its effectiveness is based on the perceived uniqueness of the product or service, and no formal laws are required. Secrecy relies on the ability of the individual or firm to withhold the knowledge asset or idea from others, but without the need for legal institutions.

In the application of virtually any IPRP regime, that which is being protected is not the good or service on offer by the firm, but access to or use of ideas – the key knowledge assets – embodied in that good or service. Each of the IPRP regimes listed above is based on the maintenance of scarcity or a requirement that the good or service be treated as scarce; the current or (predicted) future utility of the asset is assumed. Secrecy, for example, enables the originator of an idea to withhold it from public exchange, thereby maintaining scarcity (Suchman, 1989). In contrast, while patents require that the idea be revealed to the public, the originator is granted monopoly rights for a limited period of time that require the idea to be treated as scarce and enable the originator to appropriate rents from the knowledge asset. The regimes can, however, be clustered into two distinct groups based on the extent to which protection remains solely the domain of the originating individual or organisation. Secrecy and natural IP, on the one hand, are protection regimes administered and managed by the individual organisation and do not rely on collective intervention to maintain IP rights. In contrast, rather than internalising the means of protection as occurs in secrecy and natural IP, trade secret law, patent, copyright, trademark, design and geographical indication protection rely on institutionalised mechanisms, principally national legal systems. The difficulty for MNEs is that, despite the TRIPS agreement, the coverage and strength of enforcement of these IPRP regimes varies markedly between nations. While all members of the WTO were intended to enact domestic laws to implement TRIPS by January 2000, the recent Seattle round identified a number of less developed countries who wish to delay compliance (Wechsler, 2000).

National Differences in IPRP Regimes

Although a number of international agreements for IPRP exist (see Jain, 1996 for a survey of these), IPRP regimes are typically enshrined in national legislation and enforced through national bodies. For example, an MNE generally must obtain patent protection separately for each nation within which it wishes to operate, rather than being able to lodge a supra-national patent that provides IPRP in multiple countries through a single application (Baughn et al., 1997).[2] Despite significant efforts towards harmonisation, there remain substantial intercountry differences in the scope of IPRP, mechanisms used, rigour of enforcement and nature of penalties for IPR violations (Bae, 1997; Frischtak, 1995). These differences are, to a large extent, a reflection of the different socio-cultural, political and economic heritages. The extent to which a target country's economic, cultural, political and legal environment impacts negatively on or fails to protect the IPR of foreign firms is termed here the *country IPRP risk.*

Country risk is often a fundamental determinant influencing choice of location for international business activity and mode of entry and operations. To the extent that country risk is an aggregate of various risks which impact the firm's activities in another country (Werner et al., 1996), assessments are likely to differ depending on the particular measures used. The literature is replete with studies on specific aspects of country risk, such as political risk (for example, Argarwal and Ramaswami, 1992; Fatehi and Safizadeh, 1994) and exchange rate risk (for example, Luehrman, 1990; Campa, 1994). Important factors in determining national levels of IPR protection include: national cultural heritages which both guide national policy formulation and implementation and which orient business practice; the level of development; legislative and judicial frameworks and processes; and the level of technological sophistication of industrial communities. The influences of these heritages on IPRP can be illustrated through a comparison of two nations that are markedly different in terms of the IPRP afforded, and who have engaged in bitter trade disputes centred around IPRP throughout the 1990s – the United States and China.

The historical emphasis placed on IPRP in the US is evidenced by the signing of the first US patent bill by George Washington in 1790 and membership since 1887 of the Paris Convention, which was established in 1883 and covers patents, trademarks and industrial designs, among others. Indeed, The Constitution of the United States (Art.1, Sec. 8) considers a patent to be an inventor's right, not a gift granted by the State. Underpinning this 'right' is the Socratic-based twin premise that an *individual* can (1) originate or be the source of an idea, and (2) own an idea, thereby excluding others from using it (Mittlestaedt and Mittlestaedt, 1997). Value is thus placed on individual creativity, original expression and individual rewards. This approach to intellectual property rights is consistent with the high level of individualism (Hofstede, 1994) associated with the US (predominantly Christian) culture and its western European heritage: copyright and patents have been recorded as early as the fourteenth and fifteenth centuries respectively in Europe. It is also consistent with a political and economic system that emphasises individual success and competitiveness as the basis for societal welfare (Macdonald, 1998). Furthermore, in advanced countries such as the United States, where industry is losing its competitive edge in the manufacturing of traditional goods, intellectual property has become the basis for national comparative advantage (Hall, 1998; Jain, 1996), resulting in a strong interest in the enforcement of IPRs. Thus the scarcity, and hence value, of knowledge assets is supported by the country's IPRP legislation, which in turn is underpinned by the socio-cultural, economic and political heritages of the United States.

In contrast to the US, China's deeply rooted Confucian heritage does not support the claim that an individual can originate an idea or has the right to own the idea. Rather, all 'new' ideas owe a debt to past generations, and the welfare of the group is placed above 'rights' of the individual (Scarborough, 1998). The Marxist principles of common ownership reinforced the Confucian ethos in these respects, and the Communist government of China removed IPRP laws imposed by the earlier colonial rulers (Bosworth and Yang, 2000). Although China introduced its modern patent law in April 1985 (Chen, 1995) as part of China's modernisation process, conceived and popularised by the late Deng Xiaoping in 1975, the principles embodied in TRIPs do not sit well with China's cultural heritage that values continuity with the past and group identity. Central to China's modernisation process is the transfer of foreign technology and know-how to China (Chen, 1995). Although Chinese policy-makers publicly recognise the fortification of intellectual property rights as crucial to this process (Schlesinger, 1997; Tackaberry, 1998), particularly in attracting foreign investment in research and development facilities (Yeh, 1999), free access to foreign intellectual property may also be viewed as 'speeding up' the development process (Smith, 1999). Furthermore, enforcement of IPR is a resource-intensive activity, with higher standards requiring greater resources to achieve a given level of compliance (Frischtak, 1995). Less developed countries may be expected to have fewer resources to devote to such enforcement costs (Sherwood, 2000). It is thus not surprising that TRIPS may appear to some countries as a modern vehicle of Western imperialism (Smith, 1999).

These deeply rooted differences between the US and China help explain why, despite China's increased commitment to international standards in IPRP (Schlesinger, 1997) and recent acceptance by the WTO, many foreign firms continue to view the protection and enforcement climate in China as inadequate and the maintenance of scarcity of one's IP difficult (Conley, 1997; Tackaberry, 1998). Because of this, one might conclude that a firm with proprietary knowledge assets on which its competitive advantage is based would be unwise to enter into production arrangements in the Chinese market. This is not, however, the perspective of all technology-intensive firms. McGaughey et al., (2000), for example, report the case of an innovative Australian designer and constructor of advanced technology, high-speed car and passenger carrying catamarans, INCAT, that has recently entered into production in China, without formal, institutional IPRP.

Established in 1978, INCAT has been a dominant player in the world market for the past decade. In 1996, INCAT chose to enter into a joint venture arrangement with its former Hong Kong licensee, AFAI High Performance Ships Ltd (AFAI) for the construction of its 'k-class' catamaran at AFAI's shipyard in Panyu, southern China. Under this joint production arrangement, INCAT is responsible for the design of the vessel and supply to the Chinese shipyard of the major machinery and prefabricated components. INCAT is also obliged to provide its technical assistance with respect to building techniques and technology specific to 'k-class' vessels. AFAI is responsible for supplying the labour to build the hull of the vessel, and for managing the construction of the vessel and the yard. INCAT has no equity interest in the Chinese shipyard, which is a joint venture between AFAI and a Chinese partner.

Despite concerns about IPRP in China expressed by many foreign firms, INCAT has not engaged in conventional modes of protecting its knowledge assets, such as the registering of patents or designs. Nor does INCAT express significant concerns about the risk of dissemination of its IP through its contractual relationship with AFAI (McGaughey et al., 2000). The obvious question is: *How can MNEs such as INCAT protect their intellectual property on which their competitive advantage is based, in nations viewed to have weak IPRP regimes, such as China?* To understand the extent to which firms such as INCAT may internalise IPRP, rather than relying on institutional mechanisms, a more complete understanding of the fundamental characteristics that underpin and maintain the scarcity and utility of knowledge assets is essential.

THE DISTINCT NATURE AND VALUE OF KNOWLEDGE ASSETS

The past decade has seen a plethora of insights on the nature and exploitation of knowledge assets underpinning firms' competitive advantage (for example, Boisot, 1995, 1998; Boisot and Griffiths, 1999; Nonaka and Takeuchi, 1995; Nonaka et al., 1996; Nonaka and Konno, 1998; Teece, 1998). A recent conceptualisation of knowledge assets and their creation that has drawn much attention (for example, Hovenden, 1998; Macdonald, 1997) and may offer insights into the above research question is that of Max Boisot. According to Boisot (1995, 1998), both the utility and scarcity of an information good – and thus its value – can be expressed by just three dimensions: codification, abstraction and diffusion. The diffusability of any data refers to the availability of the data or a knowledge asset to a relevant population of data-processing agents. It is conditioned by an ability to structure those data and to economise on data processing and transmission costs (Boisot and Griffiths, 1999). Data structuring is a product of codification and abstraction.

Codification refers to the creation of categories and the assignment of phenomena (data) to these categories based on their attributes (for example, big, small, red, blue). Data that do not fit the classification schema are shed. Complexity, or the amount of data processing required to interpret those data, is thus reduced in the process of codification; codifying economises on the quantity of data to be processed (Boisot, 1995). As providing the classification schema maximises the identification and classification of useful data, codification also reduces the uncertainty associated with the utility of an information good and facilitates data processing. Abstraction works in tandem with codification (Boisot and Griffiths, 1999).[3] Whereas codification gives form to phenomena by grouping data into categories, abstraction gives the phenomena structure by identifying the underlying relationships between the data and thus the categories which are relevant to the data-processing task. Through understanding the structure – be it a causal or descriptive understanding – abstraction generates concepts that economise on the number of categories required to assign phenomena. Both codification and abstraction shed data and reduce complexity, and are processes by which information is extracted from data for subsequent processing in knowledge creation activities.

The relationship between codification, abstraction and diffusion is depicted by Boisot (1995, 1998) in three dimensions assembled into what he termed an Information-Space, or I-Space shown in Figure 10.1. The codification dimension is scaled according to 'algorithmic information complexity': the number of bits of information required to perform a particular data-processing task. At the uncodified end, an infinite number may be required, making data transmission costly or difficult. Uncodified knowledge is often thought of as tacit knowledge (Polanyi, 1966), knowledge that is personal and context-specific, and thus hard to formularise and share with others (Nonaka and Konno, 1998; Nonaka, et al., 1996). Codified knowledge is explicit knowledge that can be expressed in words, numbers and symbols and is more easily shared, although the level of codification can vary. The second dimension, abstraction, is scaled according to a different form of complexity: 'effective complexity'. Effective complexity is measured by the number of bits of information required to specify the regularities (causal or descriptive relationships) that characterise the data-processing task. At one end of the abstraction dimension, information is highly concrete, dealing with predominantly perceptual and local knowledge with limited application. Abstract conceptual knowledge may find general application. The third dimension, diffusability, reflects the extent to which the data are available for those who want to use it, and is a function of the degrees of codification and abstraction. It is not a measure of adoption or uptake. Diffusability can be scaled to refer to the proportion of a given population of data processing agents that can be reached with information operating at different levels of abstraction and codification. As depicted in Figure 10.1, the greater the level of codification and abstraction, the greater the diffusability.

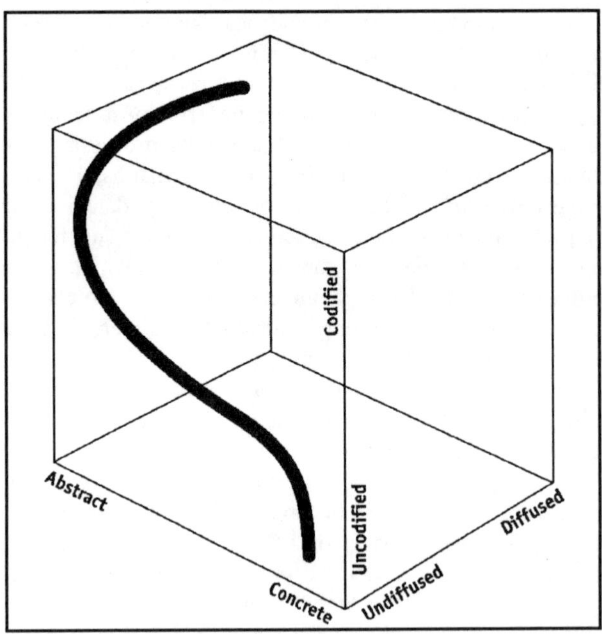

Source: Based on Boisot (1998: 28)

Figure 10.1 The diffusion curve in the I-Space

Boisot extends his use of the I-Space to its consideration as a data field. Knowledge can be located in the data field as a function of its data processing characteristics which, over time, are modified through learning. As depicted in Figure 10.2, highly personal, tacit knowledge may become more structured (codified and abstract), converting to proprietary knowledge under the control of the originator. This knowledge is not, at this point, diffused. Over time, proprietary knowledge becomes diffused and enters the public domain. Through recurrent use of this 'textbook' knowledge, it is internalised by individuals to become part of one's 'common sense' world-view. This 'common sense' knowledge is not, however, homogeneous among individuals: individuals pass the same experience through different cognitive filters based on unique personal histories. Different people put different constructions on commonly available information. A significant proportion of what is taken to be common sense is converted back into highly personal knowledge (Boisot, 1998).

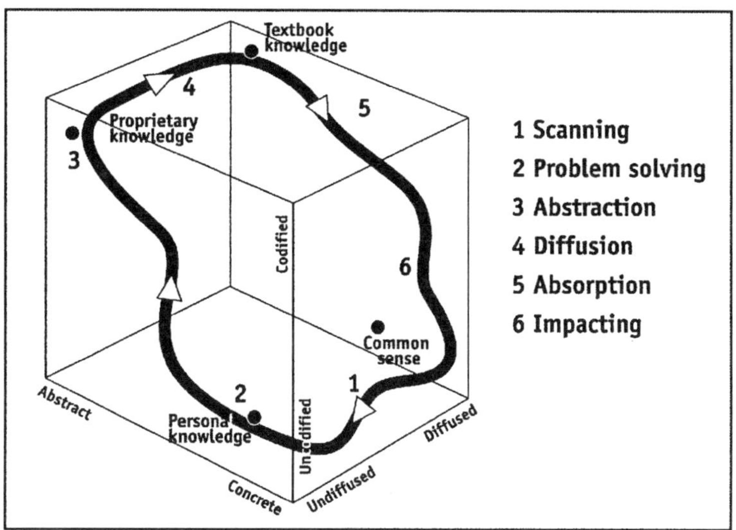

Source: Based on Boisot (1998: 59–61)

Figure 10.2 The location and flow of knowledge assets in the I-Space

New knowledge is created through the movement of information through the I-Space in a clockwise cycle known as the Social Learning Cycle (SLC) comprising the six phases listed in Figure 10.2 and described briefly in Table 10.1. Knowledge assets emerge through a two-step process of (1) generating insights through a process of extracting information from data (creating knowledge), and (2) testing the insights under different situations that enable a gradual accumulation of experiential data (applying knowledge) (Boisot, 1998). Phases one to three of the SLC correspond to the generation of insights and phases four to six to the testing of these insights. Boisot is careful to explain that the cycle depicted in Figure 10.2 is merely a schematic – many different cycle shapes are possible due to frictions or obstacles to data flows.

The transformations in knowledge assets, as they flow through the SLC, have implications for the value of that knowledge to a firm. The greater the codification and abstraction of a knowledge asset, the greater its potential utility. At the same time, however, the difficulty of maintaining its scarcity increases. Knowledge assets located in the upper, left, back corner of the I-space (that is, the proprietary knowledge in Figure 10.2) thus inhabit the region of maximum potential value, while those inhabiting the lower, right, forward corner (that is, the common sense knowledge of Figure 10.2) inhabit the minimum value zone (Boisot, 1998).

Table 10.1 Six phases of social learning cycle

Phase	Description
Scanning	Identifying threats and opportunities in generally available but 'fuzzy' data. Scanning may be rapid when data is well codified and abstract, and slower when uncodified and context-specific
Problem solving	The codification of insights from scanning, resulting in a reduction in the uncertainty initially associated with them
Abstraction	Generalising the application of newly codified insights to a broader range of situations. Problem solving and codification often work in tandem.
Diffusion	Sharing the newly created insights with a target population.
Absorption	Applying the new insights to different situations through 'learning-by-doing' such that, over time, application is guided by uncodified experience.
Impacting	The embedding of abstract knowledge in concrete practices, such as artefacts, technical or organisational rules, or behavioural patterns. Absorption and impacting often work in tandem.

Source: Based on Boisot (1998: 59–61)

STRATEGIC INTERVENTIONS IN THE SLC THROUGH IPRP REGIMES

The notion of obstacles or frictions in the SLC introduced by Boisot can be extended to explicitly consider strategic interventions in the knowledge flows and associated transformations, shifting the focus from the creation of knowledge assets in the SLC to a focus on their protection. That is, to exploit the value of one's knowledge assets, a firm may *strategically* manage their flow through timely *interventions* in the SLC. Different IPRP regimes could conceivably be applied independently or in combination throughout the SLC as such strategic interventions. IPRP regimes can be used as strategic interventions in the SLC in two fundamental ways: (1) to ensure that rents are appropriated without, from the originator's perspective, significant concern about altering the flow of information through the SLC; or (2) retarding the flow of information in the SLC. Patents and copyright provide a clear example of the former strategy, and secrecy of the latter.

Patents and Copyright

The underlying purposes of the patent and copyright systems are (1) to protect the rights of the inventor of a novel and useful product and service, and (2) to encourage a society's inventiveness, technical progress and/or creativity (Macmillan, 1998; Merges, 1988). In the case of patents, the granting of monopoly rights of control to inventors for a limited time (for example, 20 years) over how the patented invention is exploited is designed to ensure that they are rewarded for their efforts. In addition, it is intended that the invention will eventually enter the public domain for the collective good (Macdonald, 1998). Copyright is typically granted for a period of 50 to 70 years after the death of the author. Both patents and copyrights are based on the twin premise that an individual can originate an idea and that the individual has the right to exploit that idea (Mittlestaedt and Mittlestaedt, 1997).

Intellectual property that is typically granted copyright protection, such as musical, literary or dramatic works, is, by its very nature, disclosed to the public upon its presentation. It is thus highly diffusable. To be granted a patent, an invention must be codified, also resulting in higher diffusability. As knowledge assets move from the left to right in Boisot's I-Space, their potential value declines (Boisot, 1995, 1998). This notion is depicted in schematic *A* of Figure 10.3. The implementation of the legal mechanisms of copyright and patent protection, however, requires that the invention or copyrighted materials be treated as if they are scarce by enabling the originator of the knowledge asset to extract fees in, for example, the form of royalties for their use. The value of the asset is thus extended into the diffused zone of the SLC, as shown in schematic *B* of Figure 10.3. While the diffusion of the knowledge asset may in fact be increased through the codification required for patent applications, this is not a primary consideration of the originator.

The spectre of copyright infringement has increased markedly over the last decade, particularly with the ease of moving information over the internet and digital copying (*PC Week,* 1997; Ramanujapuram and Ram, 1998). This has precipitated the development of strategies designed to impede copyright infringement that are firm-based rather than reliant on political or legal institutions. One recent example is the announcement on 3 March 1999 of the joint development of a content protection framework for Digital Versatile Disk (DVD)-Audio by IBM, Intel, Matsushita Electric and

Toshiba, supported by BMG, EMI, Sony Music Entertainment, Universal Music Group and Warner Music Group (*Electronic News,* 1999). The protection framework employs watermark and encryption technologies created or identified by the four companies to protect music available on pre-recorded DVD-Audio disc which can be played on licensed players. Such interventions against illegal copying provide safeguards for the creators of artistic work, although the subsequent inadvertent disclosure of encryption keys in the above example illustrates some potential limitations.

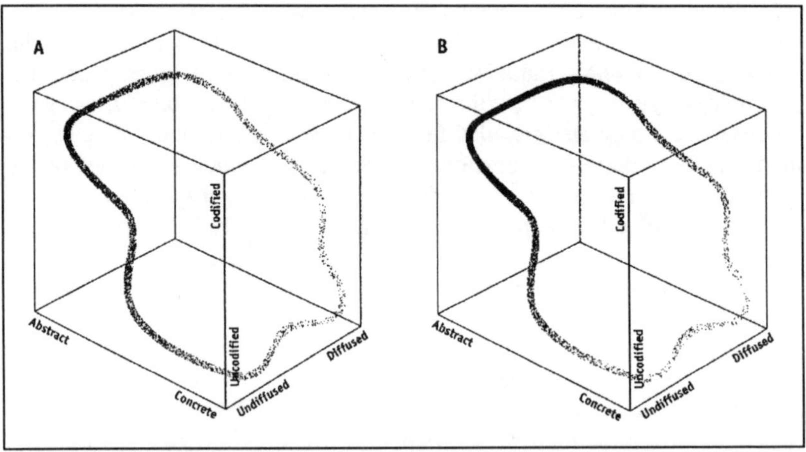

Figure 10.3 The impact of patents and copyright on the value of knowledge assets

Another example of a strategic intervention that overcomes risks of patent or design infringement is provided by Computer Design Marine (CDM) in Western Australia. CDM offers a variety of aluminium powerboats for domestic sale and export to Indonesia, Japan, Malaysia, Portugal, Thailand and the United Kingdom. The vessels can be acquired as either of CDM's two construction systems. The first construction system includes precision pre-cut and marked aluminium plate and extrusions for the hull and superstructure, along with a construction manual, drawings and information book. The purchaser undertakes the welding and construction.

The second construction system involves the sale of software only, which comprises the cutting and marking codes for the selected vessel, and is available for export markets. The low level of complexity and skills required in the welding of the cut aluminium plates (CDM, 1999) suggests that unauthorised production of these vessels would not be problematic in markets such as China. To overcome this risk, the computer software destroys itself immediately upon its having guided a cutter that has cut and checked a panel for pre-fabrication into boat assembly (*Ascent Technology Magazine,* 1998). Again, the protection of the IP is internalised by the firm rather than relying on institutional interventions.

Secrecy

In contrast to creators of literary or artistic works, inventors may have the option of employing secrecy as a means of protecting their knowledge assets embodied in either goods or services. Secrecy may also be used for knowledge assets that do not meet the requirements for award of a patent, or where risks related to patenting are perceived to be great. With secrecy, diffusion of the knowledge asset is blocked. This can be achieved by a firm in two ways, as illustrated in Figure 10.4.[4] In Figure 10.4, *A* depicts a knowledge flow where a strategic intervention prevents information that has become codified and abstract, and thus highly diffusable, from continuing along a diffusion path. The knowledge asset is withheld from the public. An example of this would be efforts by the owners of the Coca-Cola formula – a codified, written recipe – to keep it secret by limiting the numbers of individuals who at any one time know the formula. The withholding of source code, the highly codified and understandable instructions of the programmer, when selling computer software is another example.

The knowledge flow *B* in Figure 10.4 reflects a circumstance where a firm or individual has engaged in measures – intentionally or otherwise –

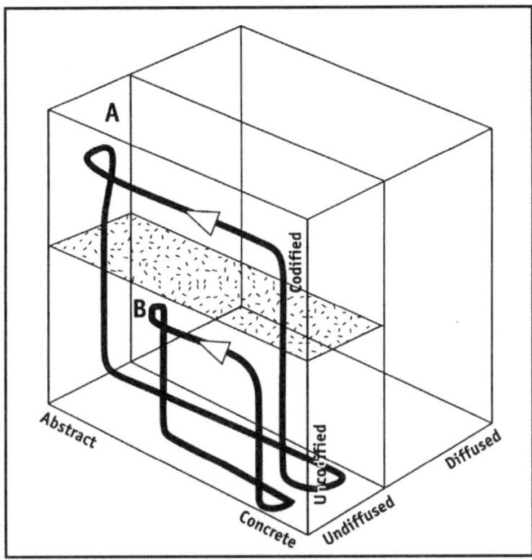

Figure 10.4 Strategic interventions in the SLC

that impede the transition of knowledge assets from a tacit, uncodified and concrete form to a codified and abstract form. The diffusability of the asset thus remains low and secrecy is maintained. Examples of this include the works of master craftspersons or artists: by never codifying the basis of their skills, master craftspersons maintain the secret of their talents. This is not always intentional: the tacit knowledge underpinning such talent may be difficult to understand and articulate, even for the holder of that knowledge (Polanyi, 1966; Teece, 1998).

BEYOND DIFFUSABILITY: TRANSPARENCY, REPLICABILITY AND COUNTRY RISK

The above examples highlight an important point: the threat to the originating firm or individual associated with dissipation of its IP is not solely contingent on diffusability, defined by Boisot to be a function of codification and abstraction. The extent to which the originating firm can strategically impede the flow or dissemination of its knowledge asset regardless of levels of codification and abstraction is clearly also important. These two factors contribute to what is termed in this chapter the *transparency* of the knowledge asset. *Transparency* refers to the extent to which others in a diffusion population can identify and understand the basis or nature of the knowledge assets or IP of an originating firm. It is a function of (1) diffusability of the knowledge asset and (2) the strength of the strategic interventions designed to withhold from others the IP of the originating firm, relative to (3) the competitors' ability to circumvent these interventions. This relativity with competitors, who may in fact operate outside the immediate industry boundaries of the originator, is important: seemingly weak mechanisms for secrecy may not be of concern if the competitors' ability to circumvent this protection is also low, resulting in the successful maintenance of secrecy. In summary, a codified, abstract knowledge asset that is not successfully kept secret has a high level of transparency, whereas the same asset if kept secret would have a lower level of transparency.

Even if a knowledge asset is highly transparent, this does not ensure that the originating firm's IP will be exploited by others. Not all competitors with the intent of exploiting the originator's IP necessarily have the capabilities or resources required to do so. In such circumstances, the threats (from competitors) to the originating firm's appropriation of rents from its knowledge assets are negligible. The extent to which actual or potential competitors can successfully replicate and use the originator's IP has been termed *replicability* in this chapter. *Replicability* is a function of (1) competitor resources and (2) competitor capabilities, particularly with reference to learning, relative to (3) the innovative capability of the originating firm. This third aspect of replicability is critical as the originator's IP is not necessarily static, but may be renewed through continual innovation. It is thus a moving target. This notion of replicability is similar to Cohen and Levinthal's (1990) concept 'absorptive capacity' (that is, a firm's ability to recognise the value of new, external information, and toassimilate and exploit it). Replicability does not, however, incorporate the capacity of a competitor to identify relevant knowledge assets. Instead, this is embodied in the notion of transparency – an aspect of a knowledge asset over which an originator has greater control.[5]

The example of INCAT, raised earlier, illustrates the utility of these two concepts – replicability and transparency – in addressing the question of how MNEs can protect their intellectual property in nations viewed to have weak IPRP regimes. A schematic of the stocks and flows of INCAT's knowledge assets is depicted in Figure 10.5. The knowledge flows depicted by both **A** and **B** in Figure 10.5 are representative of INCAT engaging in secrecy, deliberate and otherwise, to protect its IP. For example, although INCAT is required to provide a significant amount of data and technical information to its joint venture partner, AFAI, including access to the INCAT yard in Tasmania for the purpose of the technology transfer, INCAT is not required to provide its partner with the background research upon which the data and technological information are based. This codified

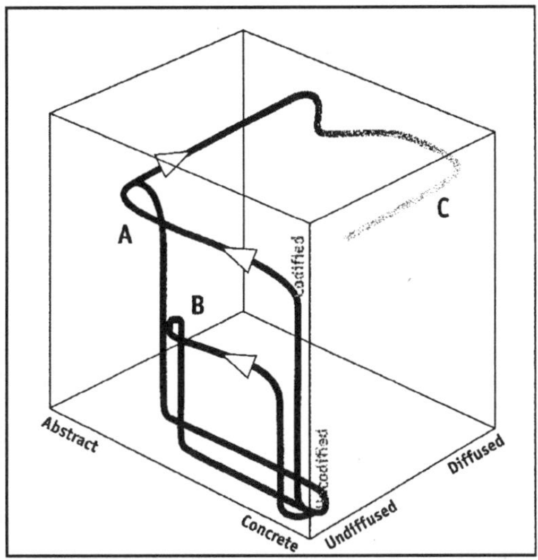

Figure 10.5 Knowledge flows in multiple SLCs of INCAT

information safeguarded by INCAT includes the principles underlying the design features of INCAT's vessels, which is critical when making alterations to a design to accommodate requests for customisation (McGaughey et al., 2000). This secrecy is reflective of **A** in Figure 10.5: the underlying principles of the design vessels are somewhat abstract and highly codified, and thus highly diffusable, but kept a secret. This codified knowledge is thus not transparent to competitors.

The knowledge assets of INCAT also comprise a vast amount of tacit knowledge accumulated over time through activities such as: tracking the problems and successes of each vessel constructed over its entire life despite changes in ownership; participation in marine advisory boards; and generating computer simulations to understand vessel performance in adverse conditions. The tacit component of INCAT's subsequent stock of knowledge, reflective of **B** in Figure 10.5, is deeply embedded in individuals within the firm and is difficult to articulate. It thus tends to diffuse slowly, if at all, and manifests itself in entrepreneurial acumen. For example, the founder of INCAT is credited with the ability to accurately assess the implications of a customer's request and design requirements *vis-à-vis* the ship's performance 'on the back of an envelope'. After determining the effects of a desired change, INCAT is able to inform the customer and redefine other specifications where necessary, thereby avoiding dissatisfaction with the end product due to incongruent expectations. This attribute draws not only on the codified mechanical principles underlying INCAT designs, but also on a degree of tacit knowledge accumulated through years of experience. The knowledge assets underpinning this entrepreneurial acumen are thus causally ambiguous and path dependent.

Causal ambiguity typically refers to a situation where the cause or source of the competitive advantage is difficult to identify (Barney, 1991; Kamoche, 1996). Hart (1995) argues that resources contributing to causal ambiguity are typically 'invisible' or tacit resources based upon accumulated experience or 'learning-by-doing', as evidenced in the case of INCAT (McGaughey et al. 2000). The historical events that have shaped a firm influence the nature and composition of the knowledge assets developed over time (Amit and Schoemaker, 1993; Dierickx and Cool, 1989; Peteraf, 1993). The causal ambiguity and path dependency of INCAT's tacit knowledge may make it not only difficult for a competitor to overcome the secrecy shrouding the originator's (INCAT's) knowledge assets but, even if overcome, also difficult to replicate.

Not all of INCAT's knowledge assets are, however, shrouded in secrecy and unreplicable. Some are highly transparent and can be copied. For example, all vessels sold by INCAT in the international market contain a complete set of plans in both paper and electronic form, which explain how the vessel was built. This information is thus highly transparent and can be easily duplicated. This phenomenon is depicted in **C** of Figure 10.5. SLC **C** reflects the selective diffusion of portions of INCAT's knowledge assets to the broader population, including competitors. The knowledge assets depicted in **C** were generated in and flow from SLC **A**, which is kept internal to INCAT. Importantly, the flow of knowledge in **C** does not progress downward in the I-Space to take full advantage of the 'absorption' and 'impacting' phases of the SLC depicted earlier in Figure 10.2. The competitors do not therefore gain the full advantages of learning-by-doing and experimentation with the diffused knowledge asset such that they can develop an intuitive sense and understanding of the technology, and thus be able to adapt it to new situations and customer requirements as can INCAT.

The failure of firms operating in SLC **C** to move down through the impacting and absorption phases of the SLC can be explained in the case of INCAT in two ways, which are not mutually exclusive. The first relates to the relative speed of learning in the respective SLCs. A key reason for INCAT's lack of concern with the diffusion of selected knowledge assets in SLC **C** is a belief that 'whatever [competitors] are stealing, they are stealing yesterday's work....' (INCAT managing director, cited in McGaughey et al., 2000). That is, INCAT believes it innovates at a faster rate than competitors who may be interested in exploiting their IP: the rate of learning in SLC **A** exceeds that of those accessing SLC **C**. Thus the IP of INCAT which competitors are attempting to replicate is a moving target, and firms operating with SLC **C** are continually 'fed' new knowledge assets from the SLC **A** of INCAT before they are able to complete their own knowledge creation process. In short, INCAT's strategy in SLC **C** reflects a belief that INCAT's learning capability exceeds that of those wishing to appropriate its knowledge assets.

The second reason competitors operating with SLC **C** may not be able to move through the absorption and impacting phases relates to Lamberton's (1998) observation, raised earlier, that new ideas or inventions are not necessarily inexpensive to imitate. Intellectual property is not comprised of discrete pieces of information, but batches and flows (Lamberton, 1998). The paper and electronic plans that explain how an INCAT vessel is built convey only part of the story. They do not convey a vast stock of tacit knowledge that was used in the vessel's creation, and is necessary for production and maintenance of, and modifications to, the vessel. Although these activities are critical to the experiential learning processes in absorption and impacting, critical knowledge for this process is retained in SLCs **A** and **B**. Recipients of the knowledge asset in SLC **C** are, in fact, only *partial* recipients of the knowledge package that comprises INCAT's IP and gives INCAT its competitive advantage. As explained by Lamberton (1998: 257), revisiting the seminal work of Arrow (1962), the outside recipients of the IP through SLC **C** '... have less knowledge than the incumbent ... and the interdependence between activities, between items or pieces of information may well mean that some parts of the jigsaw puzzles are missing.' The faster rate of learning in INCAT's SLC *A* and incomplete nature of the knowledge selectively released to the public, means that new entrants or competitors are perpetually at a disadvantage. To the extent that INCAT's vessels and associate services are considered unique by potential clients, INCAT's stocks and flows of knowledge assets approximate natural intellectual property protection.

Clearly, the proportion and nature of diffused knowledge relative to the total knowledge package, and the resource stocks (for example, of knowledge) and capabilities (for example, in learning) of the competitors relative to the originator of the IP play important roles in the perceived risks associated with a country's approach to IPRs. That is, the risks of a competitor appropriating one's IP are not just a function of the strength of a country's IPR regimes, but also the transparency and replicability of the knowledge assets – factors that the informed firm can influence through strategic interventions in its knowledge flows.

CONCLUSIONS

With the critical role of knowledge assets, and hence intellectual property, forming the basis for MNEs' competitive advantage, the importance of protecting these knowledge assets is brought to the fore. The implementation of effective strategies for protection in the face of national variations in IPRP regimes requires, however, a comprehensive understanding of not only what makes these knowledge assets valuable, but also how this value may be maintained in the face of transformations in the knowledge asset itself over time. This dynamic dimension is often not sufficiently emphasised. Using Boisot's conceptual I-space and, most notably, the concepts of codification, abstraction and diffusability as an entry point, the present chapter makes several contributions towards enhancing understanding and management of IPRP in the international arena. First, by extending the notion of 'blockages' in Boisot's (1998) Social Learning Cycle, the concept of *strategic interventions* that a firm may make in the SLC to limit the uptake of its IP by a competitor is developed. A concern with the uptake of one's IP by competitors requires consideration of not just the characteristics of the knowledge assets and the originator's interventions in the SLC, but also competitor characteristics. Through integrating insights and concepts from scholars in the fields of information economics and knowledge management with strategic management, principally the resource-based view, two additional concepts were defined and developed in this chapter: *transparency* and *replicability*. These concepts contribute to an understanding of how firms may employ firm-based regimes of IPRP, rather than relying solely on collective, institutional regimes. The utility of these concepts is illustrated through industry examples, most notably INCAT.

The application of the concepts of transparency and replicability to the understanding and management of IPRP strategies also challenges two key assumptions in the extant literature. The first assumption challenged, and flagged by Lamberton (1998), is that while information is costly to produce, it is easy and inexpensive to copy (Suchman, 1989). In circumstances where the IP on which competitive advantage is based is highly transparent (that is, others can readily identify and understand the basis or nature of the knowledge assets of the originating firm) and highly replicable (that is, others can readily replicate and use the originator's IP), the above assumption may in fact hold true. The case of INCAT, however, belies this simple scenario: recipients of INCAT's diffused knowledge asset are, in fact, only *partial* recipients of the knowledge package that gives INCAT its competitive advantage. Thus, diffusion of a portion of one's IP through, for example, the award of a patent does not necessarily mean that competitors can replicate the bundle of knowledge assets on which a firm's competitive advantage is based or, for that matter, even identify the requisite assets.

This observation also underpins the challenge to the second assumption, namely that the IP of knowledge intensive firms is at substantial risk in countries with weak institutional IPRP. To base one's foreign market entry decisions and international strategies on an assumption that countries deemed to have weak IPRP regimes are unilaterally far 'riskier' environments of operation than countries with a strong heritage of IPRP is clearly dangerous, and may impede the exploitation of very real opportunities. Importantly, this chapter highlights the dangers of over-emphasising a country's institutional mechanisms of IPRP to the exclusion of the transferability and replicability of the MNE's IP when assessing the risks to the firm's IP. If Teece (1998) is indeed correct with his assertion that the *essence* of a firm is its ability to create, transfer, assemble, integrate and exploit knowledge assets, the importance of strategic interventions in knowledge flows as a means affording the firm protection of its proprietary knowledge across borders cannot be overlooked.

Notes

1. Following Sundaram and Black (1992: 733), an inclusive definition of MNE is used is this chapter. Specifically, an MNE is defined as '...any enterprise that carries out transactions in or between two sovereign entities, operating under a system of decision making that permits influence over resources and capabilities, where the transactions are subject to influence by factors

exogenous to the home country environment of the enterprise.' Thus, references to MNEs in this chapter are not limited to firms engaged in foreign direct investment but may include, for example, exporters.

2. Exceptions to this include European patents granted by the European Patent Office (Munich) which covers member nations of the European Union (Blakeney, 1998), and the Eurasian patents granted by the Eurasian Patents Office (Moscow) that cover nine countries.
3. Boisot (1995: 60) notes, however, that codification and abstraction may work in tandem *or* independently.
4. The design of these schematics is based on the style used by Boisot (1995, 1998).
5. Replicability as used in this chapter should also not be confused with Teece's (1998) use of the term, where it is used as a synonym for absorptive capacity.

REFERENCES

Amit, R. and P.J.H. Schoemaker (1993), 'Strategic Assets and Organizational Rent', *Strategic Management Journal*, (14), 33–46.

Argarwal, S. and S.N. Ramaswami (1992), 'Choice of Foreign Market Entry Mode: Impact of Ownership, Location and Internalization Factors', *Journal of International Business Studies,* **23** (1), 1–27.

Arrow, K.J. (1962), 'Economic Welfare and the Allocation of Resources for Invention', reprinted in D.M. Lamberton (1996) (ed.) *The Economics of Communication and Information,* Cheltenham, UK: Edward Elgar.

Ascent Technology Magazine (1998), 'Great Leap Forward for Pre-fab Boats', (March), 17.

Bae, Robert (1997), 'Intellectual Property in the Pacific Rim Countries: Rights and Remedies', *American Society of International Law,* Proceedings of the Annual Meeting 1997, pp. 395–407.

Baets, W.R.J. (1998), *Organizational Learning and Knowledge Technologies in a Dynamic Environment,* Dordrecht: Kluwer Academic Publishers.

Barney, J. (1991), 'Firm Resources and Sustained Competitive Advantage', *Journal of Management*, (17), 99–120.

Baughn, C. Christopher, Michael Bixby and L. Helton Woods (1997), 'Patent Laws and the Public Good: IPR Protection in Japan and the United States', *Business Horizons*, **40** (4), 59–65.

Blakeney, Michael (1998), 'The Role of Intellectual Property Law in Regional Commercial Unions in Europe and Asia', *Prometheus*, **16** (3), 341–50.

Boisot, Max and Dorothy Griffiths (1999), 'Possession is Nine Tenths of the Law: Managing a Firm's Knowledge Base in a Regime of Weak

Appropriability', *International Journal of Technology Management*, **17** (6), 662–76.

Boisot, Max H. (1995), *Information Space: A Framework for Learning in Organisations, Institutions and Cultures,* London: Routledge.

Boisot, Max H. (1998), *Knowledge Assets: Securing Competitive Advantage in the Information Economy,* Oxford: Oxford University Press.

Bosworth, D. and D. Yang (2000), 'Intellectual Property Law, Technology Flow and Licensing Opportunities in People's Republic of China', *International Business Review*, **9** (4), 453–77.

Campa, J.M. (1994), 'Multinational Investment under Uncertainty in the Chemical Processing Industries', *Journal of International Business Studies,* **25** (3), 557–78.

CDM (1999), *Computer Design Marine Home Page*, http://www.curran.com.au/, first accessed June 1999.

Chen, M. (1995), 'Technological Transfer to China: Major Rules and Issues', *International Journal of Technology Management,* **10** (7/8), 747–56.

Cohen, W.M. and D.A. Levinthal (1990), 'Absorptive Capacity: A New Perspective on Learning and Innovation', *Administrative Science Quarterly*, **35** (1), 128–52.

Conley, J. (1997), 'Enter the Dragon', *International Business,* **10** (1), 40–44.

Correa, Carlos M. (1995), 'Intellectual Property Rights and Foreign Direct Investment', *International Journal of Technology Management*, **10** (2/3), 173–99.

de Almeida, P.R. (1995), 'The Political Economy of Intellectual Property Protection: Technological Protectionism and Transfer of Revenue among Nations', *International Journal of Technology Management*, **10** (2/3), 214–29.

Dierickx, I. and K. Cool (1989), 'Asset Stock Accumulation and the Sustainability of Competitive Advantage', *Management Science*, **35** (12), 1504–14.

Drahos, Peter (1998), 'Property Rights in Information: The Trade Paradigm', *Prometheus*, **16** (3), 245–8.

Electronic News (1999), 'DVD-Audio Moves Closer to Reality', 15 March, **45** (11), 24.

Fatehi, K. and M.H. Safizadeh (1994), 'The Effect of Sociopolitical Instability on the Flow of Different Types of Foreign Direct Investment', *Journal of Business Research*, **1** (31), 65–73.

Frischtak, Claudio R. (1995), 'Harmonisation versus Differentiation in International Property Rights Regimes', *International Journal of Technology Management*, **10** (2/3), 200–213.

Hall, P. (1998), 'Intellectual Property Rights Protection and International Trade: An Economic Survey', *Prometheus*, **16** (3), 261–73.

Hart, S.L. (1995), 'A Natural-Resource-Based-View of the Firm', *Academy of Management Review,* **20** (4), 986–1014.

Hofstede, G. (1994), *Cultures and Organisations: Software of the Mind,* Hammersmith, UK: Harper Collins.

Hovenden, Fiona (1998), 'Information Space: A Framework for Learning in Organisations, Institutions and Culture', Book Review, *Management Learning*, **29** (2), 227–31.

Jain, Subhash C. (1996), 'Problems in International Protection of Intellectual Property Rights', *Journal of International Marketing*, **4** (1), 9–32.

Kamoche, K. (1996), 'Strategic Human Resource Management within a Resource-capability View of the Firm', *Journal of Management Studies*, **33** (2), 213–33.

Kidd, J.B. (1998), 'Knowledge Creation in Japanese Manufacturing Companies in Italy', *Management Learning,* **29** (2), 131–46.

Kogut, B. and U. Zander (1993), 'Knowledge of the Firm and the Evolutionary Theory of the Multinational Corporation', *Journal of International Business Studies,* **24** (4), 625–46.

Lamberton, Don (1998), 'Intellectual Property and Trade: Economic Perspectives', *Prometheus*, **16** (3), 255–60.

Long Range Planning (1997), 'Special Issue: The Management of Intellectual Property', **30** (3), 346–441.

Luehrman, T.A. (1990), 'The Exchange Rate Exposure of a Global Competitor', *Journal of International Business Studies,* **21** (2), 225–42.

Lyles, M.A. and J.E. Salk (1996), 'Knowledge Acquisition from Foreign Parents in International Joint Ventures: An Empirical Examination in the Hungarian Context', *Journal of International Business Studies,* **27** (5), 877–904.

Macdonald, Stuart (1998), *Information for Innovation: Managing Change from an Information Perspective,* Oxford: Oxford University Press.

Macdonald, Stuart (1997), 'Information Space: A Framework for Learning in Organisations, Institutions and Culture', Book Review, *New Technology, Work and Employment*, **12** (2), 148–50.

Macmillan, Fiona (1998), 'Copyright, Culture and Private Power', *Prometheus*, **16** (3), 305–16.

McGaughey, Sara L., Peter W. Liesch and Duncan Poulson (2000), 'An Unconventional Approach to Intellectual Property Protection: The Case of an Australian Firm Transferring Shipbuilding Technologies to China', *Journal of World Business,* **35** (1), 1–20.

Merges, Robert P. (1988), 'Commercial Success and Patent Standards: Economic Perspectives on Innovation', *California Law Review*, **4** (76), 805–76.

Mittlestaedt, John D. and Robert A. Mittlestaedt (1997), 'The Protection of Intellectual Property: Issues of Origination and Ownership', *Journal of Public Policy and Marketing*, **16** (1), 14–25.

Nonaka, Ikujiro and Hirotaka Takeuchi (1995), *The Knowledge Creating Company*, New York: Oxford University Press.

Nonaka, Ikujiro and Noboru Konno (1998), 'The Concept of "Ba": Building a Foundation for Knowledge Creation', *California Management Review*, **40** (3), 40–54.

Nonaka, Ikujiro, Hirotaka Takeuchi and Katsuhiro Umemoto (1996), 'A Theory of Organisational Knowledge Creation', *International Journal of Technology Management, Special Issue on Learning and Unlearning for Technological Innovation*, **11** (7/8), 833–45.

PC Week (1997), 'It's the World's Biggest Copy Machine', 27 January, **14** (4), 109–10.

Penrose, Edith T. (1959), *The Theory of the Growth of the Firm,* Oxford: Oxford University Press.

Peteraf, M. (1993), 'The Cornerstones of Competitive Advantage: A Resource-based View', *Strategic Management Journal*, (14), 179–91.

Polanyi, M. (1966), *The Tacit Dimension,* London: Routledge & Kegan Paul.

Ramanujapuram, Arun and Prasad Ram (1998), 'Digital Content and Intellectual Property Rights', *Dr Dobbs Journal,* **23** (2), 20–24.

Sanchez, R. and A. Heene (1997), *Strategic Learning and Knowledge Management,* New York: John Wiley.

Scarborough, J. (1998), 'Comparing Chinese and Western Cultural Roots: Why East is East and…', *Business Horizons*, **4** (6), 15–25.

Schlesinger, M.N. (1997), 'Intellectual Property Law in China: Part I – Complying with TRIPs Requirements', *East Asian Executive Reports,* **19** (1), 9–20.

Sherwood, R.M. (2000), 'The TRIPS Agreement: Benefits and Costs for Developing Countries', *International Journal of Technology Management*, **19** (1/2), 57–76.

Smith, M.W. (1999), 'Bringing Developing Countries' Intellectual Property Laws to TRIPs Standards: Hurdles and Pitfalls Facing Vietnam's Efforts to Normalise an Intellectual Property Regime', *Case Western Reserve Journal of International Law*, **31** (1), 211–51.

Stigler, G.J. (1965), *Essays in the History of Economics,* Chicago: University of Chicago Press.

Suchman, Mark C. (1989), 'Invention and Ritual: Notes on the Interrelation of Magic and Intellectual Property in Preliterate Societies', *Columbia Law Review*, **89** (6), 1264–94.

Sundaram, K. Anant and J. Stewart Black (1992), 'The Environment and Internal Organisation of Multinational Enterprise', *Academy of Management Review*, **17** (4), 729–57.

Tackaberry, P. (1998), 'Intellectual Property Risks in China: Their Effect on Foreign Investment and Technology Transfer', *Journal of Asian Business*, **14** (4), 1–38.

Teece, David J. (1998), 'Capturing Value from Knowledge Assets: The New Economy, Markets for Know-how, and Intangible Assets', *California Management Review*, **40** (3), 55–79.

Werner, S., L.E. Brouthers and K.D. Brouthers (1996), 'International Risk and Perceived Environmental Uncertainty: The Dimensionality and Internal Consistency of Miller's Measure', *Journal of International Business Studies,* **27** (3), 571–87.

Wechsler, J. (2000), 'Access a Global Concern', *Pharmaceutical Executive,* **20** (3), 26–30.

Yeh, P. (1999), 'Yo, Ho, Ho and a CD Rom: The Current State of Software Piracy in the PRC', *Law and Policy in International Business*, **31** (1), 173–94.

11. Assessing Measures of Performance of International Joint Ventures: Evidence from Bangladesh

M. Yunus Ali and A.B. Sim

INTRODUCTION

The strategic importance of joint ventures has increasingly been established in recent years. Joint ventures are not only popular for firms from developed countries to enter into developing countries (Beamish, 1993; Osland and Cavusgil, 1996; Wagner, 1993), they are also popular between firms from advanced countries (Hergert and Morris, 1988; Glaister and Buckley, 1994). Despite their growing strategic importance, joint ventures have some downsides due to their apparently high rate of failure (Beamish, 1988; Kogut, 1988). What constitutes failure or successful performance is important. However, the measurement of joint venture performance is a highly debated issue in the literature and there is a lack of consensus among researchers (Parkhe, 1993). Performance measures vary from conventional financial and non-financial measures of organisational success to subjective assessment of achievement of organisational goals. Joint ventures are collaborative efforts between two or more economic units often with conflicting organisational goals and this complicates the issue. The disagreement over the use of objective measures such as stability, survival and duration and subjective measure such as partners' satisfaction with performance of the joint venture have to be resolved

Objective measures of performance were widely used in studies during the 1970s and the early 1980s (for example, Dang, 1977; Franko, 1971; Killing, 1983), but the use of subjective measures has gained greater support in recent years (Nitsch et al., 1996; Osland and Cavusgil, 1996; Yan and Gray, 1994). Despite this trend, there is no general consensus among researchers on the appropriate definition and measurement of joint venture performance. Lack of consensus exists mainly on three points:

1. the use of objective versus subjective measures of performance;
2. the use of a single global measure versus the use of a multi-item 'construct' measure of subjective assessment; and
3. the use of which joint venture party's assessment – one parent or both parents, or the joint venture manager (Schaan, 1983; Beamish, 1984).

Despite the increasing use of subjective measures in recent years some researchers still consider objective events such as 'stability' or 'survival' of a joint venture as a proxy of success (Beamish and Inkpen, 1995; Blumenthal, 1988). The use of different measurement makes it difficult to compare joint venture performance across studies and generalise results for theory development. Several recent studies, however, have attempted to resolve these issues through rigorous analysis of different measurement methods (Geringer and Hebert, 1991; Hatfield et al., 1998; Glaister and Buckley, 1998a, b), but inconsistencies still remain. These studies were undertaken in developed country contexts among joint ventures between firms from developed countries. Few studies examine these issues in the context of developing countries. This chapter will make an attempt to address these issues of measurement of joint venture performance with empirical data from joint ventures between firms from developed and developing countries as well as between firms from developing countries operating in a developing country, Bangladesh.

BACKGROUND AND HYPOTHESES

Survival, stability and duration (longevity) are widely used measures of joint venture performance in the literature (Beamish, 1993; Beamish and Inkpen, 1995; Blodgett, 1992; Franko, 1971; Harrigan, 1988; Hennart et al., 1998; Killing, 1983). Franko (1971) examined joint venture instability. A joint venture was unstable when the MNC partner's ownership was increased to a wholly-owned subsidiary, changed from minority or 50:50 to a majority position, sold out to local partner, or liquidated (Franko, 1971: 17–8). Blodgett (1992) used 'renegotiation of the contract' as a measure of instability. However, none of these researchers could specify that the changes were prompted by unsatisfactory performance of the venture. Killing (1983) defined joint venture instability in terms of liquidation (including takeover by one partner) and major reorganisation of the joint venture as a result of poor performance, and found it congruent with subjective global assessment of success (as poor, satisfactory, or good).

Harrigan (1988) used joint venture 'survival' (whether the venture was operating as 'jointly-owned venture' at the time of survey) and 'duration' (number of years the venture survived) as objective measures and joint venture 'success' in terms of subjective assessment by both parents. She found a positive association between success and survival but no significant association between success and duration.

All these measures have limitations. Termination (stability or survival) of a joint venture may not indicate failure due to poor performance (Beamish, 1984; Buckley et al., 1988) and the renegotiation of joint venture contract may indicate success of the venture which encouraged one partner to increase its stake. The change in equity position may also reflect changes in the joint venture's environment, or changes in parents' strategic objective in the joint ventures' industry rather than its poor performance (Gomes-Casseres, 1987). Beamish and Inkpen (1995) also agreed with this argument and emphasised that joint venture stability is 'only one of various factors in the performance equation' (p. 28) and stability (instability) cannot be equated with success (failure). This contention was based on their empirical findings where managers assessed a number of unstable ventures as 'successful'. A recent study by Hennart et al. (1998) made it clear that determinants of joint venture termination (in terms of overall exit as joint venture and sell-off) are not determinants of joint venture liquidation. This study found that 108 out 355 Japanese stakes in the US manufacturing affiliates were terminated (representing 30 per cent termination rate), but the hazard rate (the probability of termination of a stake in year t) for joint ventures was higher than that of wholly-owned subsidiaries. On the basis of statistical analysis of proportional hazard rates for gross termination, liquidation and sell-off this study concluded that joint venture exits can not be seen as failures because sale of an affiliate may have different significance than mere failure (Hennart et al., 1998:393).

Anderson (1990) argued that joint ventures are complex organisations that are aimed at achieving long-term non-financial objectives. Anderson proposed a 'package' approach involving a composite measure of joint venture performance where long term 'input' items (such as harmony among parents and morale) and 'output' items (such as learning, product quality, market share, profit and cash flow) are included. She argued against the use of a simple measure as it runs the risk of down-grading valuable information because managers often simplify the job of assessing performance giving very high weight to profitability.

In recent years, joint venture researchers have used perceptual assessment of performance to overcome the limitations of using the objective measures based on survival, stability, and financial criteria (Awadzi et al., 1988; Beamish, 1984; Blumenthal, 1988; Killing, 1983; Nitsch et al., 1996; Osland and Cavusgil, 1996; Schaan, 1983; Yan and Gray, 1994). This perceptual measurement varies from the use of a single item to a composite of multi-item scale. Killing (1983) used a global subjective measure where managers assessed their satisfaction with the performance of the joint ventures as poor, satisfactory or good. The major advantage of this measure is its ability to provide parents' overall global perceptual evaluation of the joint venture. Its simplicity might have encouraged other researchers to use this global subjective measure (Nitsch et al., 1996) but its simplicity is often risky. Since joint venture performance is a multidimensional measure, there is a likely risk of respondent bias towards financial profitability unless other criteria of measurement are specified (Anderson, 1990; Schaan, 1983). The following comment by a US manager raises the concern against using a single-item overall measure of joint venture performance:

> The only appropriate criterion for performance evaluation is whether or not the partners and their stakeholders are happy with the joint venture's operation. The happiness for us is measured by its profitability and market share – the two most important goals we had ....(Yan and Gray, 1994, p. 1495).

Yan and Gray claimed that these comments are representative of other respondents of their study of US–Chinese joint ventures. If this is the general sentiment of business managers, a single-item measure is likely to end up with measuring financial performance of the joint venture. This sentiment is echoed in another joint venture study in China (Osland and Cavusgil, 1996) where the US and Chinese joint venture partners reported different sets of joint venture goals but 'profit [was] a dominant goal and source of satisfaction' when assessing performance. They found that despite managers' dissatisfaction with the pace of technology transfer, level of export (for Chinese partners), product quality and lack of control over the ventures (for US partners) most ventures were rated successful as profit expectations of both parties were satisfied. These findings indicate that managers' overall satisfaction is influenced primarily by the profit criterion and is not appropriate to be used to measure joint venture performance where other long-term non-financial objectives are important.

The use of a multi-item scale to assess joint venture performance against initial projections (Blumenthal 1988) or its achievement in satisfying partners' objectives was considered by some researchers in recent years to overcome that risk of profit bias (Al-Aali, 1987; Sim and Ali, 1998; Awadzi et al, 1988). Beamish (1984) realised the need for multi-item assessment of the overall assessment of performance but he found managers' reluctance to use such criteria in their assessment. This encouraged some researchers to use an overall global performance measure rather than using a multi-scale measure. The question may arise whether multi-item measurement really matters in managers' overall assessment or not. Unfortunately only a few studies have addressed that question with some statistical rigour. The exceptions being studies by Blumenthal (1988), Geringer and Hebert

(1991), and more recently by Hatfield et al. (1998) and Glaister and Buckley (1998a). Blumenthal (1988) examined correlation between managers' general satisfaction with the joint venture performance (measured by a single item) and managers' satisfaction with JVs' performance along eleven joint venture objectives. Significant correlation between the global overall measure and nine of the eleven items indicated that the item-scale measurement criteria are reflected in the single item, but some of the items provided relatively little clue to managers' global assessment. She argued that 'joint venture goals are primarily bottom line oriented (revenue and profits) and satisfaction of bottom line goals are more important to overall satisfaction with joint ventures' (Blumenthal, 1988: 222).

Geringer and Hebert (1991) contributed significantly by comparing objective and subjective measures of joint venture performance. They found support for their hypothesised significant positive correlation between objective measures (IJV survival, duration and stability) and subjective measures of performance in terms of partners' satisfaction with IJV's performance. Their measures were an overall partners' satisfaction measure and 15 individual dimensions of assessing IJV performance against initial projection. They did not use an aggregate measure of the 15 dimensions. IJV survival and duration were found to have strong correlations with partners' satisfaction and many of the individual dimensions of IJV performance. Glaister and Buckley (1998a) replicated Geringer and Hebert's (1991) study in the UK context with some extensions. Primarily they found that Equity Joint Venture (EJV) survival was significantly related to UK partners' satisfaction with EJV performance and five of the fifteen dimensions of EJV performance. EJV duration and stability were not significantly correlated with any of the subjective measures of satisfaction. Similar but weaker correlations were found for non-equity alliances. These findings however varied from that of Geringer and Hebert (1991).

Hatfield et al. (1998) examined the measurement of joint venture performance more rigorously than the pioneering work of Geringer and Hebert (1991) and its replication by Glaister and Buckley (1998a). Instead of merely comparing objective and subjective measures of joint venture performance, they examined objective and subjective measures of performance using bivariate and multivariate analysis. Their bivariate analysis revealed that their objective measures in terms of joint venture survival and duration and subjective measures of joint venture performance (partners' goal achievement using a weighted aggregate measure and overall partners' satisfaction) were significantly and positively correlated. This lends support for Geringer and Hebert (1991) but contradicted Glaister and Buckley's (1998a) findings. These conflicting empirical results indicate the need for more research in this area. Hence this chapter's attempt to investigate these issues with the empirical data from a developing country context of Bangladesh to test the following hypotheses:

H_1: Objective measures of international joint venture performance are positively correlated with subjective measures of international joint venture performance.

H_2: Objective measures of international joint venture performance and overall assessment of performance (in terms of partners' satisfaction) are positively correlated with individual items of a perceptual composite measure (in terms of partners' goal achievement).

Hatfield et al. (1998) examined whether joint venture goal achievement, partners' overall satisfaction, joint venture duration and joint venture survival measure the same or different phenomena. They tested the hypothesis with regression analysis to examine whether one measure can explain significant amount of variances of the other measure of performance. Their results showed that these variables measured different phenomena as their R^2 were less than 0.50 indicating that 'no measure explained the majority (> 0.50) of the variance in another measure' (Hatfield et al. 1998: 363). In other words, their regression results suggest that one measure cannot be used as a perfect surrogate for the other. This exploratory analysis is an important exercise in understanding the relationship between objective and subjective measures that deserves further empirical verification. Thus the following hypothesis will also be tested in this chapter with empirical data from a developing country context of Bangladesh:

H_3: Partners' goal achievement, joint venture duration, survival and stability do not measure the same phenomenon.

Hatfield et al. (1998) also explored the multivariate relationships among subjective and objective measures of performance using multiple regression and logistic regression analysis. Using their regression results, they indicated that 'partners' goal achievement is a more precise managerial assessment measure of joint venture performance than is partners' satisfaction, and that joint venture duration and survival are subsequent outcomes affected by performance and other factors such as changes in the environment and partner firms' strategies' (Hatfield et al. 1998: 365). They also went on to argue that partners' satisfaction as a measure of performance is problematic as it is confounded by non-performance factors (such as joint venture survival which is an outcome of success or failure and other exogenous factors). Hatfield et a. concluded that partner goal achievement is a more appropriate managerial assessment measure of performance and offers more precision than overall satisfaction, and 'avoids contamination of nonperformance factors' (366). This conclusion needs to be supported by further empirical data from different contexts. Therefore, this study will examine Hatfield et al.'s conclusion with empirical data from a developing country context.

RESEARCH METHODOLOGY

Empirical data from a survey of 59 private sector IJVs in Bangladesh were used to test the research hypotheses developed in the preceding section. There were 242 joint venture projects registered with the government of Bangladesh but only 67 IJVs satisfied the sample selection criteria of (1) privately sponsored IJV and (2) at least three years in operation. Fifty-nine IJVs participated in the survey including 26 from developed countries and 33 from developing countries. In most joint ventures, one local and one foreign partner was involved. These IJVs represented a range of industries including apparel, clothing and textile, electrical and electronics, engineering, leather, rubber and plastic products, chemical and pharmaceutical, and metal fabrication. Local partners were relatively much smaller (average firm size being US$5.1 million) than the foreign parents (average firm size being US$358.5 million). Foreign parents from developing countries were smaller (60 per cent of parents' firm size was below US$10 million, average firm size being US$83.28 millions) than their counterparts from developed countries (over 50 per cent parents had a firm size over US$100 million, average firm size being US$707.77 millions). The size of the joint ventures' companies was rather small by western standards (ranging between US$400,000 and US$10 million in sales) but medium-sized firms in the host country context.

Data Collection

Data were collected using personal interviews with a structured questionnaire, which was pretested. The CEOs of the JVs were interviewed. Since joint ventures involve two or more partners, some researchers argued that both (or all) partners' assessment of performance is appropriate (Beamish, 1984; Harrigan, 1988; Schaan, 1983). This would be an ideal situation but constraint of resources, time and accessibility may limit use of assessment by all partners, such as in this study. Geringer and Herbert (1991), however, provided support for the use of Joint Venture General Managers (JVGM) as respondents when they reported significant association between partners' and JVGMs' assessment of performance and concluded that JVGMs could provide fairly reliable data on performance. Glaister and Buckley (1998a) also indicated support for the use of single source data collection.

Subjective Measures of Performance

This research adopted Schaan's (1983) definition of JV performance as 'the ability of a JV to meet the expectations of its parents' (227). Parents' expectations may include strategic goals for corporate development and learning or just the bottom line goal of earning profits. A JV may fail to meet the profitability goal of its parents but may achieve other expectations such as organisational learning, market access, technical skills and other goals.

The CEOs of IJVs in our sample were asked to evaluate the venture's performance in fulfilling parents' expectations on nine dimensions which included local market development, foreign market development, acquisition of manufacturing skills, acquisition of marketing skills, acquisition of technical skills, sales growth, market share, profits and dividend; and technical and managerial training. This list was developed from the pilot study. A 5-point Likert-type scale was used for the assessment by the respondents (1 = far short of expectation, 2 = short of expectation, 3 = about the same as expected, 4 = exceeds expectation, and 5 = far exceeds expectation). The reliability coefficient of the items (Cronbach's alpha 0.87) was found to be high and acceptable (Nunnally 1978).

These achievement levels were weighted by the importance of each goal. Respondents were also asked to rate the importance of each goal to the parents on a 5-point scale (0 = not at all important, and 4 = extremely important) and it was used as a weight in the calculation of an index[1]. The composite index of joint venture performance in terms of goal achievement (ACHIEVE) is the average of the assessment of fulfilment of partners' expectations on nine joint venture goals weighted by the importance of each goal to the parents.

In addition to the multi-item scale, a single item scale was used to assess the IJV CEOs' satisfaction with the overall performance of the IJV (PERFORM) on a 5-point Likert-type scale (where 1 = 'not at all satisfied' and 5 = 'extremely satisfied'). This is a single-item scale of satisfaction with the IJV.

Objective Measures of Performance

This research also adopted *IJV Stability, IJV Survival* and *IJV Duration* as objective measures from past studies to facilitate comparison of results

(Glaister and Buckley, 1998a; Geringer and Herbert, 1991; Harrigan, 1988; Hatfield et al., 1998). *IJV Stability* was measured using a dichotomous variable (STABILITY) to indicate whether there had been any changes in the partners' equity division in the IJV (including take-over by a parent or termination) since the formation of the joint venture. Thirty-nine of the 59 joint ventures were classified as stable. *IJV Survival* was also measured using a dichotomous variable (SURVIVAL) to indicate whether the venture survived as a joint venture at the time of the survey. Forty-seven of the 59 ventures still existed as joint ventures. *IJV Duration* (DURATION) measured the number of years the venture survived as a joint venture or until the time of the survey, whichever came first.

EMPIRICAL FINDINGS AND DISCUSSION

The correlations between objective and subjective measures of joint venture performance are presented in Table 11.1. The results in fact provide only partial support to hypothesis 1. As expected, the global measurement overall performance strongly and positively correlated with goal achievement ($r = 0.811$) and joint venture survival ($r = 0.467$). Correlation between overall performance and joint venture stability is positive but barely significant ($r = 0.234$ significant only at $p = 0.07$) which indicates that changes in equity distribution between partners do affect managers' assessment of overall performance of the joint venture but is not a critical factor. This result is marginally different from Geringer and Hebert's (1991) finding ($r = 0.28$ significant at $p < 0.05$) but closer to Glaister and Buckley's (1998) finding in the UK context ($r = 0.19$, not significant at $p < 0.1$). Overall performance is not correlated with joint venture duration (close to zero) and this contradicts findings of Geringer and Hebert (1991) and of Hatfield et al. (1998) (both reported correlation above 0.4 and significant) but lends support to Glaister and Buckley's (1998a) finding (where correlation was zero). This in fact lends support to Hennart et al. (1998), who concluded that not all short-lived joint ventures should be seen as failures. These findings indicate that managers' overall assessment of performance was strongly associated with goal achievement and survival of the joint venture, weakly associated with stability but not associated with duration of the joint venture.

Results in Table 11.1 also show that goal achievement is moderately correlated with joint venture survival ($r = 0.356$) but not correlated with the two other objective measures (joint venture duration and stability). Result shows that joint venture survival is positively correlated with joint venture stability ($r = .680$), but it is negatively correlated with joint venture duration (though the result is not significant). Joint venture duration is not at all correlated with two subjective performance measures but negatively correlated with two objective measures. Its negative correlation with joint venture stability (though significant at $p = 0.08$) indicates that the longer-surviving joint ventures are more subject to equity renegotiation by partners as a result of learning (Gomes-Casseres, 1987). Thus the bivariate statistical analysis provides mixed support to our hypothesis that subjective and objective measures are positively and significantly correlated.

Table 11.1 Spearman correlations between objective and subjective measures of performance

Performance measures	1	2	3	4	5
1. Overall performance	1.000				
2. Goal achievement	0.811***	1.000			
3. Joint venture survival	0.467***	0.356***	1.000		
4. Joint venture duration	0.068	-0.011	-0.153	1.000	
5. Joint venture stability	0.234*	-0.023	680***	0.232*	1.000

Significance level: * $p \leq .10$; ** $p \leq .05$; *** $p \leq .01$

Bivariate correlations of overall performance, joint venture survival, stability, and duration with nine individual dimensions of goal achievement were used to test hypothesis 2. Results are in Table 11.2, which partly support the hypothesis. Results show that managers' global overall performance measure (PERFORM) is positively correlated with each individual dimension of partners' goal achievement (ACHIEVE). All correlation coefficients are positive and significant at 0.05 or less. Thus this result lends significant support to Blumenthal's (1988) findings that managers' global measurement of performance is positively correlated with individual dimensions of partners' goal achievement.

The correlation coefficients (mostly above 0.5) indicate positive association and suggest that managers' assessments of these financial and non-financial goals are important contributors to their overall satisfaction with the venture performance. The single overall measure is also highly correlated with the weighted composite measure of performance ($r = 0.811$ significant at 0.01or better as shown in Table 11.1). This lends support to the argument that managers' overall assessment reflects major dimensions of performance (Beamish, 1984).

Results of this study and that of Blumenthal (1988) might suggest that a single-item overall subjective measure is sufficient. However, the multi-item composite measure has advantages over the single-item measure. On the one hand, the ordinal nature of the single-item overall measurement

Table 11.2 Spearman rank order correlations of individual dimensions of goal achievement with objective and subjective measures of JV performance

Individual dimensions of partners' goal achievement	Subjective measure Overall performance	Objective performance measures JV Survival	JV stability	JV duration
Achievement of local market development	0.354**	0.183	0.029	0.429***
Achievement of foreign market development	0.672***	0.186	0.095	-0.133
Achievement of manufacturing skill acquisition	0.385***	0.378***	0.061	-0.072
Achievement of marketing skill acquisition	0.707***	0.370***	0.048	0.172
Achievement of technical skill acquisition	0.413***	0.225*	-0.005	0.206
Achievement of sales growth	0.618***	0.247*	-0.083	0.035
Achievement of market share	0.521***	0.187	-0.020	-0.049
Achievement of profit & dividend	0.651***	0.252**	0.055	0.238*
Achievement of technical & management training	0.538***	0.303**	-0.069	0.267**

Significance level: * $p \leq .10$; ** $p \leq .05$; *** $p \leq .01$

scale has severe limitation for advanced statistical analyses. On the other hand, the weighted multi-item composite measure is an interval scale, which is more useful for statistical analyses (Beamish, 1984). Although the multi-item assessment is also measured on an ordinal point scale, the weighted composite becomes an interval scale with a theoretical range between zero and number of items times the maximum importance scale assigned to items. Thus the multi-dimensional measure is a preferred measure over the single-item overall measure for more rigorous statistical analysis.

Table 11.2 also shows correlations between the three objective measures of joint venture performance and the nine individual dimensions of the subjective measure of joint venture goal achievement. It shows that joint venture survival (SURVIVAL) is significantly correlated with six out of nine dimensions. Four of these correlation coefficients are positive and significant at p = 0.05 or less with another two significant at p = 0.10. Thus these results provide support to hypothesis 2 in terms of joint venture survival, which is similar to the findings of Geringer and Hebert (1991) and Glaister and Buckley (1998a).Results in Table 11.2 show that joint venture stability is not correlated with any of the nine individual dimensions of partners' goal achievement. These results are contrary to that of Geringer and Herbert (1991) where stability was correlated with six of the fifteen dimensions of performance (though most coefficients were around 0.2) but close to those of Glaister and Buckley (1998a) where only one out of fifteen dimensions was found significant but negative. Results of this study may support the view that joint venture stability reflects other factors such as strategic control and environmental changes (Gomes-Casseres, 1987) in addition to performance.

Bivariate relationships between joint venture duration and nine individual dimensions of partners' goal achievement do not support hypothesis 2. Only three of the nine dimensions are correlated with joint venture duration. This finding contradicts that of Geringer and Hebert (1991) but supports the finding of Glaister and Buckley (1998a) where none of the fifteen dimensions was found significantly correlated.

Following Hatfield et al. (1998) regression analysis was used to examine whether performance measures are positively and significantly related. The performance measures are positively related if standardised betas are positive and the F-values of the regression models are significant. In the absence of any predicted cause and effect relationship between any variables in this set, possible pairs of subjective and objective measures of performance and two objective measures were examined.

The results presented in Table 11.3 showed mixed support for hypothesis 1. The results are quite similar to those shown by correlation analysis discussed earlier. Survival is the most significant objective measure being correlated with all other variables. Stability is also related to all variables except goal achievement. The results are different from Hatfield et al. (1998), which showed positive relationships among all the variables, except for stability, which they did not investigate.

Table 11.3 also provides support for hypothesis 3 indicating that goal achievement, joint venture duration, survival and stability measure different phenomena. There were no significant relationships between goal achievement and stability as well as duration. The other variable pairs in Table 11.3 are significantly related but their R^2 were 0.462 or below, indicating that none of these measures explained the majority (> 0.5) of the variance in another measure. For example, while survival and goal achievement are positively related, the R^2 of 0.183 indicate that survival is affected by other factors (for example, environmental and partners' strategic factors) in addition to goal achievement. Hence goal achievement, joint venture survival, duration and stability are not substitutable measures.

Hatfield et al. (1998) argued that partner satisfaction is an overall outcome assessment, largely determined by goal achievement and other factors. His regression result showed that goal achievement and joint

Table 11.3 Regression analysis for hypothesised variable sets

Variable pairs	Standardised beta	R^2	F-value	Df
Overall performance Joint venture survival	0.546	0.298	24.25***	58
Overall performance Joint venture stability	0.306	0.094	5.90**	58
Overall performance Joint venture duration	0.046	0.002	0.123	58
Goal achievement Joint venture survival	0.427	0.183	12.72**	58
Goal achievement Joint venture stability	0.056	0.003	0.177	58
Goal achievement Joint venture duration	0.032	0.001	0.060	58
Joint venture survival Joint venture duration	-0.258	0.067	4.08**	58
Joint venture survival Joint venture stability	0.680	0.462	48.95***	58
Joint venture stability Joint venture duration	-0.257	0.066	4.02**	58

Significance level: * $p \leq .10$; ** $p \leq .05$; *** $p \leq .01$

venture survival were the significant variables determining partner satisfaction. A stepwise regression was run for our data using overall performance (in terms of satisfaction) as the dependent variable. Stepwise regression results in Table 11.4 show that partners' goal achievement and joint venture stability jointly explain 75 per cent of the variances of overall performance (74 per cent when adjusted for the population).

Results show that partners' goal achievement is a major determinant (unique R^2 0.683, significant at $p = 0.001$) while joint venture stability explained only a fraction of the variances (unique R^2 0.063, significant at $p = 0.01$). Interestingly, joint survival and duration did not enter the model. The t-value for joint venture survival at step 1 was found significant but it lost its ground when joint venture stability entered the model which indicates high collinearly between these two variables (correlation matrix in Table 11.1 shows $r = 0.68$, a moderate to high collinearly). As stability was not studied by Hatfield et al. (1998), this result cannot be compared to theirs[2].

Table 11.4 Stepwise regression analysis for overall performance of joint venture

Model 1 Variables in the model	Regression coefficient	Standardised beta	**Model 2** Variables in the model	Regression coefficient	Standardised beta
Goal achievement	0.524	0.826***	Goal achievement	0.515	0.812***
			Joint venture stability	0.542	0.251***
Model statistics			Model statistics		
R^2	0.683		R^2	0.746	
Adjusted R^2	0.677		Adjusted R^2	0.737	
F	122.81***		R^2-Change	0.063	
			Model F	82.14***	
			F-Change	13.83***	
Variables excluded	**Beta In**	**t-value**	**Variables excluded**	**Beta In**	**t-value**
Joint venture survival	0.206	2.624**	Joint venture survival	0.010	0.091
Joint venture duration	0.078	1.046	Joint venture duration	0.102	1.520
Joint venture stability	0.251	3.719**			

Significance level: * $p \leq .10$; ** $p \leq .05$; *** $p \leq .01$

However, our finding supports their argument that satisfaction (measured as overall performance here) is an overall outcome largely determined by goal achievement and other factors (stability in this study).

The above results provide support that performance (in terms of satisfaction) is an overall assessment measure, largely determined by goal achievement and to a much lesser extent by joint venture stability. As joint venture stability may reflect nonperformance factors such as adaptation to environmental changes, using overall satisfaction as a performance measure may be problematic. Furthermore, it is a general and vague concept, whose evaluation is based largely on the frame of reference or criteria used by respondents who are rating it. Hence, it is more appropriate to use goal achievement rather than overall rating of partner satisfaction, as a measure of joint venture performance as advocated by Hatfield et al. (1998). Also as goal achievement, joint venture stability, survival and duration have been shown to measure different phenomena, it is better to treat them as such (that is, as different phenomena). Joint venture stability, survival and duration should not be used as proxy measures for joint venture performance. As joint venture termination and sell-off by one partner does not mean a failure of the venture (Hennart et al., 1998), the use of these as proxy of performance is risky.

Goal achievement has other points in its favour as a preferred measure of joint venture performance. It is a more precise measure than partner satisfaction. It overcomes some of the problems involved with traditional financial measures (such as respondents' reluctance to provide confidential financial data, comparability across industry and so on). Also it is more comprehensive as it includes non-financial goals, which are often important to joint ventures. In this study, the most important goal rated is foreign market development. The use of a composite index of partners' goal achievement also allows for different combination of partners' goals, which are important to partners, to be incorporated into the measure.

SUMMARY, CONCLUSION AND LIMITATIONS

This study has provided further empirical evidence on the issues surrounding the measurement of joint venture performance from a developing country context of Bangladesh. Hypotheses 1 and 2 were partly supported which is reflective of the empirical evidence from previous research in this area. Further empirical research here is indicated. Hypothesis 3 was supported and this validated the findings of Hatfield et al. (1998). Our analysis also supports the use of goal achievement as the preferred measure of joint venture performance. However, the measure needs to be further refined and tested in other contexts to provide further evidence of its validity and applicability in measuring IJV performance.

The findings must also be tempered by several limitations of this study. Sample size and the nature of a one-country analysis are limitations. The use of joint venture general managers' assessment of performance, though supported by previous studies, is another obvious limitation. It is preferable to use multiple perspectives (with respondents from all partners and JV management) which will allow for triangulation of results. Further research is indicated along this line.

Notes

1. The use of 0 for 'not at all important' facilitated the correct weighting of achievement in a particular item. The weighted value of an item will form part of the composite of all items if its importance is non-zero. A zero-important item will not influence the composite due to its weighted zero (1 x 0 = 0) value.
2. For further comparison of results, Hatfield et al.'s (1998) analysis was replicated where joint venture stability was excluded from the model. A stepwise regression model with two objective measures and partners' goal achievement as possible determinants produced result very similar to that of Hatfield et al. Seventy-two percent of the variances (71 per cent when adjusted for the population) of overall performance was explained by partners' goal achievement (unique R^2 0.683, significant at $p = 0.001$) and joint venture survival (unique R^2 0.035, significant at $p = 0.01$). As found by Hatfield et al., joint venture duration did not enter the model indicating its insignificant impact on overall performance.

REFERENCES

Al-Aali, A.Y. (1987), *A Performance Model for American Manufacturing and Service Joint Ventures in Saudi Arabia*, Unpublished Ph.D. Dissertation, Georgia State University, USA.

Anderson, E. (1990), 'Two Firms, One Frontier: On Assessing Joint Venture Performance', *Sloan Management Review,* (Winter), 19–30.

Awadzi, W.K., B. Kedia and R. Chinta (1988), 'Strategic Implications of Cooperation and Complementary Resources in International Joint Ventures', *International Journal of Management,* **5** (2), 125–32.

Beamish, Paul W. (1988), 'Multinational Joint Ventures in Developing Countries', London: Routledge.

Beamish, Paul W. (1984), *Joint Venture Performance in Developing Countries*, Unpublished Ph.D. Dissertation, The University of Western Ontario, Canada.

Beamish, Paul W. (1993), 'The Characteristics of Joint Ventures in the People's Republic of China', *Journal of International Marketing,* (1&2), 27–48.

Beamish, P.W. and A.C. Inkpen (1995), 'Keeping International Joint Ventures Stable and Profitable', *Long Range Planning,* **28** (3), 26–36.

Blodgett, L. (1992), 'Factors in the Instability of International Joint Ventures: An Event History Analysis', *Strategic Management Journal,* **13** (6), 475–81.

Blumenthal, J.F. (1988), *Strategic and Organisational Conditions for Joint Venture Formation and Success*, Unpublished Ph.D. Dissertation, University of Southern California, USA.

Buckley, P.J., G.D. Newbould and J. Thurwell (1988), *Foreign Direct Investment by Smaller U. K. Firms,* London: Macmillan.

Dang, T. (1977), 'Ownership, Control and Performance of the Multinational Corporation: A Study of U.S. Wholly-owned Subsidiaries and Joint Ventures in the Philippines and Taiwan', Unpublished Ph.D. Dissertation, University of California.

Franko, L.G. (1971), *Joint Venture Survival in Multinational Corporations*, New York: Praeger.

Geringer, J.M. and L. Hebert (1991), 'Measuring Performance of International Joint Ventures', *Journal of International Business Studies*, **22** (2), 235–54.

Glaister, K.W. and P.J. Buckley (1998a), 'Measures of Performance in UK International Alliances', *Organisation Studies,* **19** (1), 89–118.

Glaister, K.W. and P.J. Buckley (1998b), 'Replication with Extension: Response to Geringer', *Organisation Studies,* **19** (1), 139–54

Gomes-Casseres, B. (1987), 'Joint Venture Instability: Is It a Problem?', *Columbia Journal of World Business*, (Summer), 97–101.

Harrigan, K.R. (1988), 'Strategic Alliance and Partner Asymmetries', *Management International Review*, (Special Issue), 53–72.

Hatfield, L., J.A. Pearce, R.G. Sleeth and M.W. Pitts, (1998), 'Toward Validation of Partner Goal Achievement as a Measure of Joint Venture Performance', *Journal of Managerial Issues,* **10** (3), 355–72.

Hennart, J-F, D-J. Kim and M. Zeng (1998), "The Impact of Joint Venture Status on the Longevity of Japanese Stakes in U.S. Manufacturing Affiliates, *Organization Science,* Vol. 9, Number 3 (May-June), pp 382-395.

Hergert, M. and D. Morris, (1988), 'Trends in International Collaborative Agreement', in F.J. Contractor and P. Lorrange (eds), *Competitive Strategies in International Business*, Lexington: D.C. Heath.

Killing, J.P. (1983), *Strategies for Joint Venture Success*, London: Croom Helm.

Kogut, B. (1988), 'A Study of the Life Cycle of Joint Ventures', *Management International Review*, (Special Issue), 39–52.

Nitsch, D., P. Beamish and S. Makino (1996), 'Entry Mode and Performance of Japanese FDI in Western Europe', *Management International Review,* **36** (1), 27–43.

Nunnally, J. (1978), *Psychometric Theory*, 2nd edition, New York: McGraw-Hill.

Osland, G. and S.T. Cavusgil (1996), 'Performance Issues in US–China Joint Ventures', *California Management Review*, **38** (2), 106–30.

Parkhe, A. (1993), 'Partner Nationality and the Structure-Performance Relationship in Strategic Alliances', *Organization Science*, **4** (2), 301–24.

Schaan, J.-L. (1983), *Parent Control and Joint Venture Success: The Case of Mexico,* Unpublished Ph.D. Dissertation, The University of Western Ontario, Canada.

Sim, A.B. and M.Y. Ali (1998), 'Performance of International Joint Ventures from Developed and Developing Countries – An Empirical Study in a Developing Country Context', *Journal of World Business,* **33** (4), 357–77.

Wagner, C.L. (1993), 'Perceived Correlates of Successful Joint Venture Negotiations in China: An Empirical Study', *International Journal of Management,* **10** (4), 413–21.

Yan, A. and B. Gray (1994), 'Bargaining Power, Management Control, and Performance in United States–China Joint Ventures: A Comparative Case Study', *Academy of Management Journal,* **37** (6), 1478–517.

12. Human Resource Management in Hong Kong: Convergence or Divergence?

Peter McGraw

INTRODUCTION

The last decade has witnessed an upsurge of academic and practitioner interest in international human resource management. This interest has been galvanised by a number of factors. First, the impact of globalisation and the intensification of competition associated with it have stimulated an examination of the contribution of human resource and labour management practices to competitive advantage. Sophisticated HR management techniques have been increasingly identified as potentially powerful strategic levers through which to manipulate economic performance. (Arthur, 1994; Cutcher-Gershenfeld, 1991; Gerhart and Milkovich, 1990; Huselid, 1995; Huselid and Becker, 1996; MacDuffie, 1995; Pfeffer, 1994; Wright and McMahan, 1992). HR practices are now seen as a potentially enduring form of competitive advantage since, unlike capital, technology, resources and finance, they are not easily and quickly replicated or imitated by competitors (Baird and Meshoulam, 1988; Lengnick-Hall and Lengnick-Hall, 1988). In the language of Hamel and Prahalad (1990) the outcomes of effective HR practices can be viewed as 'core capabilities'. This argument has been made in relation to both organisations and nation states and is increasingly voiced as the competitive lead times deriving from traditional factors of production become shorter due to the increased pace of diffusion.

Second, there has been a rapid growth in the number of companies that are now operating across national borders (Shenkar, 1995). Inevitably, as more companies have 'gone international' there has been an emerging dialogue relating to the problems and issues raised by 'managing across borders' (Bartlett and Ghoshal, 1989).

Third, the sustained economic growth of certain economies, most noticeably those in East Asia, has stimulated debate about the importance of culture in relation to economic dynamism, particularly in societies where Confucianism is influential (Redding, 1993).

Fourth, international comparative benchmarking of management practices, both inside and outside the firm, has become an increasingly influential driver of change in many organisations worldwide (Martin and Beaumont, 1998). This has been enabled by the increased pace of diffusion of management systems and ideologies and has been facilitated by improved communication technologies, the continued internationalisation of business and the global ascendancy of managerial paradigms such as those associated with international quality standards.

All of the factors noted above have focused attention on the practice of international management. The data presented in this chapter add to the re-emerging debate about the convergence or divergence of managerial practices as a result of globalisation, particularly HR practices. The term that is commonly used to capture this convergence is 'institutional isomorphism'. The chapter also considers staffing practices within MNCs, which are critical to the spread of institutional isomorphism, and how these relate to MNC strategy. Underlying both of these areas is the multi-faceted issue of culture, corporate and national, and how best to create cultural synergy, or at a minimum avoid cultural incompatibility. This too has recently become a major managerial concern for international organisations. (Adler, 1995; Bartlett and Ghoshal, 1989; Olie, 1995; Rosenweig and Nohria, 1994).

Convergence or Divergence

The argument for the convergence of managerial practice across borders originated in the 1950s and was traditionally associated with the ideological hegemony of structural functionalism. The convergence hypothesis was based on the, essentially ethnocentric idea, that organisations will become more homogenous in character, regardless of the environment in which they operate, as they are driven by the forces of a common 'logic of industrialism' as represented by the same (western) technologies, production systems and management systems (Olie, 1995). Ultimately, according to this view, all societies will become more and more alike as the common modes of production drive a wider modernism throughout them. This theory lost popularity during the 1970s as new, non-western, industrial societies emerged and developed their own highly successful, culturally attuned systems of management. With the decline of convergence theory came the growth of culturally relativist or divergent explanations of organisational functioning (Olie, 1995).

The argument for divergence rests on the contention that all societies are culturally unique and that this difference inevitably structures the way in which organisations function within a given society. According to this view organisations can only be properly understood in the milieu of the society in which they operate, notwithstanding superficial similarities in product, size, technology and production systems. Hofstede (1980) is perhaps the best known proponent of the cultural relativist argument and has led the way in advancing the idea that national culture influences the micro level operations of organisations, primarily in the areas of leadership styles, decision-making processes and worker motivation. In applying this concept in relation to the practice of international human resource management (HRM) Schneider (1988) has argued that the assumptions underlying HRM practices in MNCs represent the culture of the country where the organisation has its headquarters and, as such, may lack fit with the national culture of the subsidiaries. The most often used illustration of this is the incompatibility in the use of 'management by objectives' schemes in many parts of the non Anglo-Saxon world (Schneider, 1988). At a macro level the proponents of cultural relativism have argued that not only does culture influence the micro management practices of organisations but it also affects their structure and strategic processes (Hofstede, 1980; Schneider and De Meyer, 1991).

At a conceptual level, Guest (1990) has argued that HRM is a theoretical movement which is suffused with the values and ideology of the culture of the United States of America from which it originated, and thus is in itself a cultural artefact. Specifically, Guest argues that HRM revolves around three ideas, which are central to the 'American Dream', namely: the potential for human growth; the desire to improve the management of people at work; and the central role in management of leadership and culture. Hofstede (1993) has made a similar point in arguing that even the term management as it is presently used is an American invention.

Child (1981) has attempted to reconcile the convergence and divergence debate in relation to organisations by arguing that these concepts can most usefully be viewed as forces which influence organisations in different areas. Thus, for example, whilst divergent national cultures may determine leadership style, decision-making and employee motivation, organisations may show convergence in structure. In other words, although organisations in different countries are becoming more alike structurally, the behaviour of people within those organisations retains its cultural specificity. This conclusion on the convergence/divergence issue is also reflected in a quote attributed to the co-founder of the Honda Motor Corporation, Mr T. Fujisawa who is once reported to have commented that 'US and Japanese management systems are 95 per cent the same and different in all important respects'.

More recently, interest in the convergence thesis has been rekindled by, amongst others, Fukuyama (1992) who has argued that with the collapse of communism we have witnessed the triumph of capitalism and the end of ideology, which in turn has led to a global convergence of political and economic structures. As a corollary to this, however, Fukuyama has argued that cultural differences may loom larger from now on as a source of potential conflict (Fukuyama, 1995: 5). Applying this same argument to international organisations, therefore, it may be argued that while structures and policies are similar across national borders the cultural mediation of management practices will inhibit genuine institutional isomorphism. This is particularly the case in societies which are culturally 'distant' from the Anglo-American model of management such as those, like Hong Kong, where Confucianism is influential. This influence will be discussed later in this chapter.

Staffing Policies in MNCs

In addition to the issues concerning convergence and divergence, the debate about the forces that shape staffing policies internationally is further complicated if the strategic staffing issues confronting MNCs are considered. Traditionally, the main approaches to MNC staffing and decision-making have been categorised using four terms: ethnocentric, whereby local subsidiaries have limited autonomy and senior management positions are dominated by expatriates; polycentric, in which MNC subsidiaries have high levels of autonomy and are generally managed by locals; geocentric, whereby the organisation pursues a worldwide integrated business strategy and chooses staff from a global pool; and regiocentric, in which staffing and decision-making tend to gravitate towards regional centres (Ondrack, 1985). More recently authors such as Bartlett and Ghoshal (1989) have argued that such typologies do not accurately represent the internal differentiation that is evident in MNCs as they struggle with the combined pressures of being globally efficient, locally responsive and synergistic in terms of the diffusion of innovation. In other words the MNC structure is determined by the interaction of competing pressures for internal consistency on the one hand versus alignment with the local environment on the other. Moreover, the various functions of management may be affected by these pressures to different degrees. Thus in finance there may be strong pressure for centralisation whereas in marketing the requirement for local responsiveness may be paramount. In the area of HRM this issue is of critical importance as organisations struggle with the need to conform to local standards (for example, trade union recognition), to be administratively centralised and thus efficient (for example, using the same performance management system to evaluate employees globally), and to spread international best practice throughout the organisation (for example, 'best practice' management systems such as ISO standards).

Existing empirical data indicate that finance and manufacturing are likely to be centralised throughout the organisation whereas HRM tends to closely follow local practices (Kobayashi, 1982). There are three main reasons for HR practices primarily following local rather than headquarters practice. First, local labour laws or regulation may prescribe a uniform standard of employment practices. Second, labour market realities in the local market tend to preclude any practices which are too far beyond local norms. Third, MNCs may prefer to conform to local practices for reasons related to political expediency and the desire to avoid unnecessary attention (Rosenweig and Nohria, 1994).

It is important to note here, however, that MNCs following different staffing strategies may have different business strategies and hence different overall HRM strategies. Evans and Lorange (1989) have noted that ethnocentric companies tend to be HR innovators in their overseas subsidiaries, whereas polycentric firms are more likely to be adaptors to the local environment. This has implications for the debate about culture and convergence as Evans and Lorange (1989) also note that in, for example, the area of recruitment, firms which manage their workforce globally are more likely to select and recruit people in any given country who fit the company's cultural values than polycentric firms, which are more likely to recruit people whose cultural values reflect those of the country of operation.

The Influence of Culture on Management Practices in Hong Kong

As can be seen in Table 12.1, which presents Hofstede's (1993) data, Hong Kong and the USA are at opposite ends of the ranking on three out of five dimensions of culture: power distance; individualism; and long-term orientation.

Table 12.1 Hofstede's culture dimensions scores

	Hong Kong	USA
Power distance	68 H	40 L
Individualism	25 L	91 H
Masculinity	57 H	62 H
Uncertainty avoidance	29 L	46 L
Long-term orientation	96 H	29 L

A consequence of this cultural variation is claimed by authors such as Redding (1993) to be a vastly different style of management in firms, which are controlled by ethnic Chinese business people. This is explained as a manifestation, primarily, of the values of Confucianism, although the history of persecution of the Chinese by various regimes is also a factor, particularly as regards the aversion to formal written business policies.

The essence of Confucianism is thought to be encapsulated in five Chinese terms. *Jen*, or human heartedness, is about respect for others and oneself. *Chuntzu*, or 'the Superior Man' is someone who is self reliant and assured but not selfish and seeks to accommodate others as much as possible. *Li*, which can literally mean ritual, concerns proper conduct and the way that things should be done. This involves issues such as proper relationships within the family, for example, filial piety, as well as relationships between friends and superiors and subordinates. *Te*, concerns the power by which rulers should exert their influence, by moral example rather than force. Lastly, *Wen* relates to the prominence which should be given to the arts as a method of moral education and a means to achieve peace. Woven through each of these principles is the concept of social sensitivity and propriety, which is captured in the term 'face'. Face involves behaving in accordance with the customs and practices of society which facilitate co-operation and allow people to preserve dignity in social transactions and thereby retain prestige and self respect (Gannon, 1994).

Reflecting the values of Confucianism, Redding (1993) has argued that firms, which are owned and controlled by ethnic Chinese businesspeople, tend to be overwhelmingly 'patrimonial' which according to Redding (1993: 155) '...is the only word which captures adequately the themes of paternalism, hierarchy, responsibility, mutual obligation, family atmosphere, personalism and protection. Out of it (patrimonialism) flow three related themes which are in some sense expressions of it, namely: the idea that power cannot really exist unless it is connected to ownership; a distinct style of benevolently autocratic leadership; and personalistic as opposed to neutral relations.'

The consequences of this approach in terms of HR practices in ethnic Chinese businesses when compared with western owned businesses are: less extensive career development and promotion procedures, except for family members; less reliance on formal performance appraisal and feedback; a more authoritarian management style; less emphasis on the empowerment of the workforce; lower levels of staff training; low levels of explicit job analysis; a high emphasis on the management of extrinsic rewards; lower levels of welfare and fringe benefits; and a low emphasis on formal industrial relations procedure and safety management (Shaw et al., 1993).

This chapter canvasses the issues discussed above and examines line managers' perceptions of culture, HR practices and values from an original sample of 135 organisations in Hong Kong. The study takes as its starting point the previous research which suggests that HR practices are likely to vary between ethnic Chinese and Anglo-American organisations. However, this study makes a more explicit exploration of the espoused and practised values in organisations and their relationship to HR practices. In order to make comparisons the responses are divided into two sub-samples. The first sub-sample consists of 42 organisations, which are local subsidiaries of Anglo-American multinationals. The second sub-sample consists of 51 locally owned organisations. For the purposes of these comparisons, responses of managers from other than these two ownership groups are excluded from the analysis.

FINDINGS OF PREVIOUS RESEARCH STUDIES ON HR IN HONG KONG

In corroboration of Redding's work and the culturally-determined predictions about HR in ethnic Chinese organisations in Hong Kong, Saha (1987) found that HR was a non-strategic activity that was mainly concerned with administrative and payroll related tasks. However, HR did have a more influential role in larger publicly listed companies. Kirkbride and Tang (1989) confirmed the low level of influence of HR in small firms and also noted a low level of HR professionalism. In large organisations Kirkbride and Tang (1989) found that HR was mainly involved in the areas of recruitment, salary administration and training with limited discretion in HR planning. HR had little involvement in work organisation, occupational health and safety and job evaluation.

Shaw et al. (1993), in their comparison of Anglo-American and Chinese firms found that, on the whole, the cultural background of the owner of the firm was a relatively weak predictor of HR practices. However, Anglo-American firms were more likely than Chinese firms to use formal performance appraisal systems, use more technical methods to assess the value of jobs and to provide more welfare and fringe benefits. Anglo-American firms also provided more training and displayed a higher use of more formal written procedures although neither of these were statistically significant in the study (Shaw et al., 1993: 810). According to Shaw et al. (1993) the best predictors of HR in Hong Kong were firm size and the existence of specialised training units within the organisations. Moderate predictors were the existence of HR departments and the level of unionisation.

METHOD

The overall aim of this study was to add to and extend the limited research on HR practices in Hong Kong, and to investigate the primary differences between HR practices and values in ethnic Chinese and Anglo-American firms. The data reported in this study was collected via questionnaires from a convenient sample of 135 employed line managers based in Hong Kong. At the time of the surveys, the respondents were studying for a part-time Masters of Management degree, which is taught in Hong Kong by the author's university. On average, respondents had just less than ten years experience as managers. Colleagues of the author administered the surveys directly on three occasions during 1998.

The surveys consisted of 23 questions, 13 of which collected background information on the respondents and their organisations. The main part of the questionnaire consisted of three questions, each of which contained multiple items, seeking information from respondents on issues central to the study. Respondents were asked to indicate their agreement or disagreement to statements using a Lickert scale format. These questions examined espoused values in their organisations (15 items), practised values in their organisations (15 items) and HR practices in their organisations (15 items).

Three further questions asked respondents to indicate the degree of influence exercised by HR in HR matters, in ensuring strategic alignment of HR and in general business direction. Three final questions asked for qualitative information on the overall role and philosophy of HR in the organisation.

Respondents were 66 per cent female, 74 per cent private sector and 59 per cent worked for a multinational organisation. All standard industry classifications were represented in the sample with the majority coming from manufacturing (16 per cent), financial services (10 per cent) and transportation (9 per cent). Seventy two per cent of respondents worked for organisations with more than 100 employees in Hong Kong and 41 per cent worked for organisations with more than 500 employees in Hong Kong. The ownership pattern of the firms reported in the sample fell into two main groups with 39 per cent employed in organisations owned by ethnic Chinese and 31 per cent in organisations of Anglo-American origin. Comparisons of the aggregate responses of these two groups form the basis for much of the analysis that follows.

RESULTS

Respondents were asked to judge, on a 5-point continuous scale, the extent to which their organisation espoused 15 typical HR values. These values were generated from various western normative models of HR as well as material on Chinese values. In the scale used in the questionnaire, 5 indicated a very high emphasis and 1 equalled a very low emphasis. The mean responses to this question for the ethnic Chinese and Anglo-American sub groups are presented in Table 12.2.

Table 12.2 Espoused values

	Organisational ownership					
	Chinese n = 51		Anglo-American n = 42			
	Mean	s.d	Mean	s.d	t-value	sig.
Centralised decision-making	3.90	0.87	3.23	0.98	3.43	0.001***
Conformity with group behaviour/norms.	3.40	0.83	3.54	0.80	-0.86	0.392
Contribution of ideas and opinions.	3.15	0.83	3.64	0.90	-2.69	0.008*
Decentralisation of authority	2.80	0.98	3.16	0.96	-1.79	0.076
Delegation of authority	3.25	1.01	3.59	0.79	-1.76	0.081
Encourage diversity of thinking	2.90	0.98	3.52	0.89	-3.16	0.002**
Maintaining face	3.76	0.86	3.23	0.87	2.90	0.002**
Maintaining group harmony	3.92	0.96	3.54	0.86	-0.81	0.418
Hierarchical relationship	3.43	0.92	3.21	0.92	1.12	0.262
Following instructions precisely	3.45	0.90	3.66	0.92	-1.13	0.260
Respect of authority	3.66	0.71	3.54	0.94	0.69	0.490
Risk taking	2.66	1.19	3.04	1.03	-1.62	0.108
Staff involvement in decision making	2.56	0.92	3.30	0.89	-3.90	0.000***
Symbolic egalitarianism	2.74	1.01	3.35	0.69	-3.31	0.001***
Toleration of diversity	2.86	0.93	3.09	0.87	-1.22	0.224

* = significant at the .05 level ** = significant at the .005 level

*** = significant at the .001 level

The variation in means is in the expected direction in most cases with the Chinese sample reflecting a higher level of espoused values associated with centralisation, hierarchy and maintaining face while the Anglo-American organisations espoused values such as symbolic egalitarianism, diversity of thought and staff involvement. Independent sample t-tests were conducted on all of the means in Table 12.2 indicating significant differences in the six areas mentioned above.

The survey also asked respondents to nominate the extent to which their organisation practised these same 15 values. Responses to this question are summarised in Table 12.3.

Table 12.3 Values in practice

	Organisational ownership					
	Chinese n = 51		Anglo-American n = 42			
	Mean	s.d	Mean	s.d	t-value	sig.
Centralised decision-making	3.84	0.98	3.71	0.80	0.68	0.498
Conformity with group behaviour/norms	3.39	0.82	3.50	0.70	-0.66	0.506
Contribution of ideas and opinions	2.72	0.80	3.19	0.86	-2.69	0.009*
Decentralisation of authority	2.43	0.85	2.66	0.87	-1.30	0.194
Delegation of authority	2.84	1.02	3.11	0.96	1.32	0.189
Encourage diversity of thinking	2.60	0.87	3.16	0.85	-3.10	0.003**
Maintaining face	3.68	1.12	3.23	1.10	1.93	0.056
Maintaining group harmony	3.07	0.99	3.40	0.62	-1.84	0.069
Hierarchical relationship	3.50	1.04	3.45	0.96	0.27	0.786
Following instructions precisely	3.56	0.94	3.42	0.94	-1.13	0.260
Respect of authority	3.56	1.04	3.28	0.83	1.42	0.159
Risk taking	2.56	0.96	2.80	0.83	-1.27	0.206
Staff involvement in decision making	2.35	0.82	2.83	0.85	-2.76	0.007*
Symbolic egalitarianism	2.37	0.89	2.76	0.79	-2.20	0.030*
Toleration of diversity in practice	2.62	0.84	2.90	0.90	-1.52	0.131

* = significant at the .05 level ** = significant at the .005 level

Table 12.3 indicates that values in practice vary a lot more than espoused values between the two groups. For both the Chinese and Anglo-American sub-samples the means for practised values are lower than those espoused on 12 out of 15 items. This suggests that both groups espouse values that they are not seen to uphold to the same level in practice. In comparison, the Anglo-American firms showed a greater propensity to practice four values: contribution of ideas; encouragement of diversity of thinking; staff involvement in decision-making; and symbolic egalitarianism. All of these were found to be significantly different using independent sample t-tests. These results provide mild support for the expected finding that ethnic Chinese firms are more likely to espouse values associated with centralised decision-making. However, on the whole, the results indicate a relatively minor difference in practised values between the two groups. It would appear though that Chinese firms are slightly more likely to espouse certain values even if they are not seen to practice them.

In relation to HR practices, respondents were asked to rate the degree of systematic practice/informality on a 5-point continuous scale in relation to 15 key areas. Formality and informality were the terms used in order to determine whether the organisations had explicit and formal HR systems which were intended to provide uniformity of practice and could be administered impartially, or implicit systems where an individual manager could make decisions without reference to policy or procedure. Drawing on the experience of Shaw et al. (1993), who found that multiple measures of single HR practices yielded the same results, respondents were asked only to make an overall assessment of formality/informality in each of the HR areas.

Mean values for the two sub-groups are presented in Table 12.4, where 5 indicates a formal system and 1 indicates a completely informal system. As can be seen from Table 12.4 the means for HR practices between the two groups vary in the predicted direction on every item, with Anglo-American firms more likely to use formal and systematic HR processes. Independent sample t-tests indicate a significant difference on all HR practices between the two groups. The variance is particularly strong in relation to training and development, job analysis, succession planning, HR planning, employee communication, grievance procedures and employee communication. The variation is less strong in areas that are significantly influenced by external factors. Examples of this include Equal Employment Opportunity and Industrial Relations, where some conformity with minimum legal standards is required, as well as compensation and benefits where external labour market pressure inhibits too much variation. These differences are consistent with the previous research discussed earlier but more pronounced. They indicate a very substantial variation in HR practice between the two sub-groups.

Table 12.4 HR practices

	Organisational ownership					
	Chinese n = 51		Anglo-American n = 42			
	Mean	s.d	Mean	s.d	t-value	sig.
Performance appraisal	3.11	1.25	3.83	1.42	-2.56	0.012*
Recruitment and selection	3.23	1.08	3.90	0.93	-3.14	0.002**
Compensation and benefits	3.52	1.18	4.19	1.06	-2.79	0.006*
Training and development	2.58	1.29	3.54	1.21	-3.65	0.000***
Job analysis	2.46	1.14	3.42	1.19	-3.96	0.000***
Succession planning	2.39	1.12	3.21	1.07	-3.52	0.001***
HR planning	2.44	1.19	3.35	1.24	-3.54	0.001***
EEO	2.64	1.04	3.38	1.24	-3.09	0.003**
OHS	3.23	1.25	3.92	1.17	-2.72	0.008*
IR	2.60	1.04	3.38	1.24	-2.24	0.027*
Employee communication	2.74	0.93	3.33	0.84	-3.15	0.002**
Grievance procedures	2.49	1.18	3.42	1.00	-3.97	0.000***
Organisational structure	3.76	1.05	4.26	0.85	-2.46	0.016*
Promotion of diversity	2.98	1.02	3.50	0.99	-2.46	0.016*
Employee involvement	2.50	0.94	3.26	1.14	-3.46	0.001***

* = significant at the .05 level ** = significant at the .005 level
*** = significant at the .001 level

Respondents were asked three questions about the influence of HR in their organisations. Table 12.5 summarises the mean responses to the questions by group where 5 is very high and 1 is very low. HR influence on HR matters is low for the Chinese sub-sample and moderate for the Anglo-American sub-sample. The Anglo-American sub-sample reported a low/moderate strategic focus for HR whereas the ethnic Chinese sub-sample reported only a low strategic focus. In relation to HR influence in overall business direction, the Chinese sub-sample reported a low influence whereas the Anglo-American sub-sample reported a moderate influence. Independent sample t-tests were conducted on mean responses of the two sub-groups and all were found to be significantly different.

Table 12.5 Influence of HR

	Organisational ownership					
	Ethnic Chinese n = 51		Anglo-American n = 42			
	Mean	s. d.	Mean	s. d.	t-value	sig.
HR influence in employment issues	2.49	0.90	3.05	0.95	-2.85	0.005**
HR influence in business direction	2.09	0.78	2.63	1.01	-2.85	0.005**
Strategic focus of HR	2.13	0.80	2.92	1.07	-4.18	0.000***

** = significant at the .005 level

*** = significant at the .001 level

Previous research into HR practices (Shaw et al., 1993) has indicated that organisational size should be an important variable in determining the sophistication and formality of HR practices. Confirmation of this was found when a comparison of means was conducted that indicated far higher scores in organisations with more than 500 employees. In order to investigate the relative importance of this as an explanatory factor two procedures were conducted. First, a cross-tabulation procedure was done which showed a relatively even spread of organisational sizes across both sub-samples. Second, t-tests were conducted on different size categories using identical grouping variables as for the earlier analysis. Comparative results across the different size categories showed almost identical differences between the two sub-samples as the combined results for all size categories. Thus size of organisation was found to influence the practice of HR in Hong Kong, with larger organisations being more likely to have sophisticated HR practices but this was consistent across size categories within both sub-samples.

DISCUSSION AND CONCLUSION

This study has examined the extent to which the Chinese and Anglo-American sub-samples in the data contrasted in terms of espoused and practised values, HR practices and HR influence within the organisation. With reference to values, six out of fifteen were espoused to a significantly different degree by the two sub-groups. The Chinese sub-group were more likely to espouse values associated with centralised decision-making and maintaining face whereas the Anglo-American sub-group espoused values encouraging the contribution of ideas and opinions, diversity of thinking, staff involvement in decision-making and symbolic egalitarianism. Both groups were observed to practice their values less than they espoused them but there were significant differences between the sub-groups in only four areas. Anglo-American firms showed a greater propensity to seek the contribution of ideas, encourage diversity of thinking, involve staff in decision-making and practise symbolic egalitarianism. These results provide some support for the expected finding that ethnic Chinese firms are more centralised in terms of management decision-making. However, on the whole the results indicate a relatively minor difference in practised values between the two groups. It would appear that both sub-groups are slightly more likely to espouse certain values even if they are not seen to practice them and that Anglo-American firms are more likely to espouse and practice values which are supportive of the classic Anglo-American HR paradigm.

The data relating to values are, initially, quite surprising in view of the extreme variation in HR practices, where all fifteen practices varied significantly between the sub-groups, with all variations in the expected direction. This confirms the findings of previous research in the area. Consistent with this, a corresponding variation in values might also have been predicted on the basis of Redding's (1993) previous research.

On a preliminary analysis it would appear that the questions about values in organisation in Hong Kong were not particularly useful in either differentiating HR practices in firms of varying ethnic origin or for predicting the extent of difference in HR practices. A possible explanation for this may be that all of the Anglo-American organisations in the sample are following polycentric staffing practices and tailoring their HR rhetoric to local norms. However, if this were the case then it would be reasonable to expect a similar flow through into the practice of HR. Another possible explanation may lie in the fact that all respondents to the survey were of ethnic Chinese background and worked mainly with other Chinese managers who espoused and practised the values of their home country rather than those formally promoted by their organisation. Alternatively, the result may have stemmed from the questionnaire methodology that may not be best suited to collecting data on values. This is an issue that will be explored in future work on the topic.

The study supports previous research findings on HR in Hong Kong that suggests that HR tends to be a non-strategic activity, especially in ethnic Chinese firms. In particular, the study supports previous findings of a lower usage of formal and systematic HR procedures in ethnic Chinese firms. Firm size was found to be a significant influence on HR practice but within each size category ethnic origin of the employing organisation was still found to be significant in influencing HR practice.

In relation to the issue of convergence and divergence, discussed at the beginning of this chapter, the variation in HR practices would indicate that Anglo-American firms are 'exporting' some of their HR practices. The reluctance of ethnic Chinese owners to engage in formal HR practices, particularly in the planning area, would indicate that the typical Chinese organisation is still informal, implicitly structured and personalised, suggesting a pronounced divergence from the western HRM paradigm and a strong influence of the Confucian and 'overseas' heritage. Further research is required to confirm this, however, and benchmarked practices rather then perceptions should be the measure used to ascertain this.

With reference to the typologies of MNC practice it would appear that in view of the exporting of HR practices noted above, the local subsidiaries of Anglo-American MNCs are tending somewhat towards an ethnocentric policy in relation to HR.

In conclusion, this study is generally supportive of previous findings on the practice of HR in Hong Kong and reports a divergence of HR practice from the more sophisticated western models in ethnic Chinese owned organisations.

REFERENCES

Adler, N. (1995), 'Competitive Frontiers: Global Management in the 21st Century', *HR Monthly,* March, pp. 10–15.

Arthur, J.B. (1994), 'Effects of Human Resource Systems on Manufacturing Performance and Turnover', *Academy of Management Journal*, **37**, 670–87.

Baird, L. and I. Meshoulam (1988), 'Managing Two Fits of Strategic Human Resource Management', *Academy of Management Review*, **13**, 116–28.

Bartlett, C.A. and S. Ghoshal (1989), *Managing Across Borders: The Transnational Solution*, Boston, MA: Harvard Business School Press.

Child, J. (1981), 'Culture, Contingency and Capitalism in the Cross-National Study of Organisations', in L.L. Cummings and B.M. Staw (eds), *Research in Organizational Behaviour*, **Vol.3**, Greenwich: JAI Press.

Cutcher-Gershenfeld, J.C. (1991), 'The Impact on Economic Performance of a Transformation in Workplace Relations', *Industrial and Labor Relations Review*, **44**, 241–60.

Evans, P. and P. Lorange (1989), 'The Two Logics Behind Human Resource Management', in P. Evans, Y. Doz and A. Laurent (eds), *Human Resource Management in International Firms: Change, Globalization, Innovation*, London: Macmillan, pp. 501–17.

Fukuyama, F. (1992), *The End of History and the Last Man*, New York: Free Press.

Fukuyama, F. (1995), *Trust*, New York: Free Press.

Gannon, M.J. and Associates (1994), *Understanding Global Cultures: Metaphorical Journeys Through 17 Countries*, Thousand Oaks: Sage Publications.

Gerhart, B. and G.T. Milkovich (1990), 'Organizational Differences in Managerial Compensation and Firm Performance', *Academy of Management Journal*, **33**, 663–91.

Guest, D. (1990), 'Human Resource Management and the American Dream', *Journal of Management Studies*, **27** (4), 377–97.

Hamel and Prahalad (1990), 'The Core Competence of the Corporation', *Harvard Business Review*, **68** (3), 79–89.

Hofstede, G. (1980), 'Motivation, Leadership and Organization: Do American Theories Apply Abroad?' *Organizational Dynamics*, **9**, 42–63.

Hofstede, G. (1993), 'Cultural Constraints in Management Theories', *Academy of Management Executive*, **7**, 81–94.

Huselid, M.A. (1995), 'The Impact of Human Resource Management Practices on Turnover, Productivity and Corporate Financial Performance', *Academy of Management Journal*, **38**, 35–72.

Huselid, M.A. and B. Becker (1996), 'Methodological Issues in Cross-sectional and Panel Estimates of the HR-firm Performance Link', *Industrial Relations,* **35** (3), 400–423.

Kirkbride, P. and S.F.Y. Tang (1989), 'Personnel Management in Hong Kong', *Asia Pacific Human Resource Management*, **27** (2), 43–57.

Kobayashi, N. (1982), 'The Present and Future of the Japanese Multinational Enterprises', *International Studies of Man and Organisation*, **12** (1), 38–58.

Lengnick-Hall, C.A. and M.L. Lengnick-Hall (1988), 'Strategic Human Resource Management: A Review of the Literature and a Proposed Typology', *Academy of Management Review*, **13** (4), 54–70.

MacDuffie, J.P. (1995), 'Human Resource Bundles and Manufacturing Performance: Organizational Logic and Flexible Production Systems in the World Auto Industry', *Industrial and Labor Relations Review*, **48**, 197–221.

Martin, G. and P. Beaumont (1998), 'Diffusing "Best Practice" in Multinational Firms: Prospects, Practices and Contestation', *The International Journal of Human Resource Management*, **9** (4), 671–95.

Olie, R. (1995), 'The Culture Factor in Personnel and Organization Policies' in A.W. Harzing and J.V. Ruysseveldt (eds), *International Human Resource Management: An Integrated Approach*, London: Sage.

Ondrack, D.A. (1985), 'International Human-Resources Management in European and North-American Firms', *International Studies of Management and Organizations*, **15** (1), 6–32.

Pfeffer, J. (1994), *Competitive Advantage through People*, Boston, MA: Harvard Business School Press.

Redding, G. (1993), *The Spirit of Chinese Capitalism*, Berlin: DeGruyter.

Rosenweig, P.M. and N. Nohria (1994), 'Influences on Human Resource Management Practices in Multinational Corporations', *Journal of International Business Studies,* **25** (2), 229–42.

Saha, S.K. (1987), 'Human Resource Management Practices in Hong Kong', *Hong Kong Journal of Business Management*, **5**, 51–68.

Schneider, S.C. (1988), 'National vs Corporate Culture: Implications for Human Resource Management', *Human Resource Management*, **27** (2), 231–46.

Schneider, S.C. and A. De Meyer (1991), 'Interpreting and Responding to Strategic Issues: The Impact of National Culture', *Strategic Management Journal*, **12**, 307–20.

Shaw, J.B., F.Y.T. Tang, C.D. Fisher and P.S. Kirkbride (1993), 'Organizational and Environmental Factors Related to HRM Practices in Hong Kong: A Cross-cultural Expanded Replication', *International Journal of Human Resource Management*, **4** (4), 785–815.

Shenkar, O. (1995), *Global Perspectives of Human Resource Management*, Englewood Cliffs: Prentice Hall.

Sparrow, P., R.S. Schuler and S.E. Jackson (1994), 'Convergence or Divergence: Human Resource Practices and Policies for Competitive Advantage Worldwide', *International Journal of Human Resource Management*, **5** (2), 267–99.

Wright, P.M. and G.C. McMahan (1992), 'Alternative Theoretical Perspectives on Strategic Human Resource Management', *Journal of Management*, **18**, 295–320.

Index